The Making of Citizens

Why are young people apparently so alienated from the world of politics, and from traditional forms of political communication? Are familiar notions of citizenship – and traditional distinctions between the 'personal' and the 'political' – still relevant in the late modern age? What role should the news media play, both in informing young people about the world, and in encouraging their political participation?

Based on research conducted in Britain and the US, *The Making of Citizens* explores these questions through a detailed analysis both of television news programmes and interviews with young people themselves. Buckingham traces the dynamic complexities of young people's interpretations of news, and their judgements about the ways in which key social and political issues are represented. Rather than bemoaning young people's ignorance, he argues that we need to rethink what counts as political understanding in contemporary societies, suggesting that we need new forms of factual reporting that will engage more effectively with young people's changing perceptions of themselves as citizens.

The Making of Citizens provides a significant contribution to the study of media audiences and a timely intervention in contemporary debates about citizenship and political education.

David Buckingham is Professor of Education at the Institute of Education, University of London. He has conducted several major research projects on media education and on young people's relationships with electronic media. His previous books include *Children Talking Television* (Falmer Press 1993), *Cultural Studies Goes to School* (Taylor & Francis 1994) and *Teaching Popular Culture* (UCL Press 1998).

Media, Education and Culture

Series editors:
David Buckingham, Reader in Education at the Institute of Education,
University of London and Julian Sefton-Green, Media Education
Development Officer at Weekend Arts College, part of Interchange Trust.

In response to the increasing diversity of contemporary societies and the
significance of the electronic media, cultural studies has developed rigorous
and exciting approaches to pedagogy, both in schools and in higher education. At the same time, research in this area has begun to pose fundamental
questions about the political claims of much cultural studies theory, and
about the relationship between academic knowledge and lived experience.
Media, Education and Culture will extend the research and debate that is
developing in this interface between cultural studies and education.

Already published:

Teaching Popular Culture: Beyond Radical Pedagogy
Edited by David Buckingham

Digital Diversions: Youth Culture in the Age of Multimedia
Edited by Julian Sefton-Green

Teen Spirits: Music and Identity in Media Education
Chris Richards

Wired-Up: Young People and the Electronic Media
Sue Howard

Forthcoming:

Mapping the Cultural Spaces of Childhood
Claudia Mitchell and Jacqueline Reid-Walsh

Media, Popular Culture and Feminisms
Lyn Thomas

The Making of Citizens

Young People, News and Politics

David Buckingham

London and New York

First published 2000
by Routledge
2 Park Square, Milton Park, Abingdon, Oxon, OX14 4RN

Simultaneously published in the USA and Canada
by Routledge
270 Madison Ave, New York NY 10016

Routledge is an imprint of the Taylor & Francis Group

Transferred to Digital Printing 2006

© 2000 David Buckingham

Typeset in Times Ten by Florence Production, Stoodleigh, Devon.

British Library Cataloguing in Publication Data
A catalogue record for this book is available from the British Library

Library of Congress Cataloging-in-Publication Data
Buckingham, David, 1954–
    The making of citizens: young people, news, and politics / David Buckingham.
       p. cm.
    Includes bibliographical references and index.
    1. Television and children. 2. Television broadcasting of news.
    3. Children—Political activity. I. Title.

    HQ784.T4 B847 2000
    302.23´45´083—dc21

                                                            99–054252
                                                            CIP

ISBN 0–415–21460–2 (hbk)
ISBN 0–415–21461–0 (pbk)

Publisher's Note
The publisher has gone to great lengths to ensure the quality of this reprint but points out that som
imperfections in the original may be apparent
Printed and bound by CPI Antony Rowe, Eastbourne

Contents

Preface and Acknowledgements

News journalism has often been seen as an essential guarantee of democracy. Far from being a trivial daily ritual, the newspaper and the television news broadcast serve as indispensable sources of the information on which the health of civil society depends. As older social bonds gradually fall into disrepair, news has become our primary means of access to the public sphere of political debate. News journalism, it is argued, is essential to creating and sustaining an informed citizenry. Without it, we face a future of apathy, alienation and the abuse of political power.

Yet recent research suggests that television news is largely failing to fulfil these responsibilities, particularly among young people. With each new generation, interest in news media and in politics itself has steadily declined. Active citizenship, it is argued, is a thing of the past, or merely a utopian fantasy. Young people today are postmodern citizens – cynical, distracted, no longer possessed of the civic virtues and responsibilities of older generations. For them, conventional politics is merely an irrelevance: the personal has become political, the private has become the public, entertainment has become education. Among this audience, traditional news journalism has simply been the victim of its own conservatism.

This book attempts to give some empirical substance to these debates. It is centrally concerned with how young people interpret and respond to broadly 'political' stories featured on television news. As such, it addresses several interrelated issues. It offers, firstly, an analysis of young people's relationships with the public sphere of political debate – and in the process, argues for a rethinking of what we mean by 'politics' in the first place. It also provides an account of how young people relate to television news, and of the reasons why it is increasingly failing to attract the interest or attention of this audience. Finally, it analyses the dynamics of viewers' interpretations of television, looking at how they make sense of the issues that are presented and how they judge television's portrayal of those issues.

The book presents the findings of research conducted both in Britain and the United States, although it is not strictly speaking a comparative study. While it does offer an analysis of programmes themselves – and specifically of programmes explicitly aimed at this audience – its central emphasis is on how young people *talk* about what they watch. It is through analysing such talk in considerable detail that the book attempts to assess the limitations and possibilities of news as a form of political communication – and indeed, as a form of political *education* for young people.

This is the third in a series of studies of young people's relationships with television that I have undertaken over the past decade or so. Like its predecessors, *Children Talking Television* (1993) and *Moving Images* (1996), it uses approaches derived from what is now termed 'British' Cultural Studies. As such, it is not essentially concerned with the *effects* of television, or with identifying the *psychological* dynamics of viewers' relationships with it, although it does have things to say about both of these. On the contrary, its central emphasis is on the social and interpersonal processes through which the meanings of television are constructed and defined.

Audience research of this kind has attracted considerable criticism among exponents of Cultural Studies in recent years, much of it from people who seem to understand very little about the motivations for conducting it in the first place. I do not wish to add to the generalized rhetoric that has sometimes characterized this debate. Suffice it to say that audience research of the kind presented here does not represent an abandonment of 'politics', as some have alleged. While I do believe that young people are a more critical and sophisticated audience than they are often assumed to be – and in this respect, the data presented here speak for themselves – this obviously does not mean that I intend to engage in a mere celebration of the power of 'active audiences'. Indeed, in some ways this book revisits very traditional questions in media research, for example, about news bias, about the pedagogic functions of news and about the nature of 'critical' viewing. In responding to young people's apparent alienation from the domain of politics, we have to pay attention to such apparently conventional questions about public knowledge and how it is to be developed and sustained. My implicit agenda here, in other words, is primarily an *educational* one.

The book is also quite conventionally structured. The first three chapters offer a reading of previous debates and research about the relationships between young people, news media and politics. Specifically, Chapter 2 reviews research on young people's use and understanding of television news; while Chapter 3 addresses recent debates about role of the media in relation to notions of citizenship and the public sphere. Chapter 4 discusses news programmes specifically aimed at young people, concentrating on issues of content, pedagogy and address. It also introduces the four programmes (two British, two American) that were used in the research. Chapter 5 discusses the methodology of the audience study, and presents some general findings about the young people's relationships both with news and with politics. It also contains a very detailed account of some sample extracts from the interviews. Chapters 6 and 7 present an analysis of the young people's interpretations of, and responses to, a total of eight news items used in the study. These chapters are necessarily quite extensive, but they are far from merely descriptive. Finally, Chapter 8 summarizes the findings and discusses some implications of the research, both for the future of news production and for political education.

Presentations based on this research have been given at the University of Pennsylvania, New York University, the University of Wales, the University of Manchester Broadcasting Symposium and the Institute of Education, University of London. I would like to thank all those who attended for their feedback.

Articles drawing on the research have been published as follows:

'News media, political socialization and popular citizenship: Towards a new agenda', *Critical Studies in Mass Communication*, **14**(4), 1997.

'The making of citizens: Pedagogy and address in children's television news', *Journal of Educational Media*, **23**(2/3), 1997.

'Young people, politics and news media: Beyond political socialisation', *Oxford Review of Education*, **25** (1/2), 1999.

'The making of citizens: Young people, television news and the limits of politics', in *Youth and Global Media: Papers from the 29th University of Manchester Broadcasting Symposium 1998*, S. Ralph, J. Langham Brown and T. Lees (eds), Luton, John Libbey, 1999.

The US research was undertaken under the auspices of the Scholars' Program at the Annenberg School for Communications at the University of Pennsylvania, Philadelphia. I am most grateful to Professor Elihu Katz, who directed the program, for his intellectual inspiration and gastronomic generosity. I also wish to thank my fellow scholars – Dona Schwarz, Gene Burns, Mike Griffin and Crispin Sartwell – for their support; and the members of faculty who participated in our regular seminars, particularly Klaus Krippendorf and Joe Turow. Special thanks must go to Barbara Grabias for holding it all together.

The research in the US schools was partly funded by the Spencer Foundation. I am grateful to Peter Hillman, John Frangipani and their colleagues for giving me access to their students; and of course to the students themselves, whose thoughtful and perceptive observations are recorded here. Thanks again to Barbara Grabias, who helped with the fieldwork and some of the transcribing; and to Gianna Howard for supplying tapes of *Channel One News*.

The UK research was partly funded by the Nuffield Foundation. I would like to thank Marion Budd and her colleagues for giving me access to their students; and, again, the students themselves for their insightful observations. Thanks also to Molly Voysey, Betty Mitchell and Deborah Harris for their efforts in transcribing; and to Eileen Lawrence for supplying videotapes. I am especially grateful to Sara Bragg, who helped with the fieldwork and did a first coding of the transcripts. Her observations were always extremely helpful and perceptive, and her support was invaluable.

Thanks must also go to Julian Sefton-Green and Sara Bragg for their critical reading of the complete manuscript; and to my immediate colleagues Hannah Davies and Peter Kelley for bearing with me during an especially busy time. As ever, Celia, Nathan and Louis Greenwood got the worst of it: but it would not have happened without them.

Chapter One

Turning off the News?

'Young People Say No To News' ran a front page headline in the *New York Times* (13 May 1996). Reporting on a study conducted by the Pew Research Center for the People and the Press, 1996 (formerly the Times Mirror Center), the story noted a sudden decline in the percentage of people under 30 who say they regularly watch television news. Of course, young people have always been consistently less interested in news than their elders; yet, as this research suggests, the generation gap between them is growing steadily wider.

Despite this story's claim of a sudden change, young people's turn away from news journalism dates back at least 20 years. In an earlier report, symptomatically entitled *The Age of Indifference: A Study of Young Americans and How They View the News* (1990), the Times Mirror Center provided some broader historical comparisons. Irrespective of the advent of the so-called 'Information Age', the increased provision of news media and the rise in college attendance in the US, the report argues, young people are now less interested in news (particularly 'political' news) and less well-informed than their counterparts in earlier decades. Thus, the percentage of people under 30 who said they 'read a newspaper yesterday' declined from 67 per cent in 1965 to 29 per cent in 1996, while measures of information levels and news attentiveness among the young show a decline both over time and relative to older age groups. News about key events in recent political history, such as the revolutions in Eastern Europe, has, the report argues, failed to engage the younger audience.

While the Times Mirror study dates this change to the mid-1970s, other evidence suggests that the turn away from news may have begun even earlier. There is, for example, a consistent decline in newspaper readership in the US which dates back to the late 1920s (Putnam, 1995); and while some of this can be explained by the displacement to other media such as radio and television, the evidence suggests a more broad-ranging shift away from news in general. Thus, according to the Pew and Times Mirror studies, young people aged 18–30 are *also* turning off the television news to a greater degree than older generations – regular viewing of network news has declined from 52 per cent in 1965 to 22 per cent in 1996; where they do express an interest in news, this is increasingly confined to 'tabloid' TV shows such as *Hard Copy*, *Inside Edition* and *A Current Affair*.

These findings are echoed in other studies. Industry research in the US (cited by Katz, 1993) suggests that the number of young adults (18–24) reading news magazines has declined by 55 per cent in the past 14 years; while the percentage of viewers between 18 and 34 watching commercial broadcast news has dropped by 45 per cent since 1980. Again, some of these shifts can doubtless be traced to the advent of new technologies and the resulting proliferation of media sources. Viewing of news is declining fastest among owners of home computers, and specialist cable channels such as CNN have taken viewers away from the networks – although CNN's audience is also now in decline. Nevertheless, age remains a significant factor here, independent of other variables.

This declining interest in news is seen in turn to result in a decline in 'informed citizenship'. The 1990 Times Mirror study, for example, points to an increasing degree of ignorance about basic political and geographical information – again, despite a rise in college attendance. Between 1947 and 1988, for instance, the percentage of young Americans who could find Europe on a world map fell from 45 per cent to 25 per cent; while the numbers who were able to recognize well-known political figures or answer test questions about recent political events were significantly lower than those in older age groups. These kinds of findings are reported in the press with increasing regularity – although, of course, it may be a mistake to take evidence about *factual recall* as evidence of *political understanding*.

Nevertheless, the wider consequences of this situation in terms of political participation are potentially very serious. For example, there has been a decline in the proportion of young voters (18–24) who bother to turn out at national elections in the US, from 50 per cent in 1972 to 41 per cent in 1992, although the reverse is the case for the oldest age group of voters (65+). For the Times Mirror researchers, the lack of political awareness among the young leads to a kind of 'blind faith' in political leaders and in the institutions of government. According to these data, young people are actually less inclined to be critical of big business and of government, and are thus more vulnerable to political persuasion, for example by campaign advertising – although the Pew Center (1996) study also suggests that public perceptions of the credibility of television news itself are in decline.

Research from other countries paints a similar picture. In their book *Freedom's Children*, produced by the left-liberal British think-tank Demos, Helen Wilkinson and Geoff Mulgan (1995) point to an 'historic political disconnection' among the younger generation both in the UK and across Europe. Surveys in Britain, France and Germany over the past decade show that young people under 25 are significantly less likely to be registered to vote, to turn out at elections, and to be politically active than they were in earlier generations. Membership of political parties and related organizations (*including* environmental pressure groups and women's groups) is

increasingly confined to the middle aged and the elderly. While this disconnection from conventional forms of politics is particularly marked among
women, ethnic minorities and the poor, young people are consistently more
alienated than adults. This is the case even in countries like Australia, where
voting is compulsory: a 1994 poll in that country registered very high agreement with various negative statements about politicians, and showed that
young people placed greater trust in pop musicians (Hartley, 1996: 73).

Likewise, recent research suggests that young people's use of, and
interest in, news media are also comparatively low. In the UK, only 6 per
cent of young people's viewing of television comes into this category, while
their reading of newspapers focuses largely on entertainment, features and
sports pages (Harcourt and Hartland, 1992). Surveys repeatedly find that
young people have a low level of interest in media coverage of political
affairs (Walker, 1996). Given the lack of comparative historical data, it is
impossible to know whether this is simply an effect of age – and hence,
perhaps, a phase that young people pass through – or whether it is a cohort
effect that will last into adulthood, as in the US. On the face of it, the latter
would seem to be more likely.

Two further elements can be added to this picture. The first is the decline
in the provision of informational television programming for children and
young people in the wake of deregulation, both in the US and elsewhere.
In the US, the Children's Television Act (1990) explicitly required franchise
holders to provide 'educational' programming, although in the years immediately following the passing of the Act, stations attempted to circumvent
this requirement by claiming, for example, that cartoons like *The Jetsons*
could be defined as educational on the grounds that they informed children
about life in the future (see Kunkel, 1993). While this loophole has now to
some extent been closed, the business of monitoring whether the Act's
requirements are being met still appears to be largely down to individual
viewers rather than government regulatory bodies.

Even in countries with a much stronger tradition of public service broadcasting, such as the UK, the proportion of informational programming
appears to have declined relative to entertainment programming in recent
years (Blumler, 1992; Davies and Corbett, 1997) – although the measure-
ment of these categories is problematic, particularly with the emergence of
hybrid forms of 'info-tainment'. Such changes are partly dictated by the
move towards a more market-led system, and the resulting drive towards
maximizing audiences. Although factual programmes (such as the BBC
news show *Newsround*, discussed in Chapter 4, and the magazine programme
Blue Peter) remain among the most popular children's programmes, they
are generally perceived to be less likely to win good ratings, and are significantly more difficult to sell in overseas markets (see Buckingham *et al.*
1999).

The second factor to add in here is the comparative value of print media
and television as means of political learning. While researchers disagree on

the extent of *causality*, there is nevertheless a consistent *correlation* between exposure to print media and higher levels of political knowledge, as compared with exposure to television (Chaffee and Yang, 1990; Graber, 1988; Neuman, Just and Crigler, 1992; Robinson and Levy, 1986). While those who follow news in general are predictably better informed than those who do not, those who rely primarily on television news are less well-informed than those who also read newspapers. Chaffee and Yang, for example, suggest the following:

> Television is a worthy supplement to these print media, but reliance on TV alone may be associated with socialization away from politics. To say, 'I get most of my news from television', as a majority of Americans do, may be a socially acceptable way of admitting, 'I don't care much about politics' (1990: 143).

These authors go so far as to doubt whether 'television-dependent citizens' can actually be seen as citizens 'in the strong, proactive sense of that term', since they are less likely to vote, to have reasons for their voting decisions, or to be involved in or to understand political processes. If, as these authors and the surveys quoted above confirm, the move away from print media is manifested much more strongly among the young, it is not unreasonable to conclude that the knowledge gap between young and old is likely to increase exponentially. On this account, the future of news journalism – and indeed of democratic citizenship – looks bleak indeed.

Explaining and Blaming

The reasons for these developments, however, are predictably more difficult to establish. The Times Mirror researchers, for example, suggest that the turn away from 'hard news' can be seen as symptomatic of a more general 'turning inward' in US society. Yet for many commentators, it is television that is primarily to blame. Robert Putnam (1995), for example, regards the decline in newspaper readership as an indication of the decline of 'social capital' – that is, of organized social networks and the feelings of 'connectedness' they produce – which he argues has largely been caused by the rise of television. Roderick Hart (1994) similarly connects the rise of television and the slow demise of print journalism in the US to the decline in civic pride and the growth of cynicism, particularly among the young. Both appear to look back to a 'golden age' before the advent of television. (It is worth noting, however, the contrast between these arguments and the findings of the Times Mirror study on young people's tendency towards 'blind faith', p. 2.) Whatever explanation one favours, it is clear that the declining interest in news journalism is seen by many commentators as an indication of a broader social crisis, and of the failure of older generations to adequately socialize the young – a situation that most suggest is likely to continue.

Correlations among broad social phenomena of this kind typically give rise to multiple interpretations; in this case, significant questions about the *direction* of the causality remain. To what extent does the decline in interest in news media *produce* a decline in 'social capital', and to what extent is it a *symptom* of it? Does dependence on television produce political apathy, or vice-versa? Logic would suggest a spiral of causality, and a network of inter-related variables, rather than a single cause–effect relationship. Yet, as in many other areas, blaming television often seems to provide a simple explanation for all the ills of the world.

Nevertheless, serious news journalism itself is predominantly exonerated in these debates: it is represented in terms of its own self-estimation, as a neutral source of information and a fundamental guarantee of a healthy democracy. Likewise, 'democracy' seems to be defined in terms of a utopian ideal, rather than in terms of any actually existing manifestation. The possibility that an apathetic or even cynical electorate is something that might be *required* and indeed actively produced by the status quo – or indeed that cynicism might be an entirely reasonable response to the current state of democratic politics (cf. Gripsrud, 1992) – is not one that such critics seem prepared to entertain.

From this perspective, then, both news and democracy appear to be seen as constants; what has changed is people's attitudes towards them. It is not democracy – or indeed news journalism, or the relationship between them – that is the problem, but people's lack of interest in those things. The resulting implication here is that the failure is that of young people themselves. If kids do not read the *New York Times* or watch *The News Hour* on TV, then it is their fault for being so ignorant. Certainly in the case of the Times Mirror study, and less directly in Hart's book, young people are implicitly condemned for being lazier and less socially responsible than their parents; and if there have been undesirable changes in the media, such as the advent of 'tabloid television', this too can be laid at the door of the young, with their love of superficiality and sensationalism.

This view inevitably invites a counter-argument. The media critic Jon Katz (1993), writing in *Rolling Stone* magazine, blames young people's growing rejection of conventional journalism fairly and squarely on the journalists themselves. Quoting several examples of journalists' 'attacks on kid culture' – from rock and roll in the 1950s to rap music, video games and *Beavis and Butthead* in the 1990s – he argues that journalists have effectively abandoned the young, rather than the other way round. According to Katz, such attacks merely reflect journalists' growing sense of anxiety about the threats to their authority as 'guardians of the country's political life'.

Contrary to journalists' representations of them as 'TV zombies', narcotized by endless acts of violence, Katz argues that young people have a very different orientation to information from that of older generations. They are, he suggests, more appreciative of the 'breadth and variety of information' provided by new media such as cable TV and the growing specialist magazine sector; and they prefer their more 'informal' and 'ironic' style to the 'monotonously reassuring voice' of mainstream news journalism. Katz argues that young people have a broader definition of news than mainstream journalists; and he refutes the implication, which he detects in the Times Mirror study, 'that public awareness is measurable primarily in terms of news media consumption and that youthful disinterest in absorbing what-ever journalism offers reflects ignorance or indifference' (1993: 130). Ultimately, it is the failure of the established news media to connect with the forms of 'everyday politics' which are most important for this genera-tion that accounts for their declining audience. In this respect, Katz suggests, the emergence of more popular forms of news journalism – such as 'tabloid television' and 'faction' shows – could be seen as an attempt to engage more fully with the changing cultural styles and competencies of the younger audience (Sternberg, 1995).

Katz's argument clearly espouses a form of generational rhetoric, in which the unitary categories of 'young' and 'old' – or, more specifically in this case, 'kids' and 'baby boomers' – are defined against each other. A broadly optimistic historical narrative is constructed here which seems just as essentialist as the narrative of decline that it attempts to replace. The kids are now 'all right', according to Katz, just as they were previously 'all wrong'. From this perspective, the decline of traditional news journalism is not to be lamented, but on the contrary to be celebrated.

Yet despite its tendency towards polemic, this argument finds many echoes in recent academic work on the media. Researchers have increas-ingly challenged the idea that young people's lack of interest in news is somehow symptomatic of laziness or irresponsibility: on the contrary, it is argued that conventional forms of news journalism have proven signally ineffective in enabling them to 'translate' broader political events into the context of their own everyday lives (Barnhurst and Wartella, 1991). Although Katz does not mention the word 'postmodernism', it clearly underlies his emphasis on irony and diversity, and his rejection of the 'monotonously reas-suring voice' of the established news media, while his notion of media audiences as active and autonomous, and his call for more popular forms of news journalism, are increasingly common in academic Cultural Studies (e.g. Fiske, 1989, 1992). Likewise, there are many who argue that the potential of new media forms and technologies in terms of participatory democracy is significantly greater than that of more traditional forms of news journalism. Even comparatively mainstream critics are acknowledging the need to move beyond the 'classical' model of news in the wake of the 'crisis in public communication' (Blumler and Gurevitch, 1995; Dahlgren, 1995).

This debate about young people's changing relationship with news media thus raises fundamental questions about the nature and meaning of citizen-ship in contemporary societies. In preparing the ground for the empirical investigations analysed in this book, the following two chapters explore some of these questions in more detail. Chapter 2 discusses previous research on young people's use and understanding of television news, and its role in political socialization. Chapter 3 provides a critical account of recent debates about the emergence of more popular forms of news journalism, and their implications for theories of citizenship and the public sphere. As I shall argue, more positive responses to the crisis in young people's relationship with politics and with news media will need to avoid the contrasting temptations of conservative lament and postmodern celebration.

Chapter Two

Beyond Political Socialization

There has been very little research on young people's relationship with television news. On one level, this is hardly surprising. As the studies described in the previous chapter suggest, young people appear to watch very little news; and their consumption of news media in general is in decline. Yet it would be wrong to overstate this case. According to some estimates (Gunter, 1987), news and current affairs programming constitute one quarter of total broadcast output, and much of this is screened during periods when children are available to view. As previous studies have repeatedly shown, children frequently express indifference, or even considerable dislike, towards the news (Buckingham, 1996; Cullingford, 1992); yet they may often have little choice but to watch it.

Evidence on this topic is exceptionally sparse; but it would seem reasonable to conclude that insofar as young people *are* being informed about current events, television news is likely to constitute a significant source. This may be the case even with very young children. For example, Denis Howitt (1982) reports on an earlier unpublished study looking at British preschoolers' perceptions of events in Northern Ireland. While their knowledge was predictably very vague and confused, these children were aware that there was political violence taking place in Northern Ireland, and that bombs and weapons were involved – knowledge which, Howitt argues, could only have come from television. As this implies, much of young people's viewing of news may be accidental rather than purposeful, distracted rather than concentrated; as Katz (1993) suggests, they may be more inclined to absorb information 'on the fly', in fragments, during the course of other activities.

The question here is whether, and in what ways, this viewing of television news might contribute to their understanding of politics. In examining research on this issue in this chapter, we will inevitably have to ask what is meant by 'political understanding', and how that understanding is to be evaluated and assessed.

Political Socialization

Much of the research in this field has been conducted within the social-psychological paradigm of 'political socialization'. At its most neutral, political socialization is defined as 'a developmental process by which adolescents acquire cognitions, attitudes and behaviors relating to their political environment' (Atkin and Gantz, 1978: 184). The first wave of political socialization research took place in the mid-1960s. Studies such as Easton and Dennis (1969), Greenstein (1965), and Hess and Torney (1967) argue that much of the most significant political learning takes place prior to adolescence, and that the lessons learnt at that stage tend to persist into adult life. While they do not deny the possibility of later learning, all these studies suggest that the knowledge that is acquired first is that which lasts the longest.

As Sears (1990) has shown, this faith in the *persistence* of political learning has come to be challenged in more recent work; in the wake of research into personal change in later life, he suggests, childhood is now no longer seen as a uniquely formative or impressionable period, either within this field or in psychology more broadly. Nevertheless, as he argues, the judgement of persistence clearly depends upon the historical period in which the research itself is carried out. There is a certain irony in reading the early classics of political socialization research with the benefit of hindsight. Both Greenstein (1965) and Hess and Torney (1967) are based on research conducted in the US in the late 1950s and early 1960s; and both emphasize the high levels of trust children place in political leaders (and in other authority figures such as the police), and their emotional identification with the nation and its political institutions. In line with the argument for persistence, Greenstein (1965) argues that the decline from what he terms this 'political euphoria' begins only in adolescence, but that the cynicism that emerges in later life is only 'skin deep'. Likewise, Hess and Torney (1967) suggest that while respect for particular individuals may decline, respect for the roles they occupy (such as the presidency) and for political institutions more broadly does not. The extent to which these arguments still apply will be considered in due course; but these researchers' strong predictions that the presence of trust in childhood would lead to a high level of political stability were clearly being disproved even as their books were being published.

As the above definition suggests, political socialization is seen here as an essentially *psychological* issue, and in broadly functionalist terms. Greenstein (1965), for example, notes that working-class children are more likely to experience '*deeply embedded psychological impediments* to the participation in politics' (my emphasis, p. 106) when compared with their middle-class counterparts. This definition of the issue clearly supports a kind of consensual functionalism, in which the system itself is implicitly seen to be beyond question. The possibility that it might be quite logical for working-class children to have a lesser investment in political participation, since they might reasonably feel that they have little to gain from it, does not seem to occur. According to Greenstein, political socialization is generally an 'effort-less' process, which becomes visible only on those rare occasions when its performance is in some way deficient. This functionalist orientation thus reinforces a kind of conservatism, which sees it as the individual's responsi-bility to adjust to the demands of the system. The function of political socialization, according to Hess and Torney (1967) is essentially 'to rein-force and help to maintain the culture'; and they go so far as to suggest that young children should be actively sheltered from information about the more negative aspects of political life, such as corruption, and from political conflict and disagreement.

Perhaps surprisingly, neither of the studies discussed here mentions tele-vision or other forms of mediated communication. While both consider a number of potential agencies of political socialization, Greenstein (1965) argues that the more informal models provided by the family are the most significant influence, while Hess and Torney (1967) single out the school as 'the central, salient and dominant force'. The role of the media only begins to emerge on the research agenda in the early 1970s, accompanied by quite strong claims about its significance (e.g. Atkin and Gantz, 1978; Chaffee, Ward and Tipton, 1970; Conway *et al.*, 1981; Dominick, 1972; Drew and Reeves, 1980; Hollander, 1971; Rubin, 1976). Indeed, the contrast between these studies and the subsequent findings of the Times Mirror study is quite striking. Atkin and Gantz (1978), for example, claim that more than half of all children watch television news on a regular basis, and that it makes a significant contribution to their interest in and knowledge about political affairs; while Conway *et al.* (1981) argue that exposure to news and levels of political knowledge are mutually reinforcing variables, which determine political attitudes and political participation to a much greater extent than other influences such as parents, gender or education (see also Comstock and Paik, 1991).

Broadly speaking, subsequent research has come to qualify some of these claims. First, as I have noted, a distinction has increasingly been drawn between television and other news sources. Television news is frequently seen to represent children's first contact with the world of politics, and serves as a bridge to the world of political affairs right through to adolescence: at this stage, high exposure to television news is correlated with high levels of political knowledge (Atkin, 1981). Once we move into early adulthood, however, a reliance on television is increasingly associated with lower levels of political knowledge, and a less enthusiastic orientation towards politics, and a growing 'information gap' emerges between those who use television *and* print media and those who use television alone (Chaffee and Yang, 1990).

Secondly, attention has increasingly been drawn to the significance of other variables, and to the relationships between them, in the political communication process. Thus, studies have drawn attention to factors such as family communication patterns (Dennis, 1986; Liebes, 1992) and their relationship with ethnicity (Austin and Nelson, 1993; Chaffee and Yang, 1990) in mediating political communications. In general, high levels of news media use are correlated with high levels of political participation, although the influence of parents, older siblings, peers or community factors is recognized as more significant (Andreyenkov *et al.*, 1989; Chaffee and Yang, 1990; Robinson *et al.*, 1989).

These findings implicitly point to the need for a more fully developed *social* theory of political understanding, yet the kind of psychological functionalism identified above remains an abiding characteristic even of more recent work. Austin and Nelson (1993), for example, note the connection between a lack of political knowledge and a lack of 'self-efficacy' or political disaffection. The implication here is clear. Political disaffection is a psychological dysfunction caused by lack of information, rather than a result of the shortcomings of the political system itself: all we have to do is provide the information and disaffection will disappear. Yet as these authors admit, this kind of correlational study is unable to specify the direction of any causality. It could equally be the case that disaffection produces a lack of interest, which leads in turn to a lack of knowledge.

Several general observations can be made about this body of research. The first concerns the reliability of the data. In many cases, these studies use children's self-reports as a measure of their television viewing, or parents' reports of their children's viewing – reports that must be questioned in terms of their accuracy. While this problem is difficult to avoid in television research, a more serious issue is raised by the way in which *relative* significance is then assigned to different sources of political information. Like adults, children may define television as their 'main source' (see Dominick, 1972), but the fact that they do so does not necessarily mean that it is (cf. Robinson and Levy, 1986). Likewise, broad correlations between global figures of amounts of viewing (for example, in making distinctions between 'light viewers' and 'heavy viewers') and levels of political knowledge do not tell us a great deal about what is actually taking place in viewers' encounters with news as a genre, let alone with specific news formats or items.

This leads on to a second, more significant, problem. The question of how much – and indeed how and what – young people actually *learn* from television news has been addressed here in very limited terms. 'Political knowledge' tends to be measured in terms of the recall of factual information, often through multiple choice tests – an approach that is shared with many of the broader surveys which have reached pessimistic conclusions about young people's ignorance of politics, described in Chapter 1. Yet the ability to identify a given political leader, or to answer test questions about recent events, clearly tells us very little about political *understanding*. It is surely necessary to distinguish between the recall of factual information and the conceptual understanding of political themes; being able to identify Nicolae Ceausescu or Adolf Hitler is clearly a different kind of phenomenon from being able to comprehend the meaning of totalitarianism. Political understandings (or at least political opinions) can to some extent be formed in the absence of political information, yet it is equally possible to develop a knowledge of political information without necessarily gaining anything by way of political understanding.

Finally, there are distinct limitations in the theoretical notion of 'socialization' itself. As I have argued, the dominant notion of political socialization is highly functionalist; it implies that children are simply passive recipients of adults' attempts to mould them into their allotted social roles. As James and Prout (1990) have argued, socialization theory implicitly regards childhood as a kind of rehearsal for adult life, a period in which children are gradually made to conform to adult norms. This approach ignores the extent to which children are active participants in constructing their own social lives and identities, and neglects the potential for resistance and negotiation that characterizes the process.

This implicitly normative approach has been criticized by some political socialization researchers themselves. R. W. Connell's (1971) early study is an important exception to the overall tendency in the field. Connell's approach is partly based on developmental psychology: he draws up a plan of the 'ages and stages' of children's political development, which reflects more general developmental shifts, for example in the growth of logical thinking and the ability to 'decentre'. However, Connell also draws attention to the affective and social aspects of political understanding, and directly challenges what he calls the 'production line approach' of political socialization research. While children are dependent upon political information that has already been processed by adults, Connell argues that they do not simply reproduce adult ideas. On the contrary, they are active agents, selectively appropriating what is available; socialization is not a passive process, but a matter of 'conscious creative activity' on the part of children themselves. At the same time, Connell emphasizes that the development of political beliefs should be regarded 'not as a mechanical function, but as a contingent, historical process': it is about traditions of thinking that are communicated across generations (for example, in the form of beliefs about threats of invasion by other nations). In a sense, Connell appears to affirm children's originality and simultaneously to deny it; children do indeed make meaning, but they do so under conditions that are not of their own choosing.

This more interpretivist approach has become increasingly common in studies of young people's understanding of politics (see Bhavnani, 1991; Stevens, 1982), and of television news (see Buckingham, 1996; Gillespie, 1995). The emphasis here is on the ways in which meanings are socially constructed and negotiated; and rather than judging young people in terms of their perceived inadequacies in relation to 'adult' norms, these studies attempt to engage with young people's interpretations on their own terms. Within political socialization research itself, several recent studies have echoed Connell's criticisms of functionalism. Ichilov (1990), for example, argues that political socialization research has largely been driven by a perceived need to socialize young people into political orientations that parents and adult society applaud; while DiRenzo (1990) suggests that socializing children only in terms of the demands of today's society may result in 'cognitive ambiguity' and anomie, as the roles and lessons of socialization are rendered obsolete in the face of accelerating social change. Here again, these arguments raise more fundamental questions about the changing nature of citizenship in contemporary societies that will be addressed in more detail in due course.

Learning from News

More detailed studies of viewers' 'information processing' of television news also appear to tell a different story from that of political socialization research. Here again, there has been very little research specifically concerned with children; although there have been a few experimental studies of the effects of different presentational formats – for example, the contribution of film (Drew and Reese, 1984), the role of editing (Davies *et al.*, 1985) and of story sequencing (Clifford *et al.*, 1995). These studies tend to confirm what has become almost a truism of research on adults' learning from news, namely that viewers understand and learn comparatively little from what they watch. The reasons for this are typically seen to involve a combination of textual factors (such as the brevity of news items, or the frequent lack of connection between visual and verbal material) and audience factors (such as viewers' lack of attention or knowledge of background information). In broad terms, research in this field directly challenges the idea that television news makes a significant contribution to the development of viewers' political knowledge and understanding.

Robinson and Levy (1986), for example, argue that television news 'has a rather dismal record as a medium of information'; a very small proportion of the stories that journalists themselves rank as most important are actually getting through to the audience. Viewers consistently nominate television as their 'main source' of information about the world, yet the evidence suggests otherwise:

> Watching the news may produce an experience of having been informed. But it is only a false sense of knowledge, for it is based only on a vaguely understood jumble of visual and auditory stimuli that leave few traces in long-term memory (1986: 17–18).

Likewise, Barrie Gunter (1987) finds that viewers quickly forget most of what they see, and that they often fail to comprehend it in the first place. In general, TV news appears to be more effective in imparting information about key personalities than in communicating details about the main stories;

even when viewers can recall what happened or who was involved, they are much less able to retain information about the causes and consequences of events. As Gunter and others (see Drew and Reeves, 1980) suggest, viewers typically invest little cognitive effort in viewing; they frequently fail to concentrate or pay attention, and are easily distracted.

However, as in the political socialization research, the question of how much – and indeed how and what – people *learn* from television news has tended to be conceived in very limited terms. 'Knowledge' tends to be measured here in terms of the recall of decontextualized factual information. As Robinson and Levy (1986) acknowledge, using measures of this kind almost inevitably leads researchers to underestimate levels of public knowledge (see also Gamson, 1992; Neuman *et al.*, 1992). Clearly, recall should not be confused with comprehension; the fact that viewers may not be able to remember particular items of factual information does not necessarily mean that they did not understand, or that they did not learn from, what they saw. Nor, indeed, does it mean that they have not been influenced (Philo, 1990).

Doris Graber (1988) offers a more complex account of how viewers understand news media, which is not limited to factual recall. Graber broadly confirms the conclusion that viewers' recall and comprehension of news are not impressive: viewers pay attention very selectively, are often confused and tend to forget much of what they have seen. Yet she also argues that viewers' failure to recall particular items of information does not necessarily mean that they have not learnt anything. They may forget the detail, but they may nevertheless have grasped the meaning.

Graber argues that people are generally 'cognitive misers' – that is, they opt for an approach to new information that they believe will involve the least mental effort on their part (cf. Just *et al.*, 1992). In their attempts to make sense of the vast amount of news material they encounter, viewers typically decide to pay attention to only a small amount of the available information. They gradually develop a backlog of information about political campaigns, for example, against which new information tends to act as a filler or refresher for their existing perceptions. From her analysis of news content, Graber argues that the pattern of news coverage is extremely stable, and as such is particularly susceptible to cognitive economies of this kind. Viewers recognize that most of what they see on the news is repetition, and they scan in order to select the information that is most relevant to them – an approach that Graber clearly feels is reasonable, given the fact that most people are unlikely to be more than peripherally involved in politics:

> From the standpoint of average Americans, haphazard news processing is quite satisfactory. Interest in news is comparatively low. Therefore it does not justify great expenditure in time and effort when things have a higher priority for the individual. But despite lukewarm interest in news, average Americans want to keep

informed because they have been socialized to consider this a civic responsibility. Many of them also want daily reassurance that they are not missing news items that might be personally significant. This combination of normative and personal pressures impels people to give at least cursory attention to news on a regular basis (1988: 251).

In some senses, of course, this might be seen to explain – and even to justify – the apathy that has been so widely criticized elsewhere; it implies that 'civic responsibility' is little more than a necessary ritual, and that making the minimum effort is an entirely reasonable response. Why, Graber asks, 'when shared stereotypes suffice', should people bother to 'go to the trouble of thinking independently' (1988: 214)?

Obviously, all these studies conceive of learning from news as an essentially psychological process. Their focus is on individual cognition, and on the internal 'processing' of information. Insofar as the social dimensions of learning are addressed, this is principally in terms of measurable demographic variables such as social class, gender and education, which are seen to 'influence' cognition from outside, as it were. Indeed, these variables are predominantly conceptualized here as 'individual differences'. Graber (1988) argues that such 'spurious variables' have very little explanatory significance; even factors such as educational attainment and interest in politics affect only the *quantity* of processing, rather than its basic nature. While Graber argues for the significance of individuals' 'belief infrastructures' – for example, their belief in tolerance, or their level of satisfaction with life – and their 'lifestyles', these are again seen to be inherently individual rather than social phenomena. Likewise, social interaction or interpersonal communication are conceptualized as variables that intervene between the screen and the viewer's mind; the complex interactions between media communication and interpersonal communication are largely ignored. Here again, there is a need for a more developed *social* theory of learning.

One further consequence of this cognitivist emphasis is the general neglect of the *emotional* dimensions of news – whether this relates to its ability to entertain, to reassure, to outrage or to disturb. Graber (1988), for example, tends to represent individuals as wholly rational beings, constantly making calculations about the most economical course of intellectual action – although she also acknowledges that people tend to use 'morselized' schemata, rather than integrating them into one overarching system of interrelated beliefs, and as such they may tend to be inconsistent. Yet news may possess a degree of credibility and 'power' that bypasses rational judgement, and that may derive partly from its use of images. To reduce viewers' responses to news to a kind of algorithm, with logical choices at each stage, as Graber's analysis tends to do, is surely to oversimplify the process.

Despite the limitations of these studies, and the differences of emphasis between them, they do paint a fairly consistent picture of the *extent* of viewers' learning from news. It is a picture that is outwardly quite at odds with the self-image of news journalism. At least on this evidence, news (and television news in particular) appears to be a very long way from fulfilling its historic mission of producing an informed citizenry – not only among young people, but also among the population at large.

Beyond Information

Research in this field thus points to a fundamental conundrum. Viewers themselves appear to look to television news as a significant source of information about the world and frequently claim that they trust it above any other source. Yet research consistently suggests that it is comparatively ineffective in actually communicating. So why, one might well ask, do people continue to watch it?

A related problem is raised when we compare the two kinds of research that have been considered in this chapter. Broadly speaking, the political socialization research suggests that television has an important – and for some researchers, pre-eminent – role in the development of young people's political understanding. Yet on the other hand, the research on learning from television suggests that even adults have difficulty in remembering and making sense of what they watch. So how can viewers be informed or influenced by something they do not even appear to understand?

One answer to both questions here might be that news creates a kind of *illusion* of being informed. A somewhat cynical interpretation of Graber's argument, for example, might suggest that viewers tune in to the news because it enables them to feel that they have discharged their responsibilities as citizens, albeit in a fairly disengaged and painless manner. In terms of influence, this would imply that news induces a generalized feeling of belonging and stability, and thereby reinforces the status quo – and that it can do so without us having to consciously assent to any particular position, or to make the effort to ingest complex factual information. News reassures us that the world is pretty much as it was yesterday, and that our place within it remains the same. From this perspective, news might be seen as a kind of social palliative – not a guarantee of active citizenship, but a substitute for it. Furthermore, it could well be argued that young people experience much less of a sense of 'civic responsibility' than adults, not least because of their relative lack of social power; and hence they are less likely to be motivated to watch the news in the first place.

While this conclusion is far from warranted – at least on the evidence reviewed thus far – it does raise the possibility that the 'effects' of news are not simply a matter of its status as *information*. As Robinson and Levy (1986) point out, much of the research in this field adopts a 'transportation theory' of communication, that defines news as simply a means of 'information transfer'. By contrast, they argue for a wider view of news as a generic cultural form and of news reception as a kind of ritual. Likewise,

Dahlgren (1986, 1992) offers an important critique of 'rationalistic' arguments about the reception of news, suggesting that this may leave 'central elements of the TV news process lingering in the shadows'. The key questions here, Dahlgren suggests, are to do with how news establishes its own credibility and coherence, and thereby creates 'forms of consciousness' and 'structures of feeling', rather than how accurately it communicates particular items of information. Instead of regarding the rhetorical elements of news as a distraction from its main purpose, we should be analysing how it uses 'fictional' tropes such as narrative and characterization, and the often stylized and symbolic features of its discourse (see also Hartley, 1996).

This is not to suggest that information is simply an irrelevance – although it is to imply that information cannot be seen as a given commodity that is simply contained in the text, and that is thereby transmitted or delivered to the viewer. On the contrary, the emphasis here is on how the text situates the viewer in relation to 'information' – or, perhaps more accurately, to do with how it defines and constructs the experience of 'becoming informed'. In other words, this perspective draws attention to the *pedagogy* of news – that is, to the social relations of teaching and learning it attempts to establish.

As I shall argue in the following two chapters, there are some dangers with this position. There is a risk of a kind of abstract formalism, that focuses on the operations of particular textual devices at the expense of considering how they represent the real world. The focus on news as a textual or discursive apparatus can lead to an unwarranted degree of generalization, where the different ways in which a particular issue is treated or framed come to be seen as mere refinements. On this account, 'news' becomes a unitary genre with unitary – and extremely general – effects. In the process, questions about 'information' – and hence about levels of public knowledge – may appear simply irrelevant.

Nevertheless, this more 'culturalist' approach to television news does help to explain some of the motivations of viewing, and the pleasures it involves. In terms of my broader interests here, it also suggests a rather different approach to questions about the nature of citizenship. Rather than attempting to measure the effectiveness of news in communicating political information, we should be asking how it enables viewers to construct and define their relationship with the public sphere. How do news programmes 'position' viewers in relation to the social order – for example, in relation to the sources of power in society, or in relation to particular social groupings? How do they enable viewers to conceive of the relations between the 'personal' and the 'political'? How do they invite viewers to make sense of the wider national and international arena, and to make connections with their own direct experience? How, ultimately, do they establish what it *means* to be a 'citizen'?

While acknowledging the limitations of a great deal of research on young people's relationship with news, it would be a mistake to abandon the central concern with information – or, more accurately, with political *understanding*. Of course, it is vital that researchers do not simply accept news journalism at its own self-estimation, as a more or less effective vehicle for transmitting 'facts'. The more general functions and pleasures of news viewing have undoubtedly been neglected, and it may be that productive alternatives to traditional news journalism will be more explicit about the 'cultural' dimensions of the genre, and adopt more 'popular' forms. Yet if news is to play a role in developing political understanding, it surely cannot abandon its responsibility to educate and to inform, and researchers should continue to assess how far that responsibility is being fulfilled.

Chapter Three

Popularity, Postmodernity and the Public Sphere

Advocates of news journalism have frequently proclaimed its grand educational and political mission. From this perspective, the news media are regarded as 'the vital arteries through which the information which is our democratic life-blood flows between rulers and ruled' (Golding, 1994). Far from being merely an entertaining pastime or an empty ritual, news is seen as nothing less than a fundamental guarantee of a healthy democracy.

Yet as we have seen, there is a widespread belief that the news media are no longer fulfilling their historic role of producing 'informed citizens'. We are, it is argued, entering a state of political apathy, for which television entertainment is principally to blame. Traditional notions of citizenship are no longer relevant, as viewers zap distractedly between commercial messages and superficial entertainment, substituting vicarious experience for authentic social interaction and community life. And while we adults may still possess the potential for civic responsibility and political participation, the new generation of television zombies is simply ignorant – and what is more, could not care less about the fact.

Such criticisms rest on an alternative conceptualization of the 'public sphere' as a domain of open, rational communication. Yet it is precisely this idea – and indeed, the classical notion of the informed citizen on which it rests – that has been widely questioned in recent years. This challenge arises not only from the charge that such notions are outdated or irrelevant to contemporary societies, but also from the accusation that they were never anything more than imaginary. Meanwhile, the distinction between the public and the private, and hence between the personal and the political, has been seen to reflect an implicit gender bias that has been systematically undermined by contemporary feminism.

This chapter provides an introduction to these debates, and their implications for news journalism. As we shall see, several critics have argued that news should actively embrace more popular, entertaining formats that will enable it to engage more directly with private or personal concerns, while others have seen this as merely symptomatic of the decline of democratic societies. Yet these debates implicitly raise more fundamental questions about the meaning of citizenship, and indeed of politics itself – questions which, I will argue, apply with particular force to young people.

The Decline of the Public Sphere

The most celebrated account of the decline of the bourgeois public sphere can of course be found in the work of the German theorist Jurgen Habermas (1962/1989). Habermas's work has been the subject of a great deal of explanatory and critical commentary (see Calhoun, 1992; Dahlgren, 1992, 1995; Peters, 1993), so I shall attempt only a brief summary of the argument here.

Habermas argues that the public sphere emerged in the eighteenth century as part of a series of historic shifts in relations between the public and the private. These begin with the decline in the 'representative' conception of publicity that was apparent in the Middle Ages, where political power was literally embodied in the figure of the lord and physically displayed before the people. Following the decline of the regal court and the emergence of parliaments and the judiciary, we eventually arrive at the foundation of 'civil society' in the eighteenth century. The bourgeois public sphere that emerges is, according to Habermas, 'a domain of private autonomy ... opposed to the state'. It is 'a forum in which the private people, come together to form a public, readied themselves to compel public authority to legitimate itself before public opinion' (1962/89: 25–6).

In the proliferation of coffee houses in eighteenth century London, Habermas finds a 'parity of the educated', in which 'rational critical public debate' emerges from the world of letters and steadily extends to the field of politics. Here, and in other institutions of the public sphere such as parliament, Habermas argues that debate serves as a way of mediating between the interests of potentially conflicting social groups – not only between the landed gentry and the moneyed classes, but also between the financial and manufacturing fractions of capital – on the basis of 'general and abstract laws'. The 'fourth estate' of the press plays a crucial role here as a vehicle for information and critical commentary on the actions of the state. Rather than delegating decision-making to parliament, the press enabled the public to become a 'permanent critical commentator' on political issues.

In the contemporary era, however, the potential for this kind of free, democratic communication has steadily declined. Habermas points to the commercialization of the media, the growing importance of advertising and public relations, and the concentration of ownership as evidence of a retreat from the civic role of the eighteenth century press. Culture, he argues, has become a commodity to be consumed: rational, critical debate has given way to the 'soft compulsion of constant consumption training' (1962/1989). The sphere of politics has become an extension of this consumer culture: political images are increasingly 'sold' to the 'undecided voter', a process that inevitably results in conformity. Parliament, for example, has been transformed from a locus of debate to a stage for government public relations. In the process, the public sphere has been 're-feudalised', or returned to a 'representative' conception of political power, in which image and the spectacle of publicity have replaced genuine debate. Like the media, the state itself increasingly addresses the public as consumers rather than as active citizens – or, to use C. Wright Mills's (1956) terms, as a 'mass' rather than a 'public'.

Habermas is pessimistic about the possibilities for a revival of a genuinely critical public sphere, yet he nevertheless holds it out as a desirable ideal. Unlike poststructuralist and postmodernist thinkers such as Foucault, Habermas regards critical discourse not as a disciplinary tool, but as an embodiment of public reason. In his more recent work (Habermas, 1987), he is keen to sustain the Enlightenment ideal of rational communication – the 'utopia of reason' – while recognizing that it was only ever partially achieved. The Enlightenment is, he argues, 'an incomplete project', not an illusory metanarrative.

Rethinking the Public Sphere

Among the extensive discussions and critiques of Habermas's account, one can identify four key points of debate. First, there is the issue of historical accuracy. As I have noted, public debates about the media are often chronically afflicted by notions of a 'golden age' – a period whose exact location is frequently left vague. While Habermas is not immune from this, his 'golden age' does at least have the advantage of historical precision – even if, as Corner (1995) points out, it reflects 'exceptionally limited socio-political conditions'. On the other hand, Habermas's characterization of contemporary society could be accused of a degree of romantic pessimism; he frequently lapses into the more grandiose rhetoric of 'mass society' theory, with little sense of a precise social or historical location. To equate the operation of political power in contemporary industrialized societies with that of the absolutist state of the Middle Ages, for example, or to imply a wholesale distinction between 'culture' and 'commerce', is to ignore the complexity of the historical evidence.

The second area of debate concerns the *exclusions* from Habermas's conception of the public sphere. The 'public' of Habermas's eighteenth-century ideal was in fact (as he himself acknowledges) highly restricted in terms of social class and gender: there were very limited degrees of basic literacy and political rights among the population at large. Yet these exclusions have more far-reaching manifestations, as feminist critics have pointed out. As Nancy Fraser (1989) argues, Habermas's fundamental distinction between public and private – or, in his later work, between 'system world' and 'life world' (Habermas, 1987) – is highly problematic. His failure to question the segregation of the (masculine) public sphere from the (feminine) private world of child-rearing and domestic labour leads Habermas to exaggerate the differences and to occlude the similarities between these two domains. This has particular implications in terms of media research, as van Zoonen (1991) indicates, through its privileging of rationalistic readings of the media and its suspicion of emotional response.

More recent work – including, to some extent, Habermas's own (see Habermas, 1987) – has pointed to the need for a more plural conception of public spheres, in which dissent and conflict are positively encouraged. The possibility, for example, of 'oppositional', 'informal' or 'proletarian' public spheres – of other possible networks for exchanging information or means of cultural expression – is crucial in the light of the increasing social hetero-geneity and globalization of contemporary societies (Dahlgren, 1991). Nevertheless, such arguments appear to leave intact the fundamental distinc-tion between public and private.

This leads on to a third problem with Habermas's account. As Peters (1993) points out, Habermas's conception of communication is a resolutely sober affair, that seems to be informed by a Puritanical notion of self-disclo-sure. There is no place in his model for the 'irrational' side of language, for rhetoric or narrative, nor indeed for aesthetics, for ceremony or for ritual – in fact, for precisely those elements that characterize popular cultural forms. 'Information', it would appear, can and should remain uncontami-nated by 'entertainment'. Like the self-legitimating rhetoric of mainstream news journalism, Habermas's account is ultimately based on an Enlighten-ment epistemology – on a belief in objective truth, in scientific rationality, and in knowledge as an unmediated representation of the world (Dahlgren, 1992). This fantasy of undistorted, authentic communication is one which, as Peters argues, 'leaves us both with an impoverished account of how communication in fact works and impedes the imagination of alternative forms of participatory media' (1993: 565). The possibility that political consciousness might be developed through means other than rational conver-sation – for example, through symbolic or emotional appeals – is one that Habermas regards with considerable suspicion.

The final point of contention here concerns Habermas's conception of the nature and effects of the media themselves. Despite the claims of some of his advocates (see Peters, 1993), Habermas's view of media effects is imbued with the 'cultural pessimism' often identified with the work of Adorno (see Adorno and Horkheimer, 1979). Thus, Habermas (1962/1989, Chapter 18) argues that the mass media have 'hollowed out' the authentic privacy of bourgeois family life and replaced it by 'pseudo-privacy'; that 'true interiority' has been replaced by a spurious form of 'familiarity'; that the media have undermined social interaction and destroyed critical debate; and that the pleasures they afford are merely 'inconsequential', easy and immediate rewards. Meanwhile, he bemoans the decline of book reading, which he sees as the guarantee of a genuine public sphere, as compared with the predigested, irrational, depoliticized domain constructed by popular journalism and the visual media.

The problems with this familiar lament have been widely rehearsed elsewhere, not only in terms of the lack of supporting evidence but also in terms of the gloomy determinism that informs it. The notion of audiences as passive dupes of media manipulation is one that cannot be sustained – although that is not to say that it should simply be replaced by a celebration of their autonomy and freedom. As Peters (1993) indicates, this kind of debate about media audiences is essentially a debate about democracy by other means – which accounts for its often sharply polarized political inflection. The basic terms of this debate – with its binary opposition between 'active' and 'passive' – hark back to debates about the nature of citizenship that begin in the late eighteenth century. As I shall argue, a more contemporary notion of citizenship will need to move beyond these rather absolutist distinctions.

Ultimately, Habermas's account of the decline of the public sphere is rather more than a work of historical sociology. On the contrary, it seeks to provide a theory of the production of subjectivity – an account of how society produces the subject position 'citizen', and hence defines what it means to participate in public life. As is clear from Habermas's account of the 'institutionalization of privateness' in the eighteenth-century nuclear family, this process is not a matter of inexorable determination at the hands of disembodied social forces; on the contrary, it is one in which individuals are actively and reflexively involved. Nevertheless, Habermas's 'ideal citizen' is conceived in highly reductive terms, as a rational public individual who dutifully exercises his civic responsibilities (gender intended), while eschewing such dubious practices as story-telling or entertainment. While it may provide a basis for a critique of existing social conditions and practices, therefore, Habermas's argument is ultimately both utopian and highly normative.

News and/as Popular Culture: Terms of Debate

These criticisms of Habermas's notion of the public sphere give rise to some significant questions, particularly about young people's apparent alienation from news media. What are the consequences of rejecting Habermas's rationalistic position, and his distinction between 'public' and 'private', particularly when it comes to news journalism? To what extent does this rejection necessarily lead to more participatory or democratic possibilities – or indeed, to more effective forms of political communication? And what potential might be offered here by newly emergent 'popular' forms of news journalism – forms which, as I have noted, appear to have a particular appeal for the young, and for others traditionally alienated from conventional forms of political discourse?

Debates on these issues are starkly polarized. On the one hand, there is a modified version of the Habermasian position. Colin Sparks (1988, 1991,

1992), for example, bemoans the growing separation between the 'quality' and the 'popular' press in Britain, and the former's decline in the face of increasing commercialization. The popular tabloids are accused of giving priority to 'the immediate issues of daily life' – most obviously in the form of so-called 'human interest stories' – at the expense of considering serious political issues. 'Entertainment' is gradually replacing 'information'. As the key institutions of the public sphere fall into decline, Sparks argues, 'the disparate pursuits of the individual come to occupy the space once filled by the citizen' (1991: 71). As societies diversify and audiences fragment, the sphere of the private individual is thus inexorably identified with political quietism and with the growth of ideological control.

On the other hand, John Fiske (1989, 1992) offers a direct challenge to the Habermasian approach, which is clearly influenced by feminist theory. Fiske characterizes the discourse of news as 'literate, homogenising and textually authoritarian' (1989: 194), and challenges the 'subjected, believing, reading relations' (1992: 59) that it attempts to foster. This leads him to focus attention on the ways in which this illusion of ideological control appears to break down. Thus, he describes how the 'realist' discourse of the news anchor attempts to 'repress' the chaos of 'unruly' events by clawing them back into the 'safe, socio-central sense of the studio' (1989: 154). For Fiske, such attempts will only ever achieve partial success, leaving a residual 'openness' that can be exploited by the 'undisciplined' reader, who can learn to 'treat news texts with the same freedom and irreverence that they do fictional ones' (1989: 177).

These two positions offer very different constructions of the role of the audience – and hence of the 'citizen' – which in turn reflect broader political differences. Fiske's 'ideal reader' is one who has little respect for the authority of news, and whose reading is led not by a sense of civic duty but by a hedonistic search for 'pleasure'. The tabloid news, he argues, produces a 'disbelieving subject'; its tone is one of 'sceptical laughter', its pleasure that of 'not being taken in' (cf. Bird, 1990, 1992). By contrast, Sparks's ideal reader is close to Habermas's rational citizen, eschewing entertainment and 'human interest' for an objective analysis of issues of public concern.

The crucial test of news, for Fiske, is not its informational accuracy, but the extent to which it enables readers to perceive its *relevance* to their everyday lives; and it is this quality of relevance that is the condition of pleasure and of popularity. Sparks is also concerned about the need for readers to establish relevance, but he ultimately sees the potential for political action not in 'everyday life' but in collective political organization. From this perspective, the role of the news is not to entertain but to 'provide the intellectual material for self-liberation' (Sparks, 1992: 42). By contrast, Fiske's conception of the political consequences of his ideal mode of viewing seems exceptionally vague and all-inclusive.

In different ways, both perspectives appear to ignore what is known about viewers' motivations for watching news in the first place. If Sparks's rationalistic view of news as a means of 'self-liberation' is (perhaps self-consciously) utopian, so too is Fiske's hedonistic approach. Despite Fiske's assertions, most viewers seek out the news at least partly in order to become informed about the world; and it is surely not unjustifiable to ask whether it is being effective in this respect. Fiske's argument that the news is 'essentially fictional' (Fiske, 1987: 308) not only trivializes the very real issues with which it is concerned, but also appears to neglect the reasons why people watch it in the first place.

Tabloid Culture: An Alternative Public Sphere?

Rather than simply bemoaning the loss of the bourgeois public sphere – or irreverently celebrating it – the need for viable contemporary alternatives remains. Where Fiske and Sparks seem to concur in this respect is in their recognition that 'serious' news – and indeed, the official discourse of 'politics' – largely fail to connect with the lived experiences of the majority. As I have noted, there is certainly evidence that these feelings of alienation apply particularly, and *increasingly*, to the young. Fiske describes this situation as follows:

> Historically, the people have been distanced from the power-bloc, their ability to influence its actions and policies minimised as the nation-state and the institutions within it become larger, more elaborated, more unknowable. It should not be surprising then, that this alienation results in popular apathy at the polling booth, and an absence of popular interest (in all meanings of the word, material and semiotic) in the official activities of the power-bloc. Nor should we be surprised that official knowledge puts the blame for such behaviour on the people ... (1992: 60).

Fiske's opposition here between 'the people' and 'the power-bloc' is perhaps unduly simplistic. Nevertheless, the most challenging part of his argument is the idea that 'apathy' should be seen not as evidence of systemic dysfunction, nor indeed of laziness or ignorance on the part of the population at large, but on the contrary as a phenomenon that is actively in the interests of the powerful, however much they might appear to deplore it.

Yet the question of how connections might be drawn between what Fiske terms the 'micro-politics' of everyday life and the 'macro-politics' of social structure and political action is a complex one. Fiske's answer is that we should concentrate on the 'micro' level, on what might be termed 'personal politics'; for it is in the struggle to gain power over one's 'immediate conditions of existence' that popular control can most effectively be exercised (Fiske, 1992: 58, 60). In terms of the media, Fiske's response is therefore to argue that news should become *more* 'popular' and *more* entertaining, rather than falling back on traditional notions of objectivity and social responsibility. Thus, he argues that news should take on some of the forms and strategies of tabloid journalism or soap opera – genres often identified with a female audience – as a means of engaging with readers' everyday lived experiences. The educational functions of news are, he argues, not the only criteria by which it should be judged. In this respect, his arguments are echoed by those of Katz (1993), discussed in Chapter 1: both imply that 'serious' news has a great deal to learn from the more informal, less 'monotonously reassuring' approaches of popular forms.

On the other hand, there are many who argue that this is very far from being a progressive development: the 'tabloidization' of the press or of television news is seen to be symptomatic of cultural decline, rather than of a burgeoning of popular political debate. The Times Mirror Center (1990) study, for example, offers a typical condemnation of the 'quasi-news' of *People* magazine and *A Current Affair*; and of course, 'serious' news journalists themselves are frequently keen to distinguish between their own work and that of their colleagues on the downmarket tabloids – even if there is in fact considerable overlap between them (Bird, 1992).

Analyses of these popular non-fictional forms have emphasized some of their political potential in this respect, although not without a degree of ambivalence. Connell (1991, 1992), for example, argues that the stories of the misfortunes of the rich and famous that are so frequently featured in the British tabloid press speak to a resentment against the dominant social order among their working-class readers. Yet he also suggests that this may simply reflect readers' desire to gain access to the benefits that that order makes available, rather than any more fundamental desire to challenge it. Likewise, other commentators have pointed to the combination of political cynicism and moral conservatism that characterizes many of these popular forms of news (Bird, 1992; Knight, 1989). Meanwhile, Livingstone and Lunt (1994) argue that television talk shows like *Oprah* and *Kilroy* may provide one model of an 'oppositional public sphere', in which experts and official voices are challenged and called to account. Yet the space that is opened up here is a highly bounded and regulated one, which may offer an illusion of participation rather than an opportunity for genuine critique.

Of course, the world of tabloid media culture is a very long way from the rational utopia of Habermas's public sphere. The implied viewer of *Oprah* or reader of *The National Enquirer* would have little in common with Habermas's public-spirited citizen – not least in terms of class or gender. Yet all these studies offer a productive challenge to narrow definitions of what counts as 'serious' journalism, and indeed as 'politics', and they question the view that the audience for popular forms is necessarily ignorant and culturally deprived. The Habermasian notion that audiences simply consume what they are offered and thereby lapse into an irrational, depoliticized state of mind, is effectively refuted.

Nevertheless, there is some doubt about the *consequences* of such audience 'activity', particularly in terms of political action or participation. In this respect, the potential of these new forms of popular journalism is distinctly limited. While there is undoubtedly a 'personal politics' in such material, it is clearly far from wholeheartedly progressive; and while there may even be a form of 'class politics' here, it is (crucially) one that is rarely articulated as such. *Oprah* or *The Sun* may well give voice to a degree of resentment against the powerful, but the crucial question is what they propose we should *do* about it.

The key point here is that 'micro-politics' should not come to be seen as a *substitute* for 'macro-politics'. On the contrary, the challenge is surely to find ways of building connections between the two. In this respect, Fiske's implied polarity between the 'educational' and the 'popular', between 'informing' people and making things 'relevant' to them, seems highly dubious. Certainly, it is hard to see how one might go about making things 'relevant' without simultaneously informing people about them, unless one wishes to remain on the level of instant punditry. Ultimately, the problem with much of this debate is that the issues come to be posed in such binary terms – as a matter of 'the people' versus the 'power bloc'; of 'activity' versus 'passivity'; and of 'popularity' versus the dead hand of 'seriousness'. Merely inverting the terms of these polarities does not enable us to address the problems that are at stake.

As John Corner (1995) has indicated, these debates cannot be carried out productively in the abstract, or simply in relation to texts. My own study suggests that Habermasian distinctions between information and entertainment, between reason and emotion, and between public and private, cannot meaningfully be sustained in the light of the complex ways in which audiences make sense of, and respond to, what they watch. Young people's interpretations of television news indicate that they do not simply adopt the position of the dutiful seeker of information or the deferential 'good citizen'. For some, their sense of exclusion and alienation from the adult sphere of political debate connects with a more general perception of their own powerlessness, to which a stance of boredom and deliberate ignorance may well represent a strategic response. At the same time, young people may be struggling to connect their everyday understandings with the official discourses of politics, albeit in ways that are not always successful. In this sense, the relationship between the 'personal' and the 'political' is not simply given, but discursively constructed by readers themselves.

Citizenship and the Spectre of Postmodernity

Habermas's account of the demise of the bourgeois public sphere clearly relates to a set of broader claims about the historical fate of modernity and of the Enlightenment project. The concept of 'postmodernity' has long since lost its fashionable gloss, yet it does provide a shorthand label for some very fundamental historical changes, many of which have occurred in the decades since Habermas's original analysis (see Harvey, 1989). These changes have led in turn to a widespread questioning of the fundamental epistemological and political assumptions on which traditional notions of citizenship are based. Again, this is not the place for a detailed discussion of such claims, yet any speculation about the future of citizenship cannot avoid taking account of the different forms of postmodernist analysis.

Broadly speaking, it is possible to identify two contrasting versions of 'postmodern citizenship'. The first is essentially pessimistic. Philip Wexler (1990), for example, provides a representative analysis of the 'death of citizenship' that explicitly draws on Habermas's critical response to postmodernity. Citizenship, he argues, had 'its best hour' in the eighteenth century, during the Enlightenment. According to Wexler, the postmodern 'semiotic society' has effectively 'killed the Enlightenment's modern individual, first by commodification, then by communication' (1990: 165). In the process, he argues, the sense of social belonging and personal autonomy that are the prerequisites for citizenship have disintegrated and passed away. All that remains is an illusory sense of self-determination and identity, achieved through passive consumption.

At the same time, however, Wexler detects a bifurcation between two classes, which adapt in different ways to the fragmentation induced by the semiotic society. The 'first' class is 'the so-called new middle class', while the second or 'other' class, is 'comprised of youth, poor and unemployed people, minorities, domestically laboring women and the aged' (1990: 171). While the first class engages in 'ego bolstering' or 'self-centered narrative reconstitution', drawing on a range of cultural resources in order to construct an orderly life, the other class looks primarily to television as a form of compensation for the decline in solidarity:

> The new middle class watches television, but television is not its first life. The 'other' class lives from television, which repays it by surrendering the capacity for attention that it produces. Here, the ego is more splattered than bolstered, drawing its strength not only from a direct dynamic relation to television, but through videated binding with its commodified television family of stars (1990: 172).

There are certainly parallels between Wexler's lament for the decline of 'solidarity' and the more conservative perspectives of commentators such as Putnam (1995) and Hart (1994), discussed in Chapter 1. Nevertheless, Wexler clearly implies that there is no going back to a past golden age or to the basic assumptions of the Enlightenment model. Albeit in highly general terms, he points to the need for a form of 'semiotic citizenship' which is appropriate to changed circumstances, and which will build upon the new forms of collective identity that have emerged, for example in the women's movement. Whether such new ideas of citizenship will simply be absorbed into the 'superficiality' of postmodern culture is a question he leaves open.

Wexler's pessimistic analysis of 'postmodern citizenship' can be contrasted with the more optimistic approach of other commentators. Instances of this can be found in a broad range of disciplines, from cultural studies (see Collins, 1989) and social psychology (see DiRenzo, 1990; Gergen, 1991) to political science (see Gibbins, 1989). From this perspective, the erosion of old structures and the loosening of traditional bonds is seen to give rise not so much to a state of instability and anomie, as to new opportunities for identity formation. Such accounts point to the growing diversity of public spheres, resulting in part from the advent of new media and communications technologies. Far from guaranteeing homogeneity, postmodern culture is seen to provide a proliferation of new values, lifestyles and social movements. Far from 'depoliticizing', it offers a new, more pluralistic, political culture, which is anarchic, stylized and essentially ironic (Gibbins, 1989). Far from enforcing consumerism and commodification, it has paved the way for a 'post-materialist' politics, in which new social movements have taken the place of old class and party alignments (Inglehart, 1977), and consumption and lifestyle have become important domains of political action (Nava, 1992).

These arguments relate in turn to much broader debates about the nature of citizenship in capitalist democracies. Thus, some authors have appropriated T.H. Marshall's 'classic' theory of citizenship, arguing that there has been a gradual extension of universalistic norms of social membership and participation, for example, in the case of the British welfare state (Barbalet, 1988; Marshall, 1977; Turner, 1986, 1993). From this perspective, postmodernity may represent a continuing development of this process, breaking down traditional forms of hierarchy and fostering new forms of cultural pluralism (Turner, 1994). On the other hand, such arguments clearly neglect the growing material inequalities in many democratic societies, not least in the sphere of information and culture (see Murdock and Golding, 1989).

John Hartley (1996) provides a vindication of popular journalism in these terms, which directly challenges the Habermasian account of the decline of the public sphere. According to Hartley, old distinctions between public and private, male and female, fact and fiction, politics and culture, news and entertainment, need to be fundamentally rethought in the context of the postmodern 'mediasphere'. Hartley points to the significance of the popular press around the time of the French revolution, and argues that contemporary journalism is still 'riding the wave' of democratization that was set in motion at that time. He also seeks to align popular journalism with new social movements such as feminism and environmentalism – all of which, he suggests, have their origins in what used to be seen as the private sphere. Thus, for example, the *Vogue* special edition on Nelson Mandela is seen not as a dangerous aestheticization of politics, but as a fruitful challenge to outmoded distinctions between public and private. Hartley's optimistic view of the extension of citizenship in postmodernity provides a direct contrast with the gloomy pessimism of Wexler, although he remains extremely vague about how these new forms of political consciousness – and particularly of political *action* – might arise from the practice of 'popular readership'.

Finally, there are those who regard the whole idea of citizenship with considerable suspicion. Toby Miller (1993), for example, is attracted by the radical anti-essentialism that is entailed in the notion of postmodern citizenship, with its emphasis on the diversity, plurality and fluidity of social identities. Yet he also questions the notion of citizenship itself, on the grounds that it inevitably positions the self in public terms, as a member of a 'collective social body' that must necessarily be bound by the 'general will'. In this respect, Miller argues, citizenship must inevitably function as a 'technology of subjection', a disciplinary apparatus, that denies cultural difference in the interests of a singular, apparently unifying ideal of national identity and civic virtue. Education, for example, seeks to induce a sense of 'ethical incompleteness' that individuals must strive to overcome through forms of self-regulation (Hunter, 1994). In this way, Miller argues, the citizen is produced as a 'well-tempered subject', 'a polite and obedient servant of etiquette, within limited definitions of acceptable behaviour'. On this account, citizenship comes to be seen not as a matter of free democratic participation, but on the contrary as a means whereby governments continue to regulate populations, albeit in the name of the public good.

Postmodern Citizenship: Limits of the Evidence

Despite their differences, the contrasting positions outlined here share the view that we are living through a process of fundamental qualitative change, in which traditional notions of citizenship have effectively been surpassed. Yet as Gilbert (1992) argues, both advocates and opponents of postmodernism tend to exaggerate its novelty in their choice of issues and exemplars, and to underestimate the continuing relevance of traditional forms of culture and political activity. These questions are highly significant in evaluating postmodernist accounts of the role of the media – which are inextricably entailed both in optimistic and pessimistic analyses of postmodern citizenship.

In practice, the extent to which the media are seen as a symptom or as a cause of these wider developments often remains unclear, and there are significant dangers in the attempt to 'read off' broader changes – for example, in epistemology or identity or society – from the analysis of media forms. In the case of media audiences, postmodernist theory seems to have sanctioned a return to the globalizing rhetoric of Adorno and his colleagues – a rhetoric that transparently fails to account for the diverse ways in which audiences read and appropriate media forms. Wexler's absurdly hyperbolic account of television viewing (p. 30 above) is a typical case in point. On the other hand, Hartley's enthusiastic advocacy of 'popular readership' is equally lacking in evidence about real readers.

The claims for generational change here are also open to debate. As Gilbert (1992) points out, the defining forms of 'postmodern culture' – MTV, for example, or digital technology – are characteristically identified with the young. Yet the differences between these forms and those which preceded them may be little more than superficial, particularly if we take account of how they are interpreted and used. Likewise, the evidence that young people possess fundamentally different political or cultural values from their parents – or, more pertinently, that those differences tend to be *lasting* – is highly questionable. The generally celebratory approach that has characterized sociological studies of youth culture, for example, has tended to emphasize more spectacular forms of resistance to adult authority and to underestimate the considerable conservatism of the young (Fornas and Bolin, 1995). Similarly, the claim that young people's political beliefs or lifestyle choices are less 'materialist' than those of their parents, or that well-established forms of social differentiation have disappeared in a flowering of new cultural identities, has been significantly questioned (Reimer, 1989).

The Limits of 'Politics'

Clearly, there is a need for much more systematic research on the implications of these changes, both for young people's relationships with the news media and with the sphere of political debate. If, as postmodern theorists tend to suggest, young people are growing up amid radically different conceptions of time and space, or with different conceptions of the relationship between the public and the private, to what extent is this leading to radically altered notions of what *counts* as 'politics' in the first place?

In a detailed empirical study of working-class youth in Britain, Kum-Kum Bhavnani (1991) finds substantial evidence of alienation from politics as conventionally defined. Yet, as she indicates, young people's views about issues such as unemployment, racism and marriage could be seen as at least implicitly 'political'. Bhavnani therefore argues for a more inclusive notion of politics, that is not confined to the actions of governments or political parties. Most critics would probably accept that the activities of new social movements are 'political', although Bhavnani also argues for a broader definition of politics 'which includes daily experience'. Politics, she argues, 'can be defined as the means by which human beings regulate, attempt to regulate and challenge with a view to changing unequal power relationships' (1991: 52).

While it does represent a potentially valuable shift, this more inclusive definition also raises some significant questions. In practice, there is likely to be significant variation in what individuals themselves conceive of as 'political' – or indeed as 'public' or 'private'. What researchers or political activists conceive of as 'political' in the experiences of ordinary people may not be the same as what those people themselves would see as 'political'. Thus, the emphasis on the private and the personal that characterizes much popular journalism can indeed be seen as political, if we choose to interpret it in this way. The question that remains unanswered by much of the analysis considered in this chapter is whether ordinary readers or viewers do so, too.

Ultimately, much of this debate turns on the familiar feminist adage 'the personal is political'. I would argue that 'personal' issues can *become* political by virtue of the discourses in which they are framed and defined – and particularly by virtue of discourses that define *individual* experiences in terms of wider *collective* or *social* categories. In other words, the same actions or experiences can be defined as 'political' or as 'not political', depending upon how they are interpreted. Of course, the characteristic strategy of many new social movements is one in which issues previously seen as personal are effectively redefined or reframed as political. Yet the personal is not *automatically* political. On the contrary, it only *becomes* political insofar as it is consciously *defined* as political, and that process of definition is inevitably one of contest and struggle.

While a more inclusive definition of politics is thus of considerable value, it is positively dangerous if it leads merely to the banal conclusion that 'everything is political'. Simply to celebrate the domain of the personal and the subjective, as though it were inherently and inevitably political – as seems to be implied by some forms of postmodernist or feminist theory – is little more than a recipe for political quietism. Ultimately, we need to sustain meaningful distinctions between the 'personal' and the 'political', or the 'private' and the 'public', if we wish to avoid lapsing into political incoherence. The central *educational* issue remains that of building connections between these domains – between the 'micro-politics' of everyday life and the 'macro-politics' of political institutions and of collective political action. It is this educational dimension that is my fundamental concern in the following chapters.

Chapter Four

Creating Citizens: News, Pedagogy and Empowerment

In recent years, television news seems to have been undergoing a crisis of confidence. Faced with declining audiences and increasing competition for ratings, the balance between 'information' and 'entertainment', always an unsteady one, has begun to shift. Thus, we have seen the emergence of 'tabloid television', 'reality TV' and audience–participation talk shows, and increasing experimentation with traditional news formats. For producers, there are significant questions here about how to engage and retain the audience, while simultaneously explaining complex events at an appropriate level. Yet these developments in the genre also pose more fundamental questions about how television addresses and constitutes the viewer as a citizen and as a potential participant in the public sphere of social and political debate.

These questions and dilemmas are even more acute in relation to young people, and to news programmes produced specifically for them. Where adults may retain some sense of civic duty – a sense of their responsibility as 'good citizens' – and hence some degree of motivation to keep up with the news (Graber, 1988), children and young people may experience no such impulses. To a greater extent perhaps than adults, they have to be enticed to watch. They have to be entertained as well as informed, in ways that reflect their existing enthusiasms and cultural experiences. They have to be given more of the 'background' in order that they can understand the 'foreground' of news events. All along the line, assumptions have to be made about their interests, their experiences, their existing knowledge and their cognitive abilities, as distinct from those of adults. Yet the evidence would suggest that, as in children's television more broadly, such assumptions are typically made on the basis of professional intuition rather than sustained research (Wartella, 1994). For all these reasons, producing news for young people is bound to be a difficult and problematic process.

The earliest television news programmes specifically designed for children and young people date back to the 1950s, when the BBC first screened *Children's Newsreel*. More contemporary examples of the genre began in the 1970s, with the advent of CBS's *In the News* in the USA and the BBC's *Newsround* in the UK. While several programmes have come and gone since that time, many major national networks have at some point provided a news or news magazine programme for the younger audience. In the UK, for example, Channel 4 currently offers *First Edition*, a weekly bulletin for schools, while *Newsround* continues as one of the BBC's longest-running children's programmes. Both the BBC and Channel 4 also produce access programmes for the younger audience, in the form of *As Seen on TV* and *Wise Up*, which regularly feature issues in the news. There are equivalent programmes in a number of other European countries, including Holland, Austria and Germany. Meanwhile, in the more commercial context of the USA, the children's channel Nickelodeon offers *Nick News*, which is also syndicated to numerous local network stations, and CNN offers a daily edition of *Newsroom*, which (like *Nick News*) is also provided commercial-free as part of the Cable in the Classroom scheme. In addition, 40 per cent of US schools subscribe to Channel One, a service that provides a daily bulletin of news and commercials and is apparently watched by a captive audience of 12 million young people.

Recent legislation in this field (the Broadcasting Act in the UK and the Children's Television Act in the USA, both passed in 1990) actively requires the provision of 'educational' and/or 'informative' programming for children – which, at least in the USA, has historically been in short supply (Kunkel, 1993). Nevertheless, as I have noted, the position of factual programming for children continues to be under threat, not least as a result of the proliferation of new channels, the growth of commercialism and the governmental commitment to deregulation (see Blumler, 1992; Buckingham, 1995b).

In this chapter, I provide a comparative analysis of five of these productions, namely *Newsround*, *First Edition*, *Nick News*, *Channel One News* and *Wise Up*. With the exception of *Newsround*, it was from these programmes that extracts were drawn for the audience research reported in Chapters 6 and 7. While I do focus to some extent on content – that is, on *what* these programmes are attempting to teach – my central emphasis is on *how* they teach, on their pedagogy. My concern is thus not so much with issues of representation or bias, which have traditionally been the focus of research on news, as with how these programmes address and thereby attempt to position their viewers (cf. Buckingham, 1987a, 1987b, 1995a). My analysis therefore focuses on the programmes' implicit assumptions about their viewers – about what young people are, and about what they should be. As I shall indicate, these assumptions are manifested not only in the selection of content – and hence in the nomination of topics which young people are (or should be) interested in; but also in the programmes' formal devices, such as the roles of presenters, the mise-en-scène and the use of narrative. In this latter respect, my analysis owes more to work on non-fictional forms in Film Studies (see Nichols, 1981; Stam, 1983) than it does to more conventional social science perspectives.

Following an outline of the five programmes, I focus on three key points of comparison. I consider first how the programmes define the interests of young people, or what is seen to be appropriate for them, through their selection and framing of areas of content. Secondly, I look at how the programmes address and target their audience through the use of visual and verbal 'language'. Finally, I consider questions of agency and voice: whose voices are heard within these programmes, and how are they sanctioned to speak? To what extent do these programmes seek to empower young people as active citizens?

While comparing these programmes with each other, I am also implicitly comparing them with 'adult' news – and perhaps in the process, I am bound to represent 'adult' news as more homogeneous than it actually is. Nevertheless, my main concern here is to define what marks these programmes out as *young people's* news – that is, as texts specifically designed for this audience. A central assumption here is that the *child* or the *young person* is itself a relative, not an absolute, category, which is defined partly in relation to the *adult*. These programmes do not reflect some timeless or objective nature of childhood, or some pre-given definition of young people's interests and concerns. On the contrary, it is through the discursive relationships between adults and children – not least on television – that the subject position of 'the child' is constructed and negotiated (see Buckingham, 1995a; Rose, 1984). These news programmes are, in this respect, merely one of the many arenas in which this ongoing definition of childhood and youth is rehearsed and accomplished.

News for Young Audiences: Five Case Studies

The five programmes I consider in this chapter derive from very different institutional contexts, each of which embodies a distinctive construction of the child audience. The programmes target slightly different (though overlapping) audiences; and there are also significant differences between them in terms of both form and content. In each case, I have analysed at least five hours of broadcasts, taped during the autumn and winter of 1995 (*Newsround, Nick News, Channel One News*) and during the spring and autumn of 1997 (*First Edition, Wise Up*).

Newsround is a ten-minute news bulletin, broadcast thrice weekly by the BBC during its weekday children's sequence at around 5.00 p.m. The programme reaches an average of 18 per cent of 4–15 year olds, although its primary target audience is in the 7–12 age group. Each edition contains an average of five major items, generally in the form of a correspondent's film report; and these are supplemented by a 'Newswrap' containing three or four shorter stories. The show uses a single presenter, and of the current regulars, one is male and one is female.

Newsround belongs to the established tradition of British public service broadcasting. While it has not quite attained the 'flagship' status of the magazine programme *Blue Peter*, its longevity and its central location in the children's schedules do lend it a distinctly official air, not unlike that of the mid-evening news. At the same time, *Newsround* could be seen as an instance of a 'modernized' public service. Like *Blue Peter*, it has worked hard to throw off the legacy of paternalism: it consciously attempts to address children on their own level and to reflect what it perceives to be contemporary children's concerns (Buckingham, 1995a; Home, 1993). Nevertheless, the programme routinely tackles hard news stories, and has not avoided controversial issues. In the sample of programmes analysed here, for example, topics included ecology and conservation, the budget, the dangers of the drug ecstasy, the war in Bosnia, and the death of Israeli Premier Rabin.

First Edition is a 15-minute weekly news bulletin produced for use in schools and screened in Britain on Channel 4. Usually presented by Jon Snow, one of the regular newsreaders on Channel 4 evening news, it is described as being aimed at 8–12-year-olds, although its target audience would appear to be somewhat older than that of *Newsround*. Each edition contains an average of three items, which means that they are significantly longer than those on *Newsround*. Items are generally presented by specialist correspondents from Channel 4's evening news, although young people are occasionally used as presenters of access-type reports. Each edition also features a studio interview, in which an adult 'expert' is questioned by a young guest interviewer.

As a schools programme, *First Edition* is somewhat more narrowly 'serious' in its content and presentation than *Newsround*. While it does feature occasional items concerned with young people's hobbies or leisure interests, its agenda is largely drawn from topical issues in the news. Among the sample analysed here, for example, there were stories on the Louise Woodward case, the 1997 election, the handover of Hong Kong and the campaign to ban fox hunting, all of which featured extensively in the mainstream news. At least one item each week is supplemented with further information published in the education supplement of the *Guardian* newspaper.

Wise Up is also screened by Channel 4, and appears weekly in the middle of its children's sequence on Sunday mornings. Like *Nick News* (discussed below), it is not strictly a news programme, although it routinely features issues that are covered in the mainstream news; as such, it provides an interesting contrast with the other programmes considered here, particularly in terms of its style. *Wise Up* is essentially a children's access programme: young people (mostly teenagers) devise, script and present the items, and have some say in the editing. Each show lasts 25 minutes, and contains an average of nine or ten items. Some are comparatively short, particularly regular items such as '29 seconds of fame' (which features new young bands or rappers), or 'vox pop' items in which young people describe their best homework excuses or the worst food they have ever eaten. The more serious items tend to be longer: among those featured in my sample were items on racism in the police, youth crime, alcoholism and the under-funding of schools.

Wise Up is often promoted as an innovative form of children's broadcasting, and has won several industry awards. In fact, it does have precedents: both the BBC's children's access show *As Seen on TV* and BBC2's *Teenage Video Diaries* pre-date it. Nevertheless, *Wise Up* is often seen as an instance of Channel 4's distinctive remit to innovate and to serve minorities (although in fact it is one of the Channel's few home-produced children's programmes). Its producer and commissioning editor have described it as a means of 'giving children a voice' (see Buckingham *et al.*, 1999: Chapter 6); as we shall see, this often involves them directly challenging the authority of adults.

Nick News is a weekly news magazine programme which has been broadcast by the cable channel Nickelodeon in the US since 1991. It airs at 8.00 p.m. on a Sunday evening, although it is repeated on Saturday mornings on Nickelodeon and early on weekday mornings on other networks. Following the implementation of the Children's Television Act (1990), which required stations to provide 'educational' programming for children, the show was hastily purchased by stations covering more than 90 per cent of US markets. *Nick News* has approximately the same target age group as *Newsround*, although it tends to be skewed more towards the older end. Each half-hour edition typically includes five segments: two more 'serious' items, generally of around 6–7 minutes each, are balanced with a 'lighter' item of a similar length (often with a cultural or musical theme) and two shorter items, of which one is generally a viewer's 'video letter'. All items are in the form of film reports, although they use participants' voice-over rather than correspondents in the manner of *Newsround* or *First Edition*. The items are introduced and linked by Linda Ellerbee, a former network newscaster, and the show is produced by her company, Lucky Duck Productions.

Nickelodeon has been a triumph of niche marketing; despite the fact that it is not available in all homes, it accounts for over one third of all children's viewing in the US. In its promotional material, advertising and programming, Nickelodeon is imbued with a rhetoric about the 'empowerment' of children: it announces itself as a 'kid zone', set against the boring world of adults (Kinder, 1995; Laybourne, 1993). As we shall see, this apparently 'child-centred' ethos also informs *Nick News*. Like *Newsround*, *Nick News* has not avoided controversial issues or 'hard' news; although as a weekly programme (and one that is frequently repeated) it is much less able to be topical. In the sample analysed here, there were items on nuclear war, affirmative action, militia groups, the war in Bosnia and the wider issues raised by the O. J. Simpson murder trial.

Finally, *Channel One News* is a ten-minute daily news show which is transmitted via satellite to US schools. The show is automatically recorded and then used later in the day, often in a homeroom or tutorial period. Schools who subscribe to Channel One are given around $50,000 worth of 'free' equipment, including the satellite receiving dish, a monitor for every classroom and cabling for the entire school. The 'catch', of course, is the advertising: each bulletin carries an additional two minutes of commercials for products specifically targeted at the teen market, such as soft drinks, snack food and sportswear. Subscriber schools sign a contract which guarantees that the programme will be shown to 90 per cent of students on 90 per cent of the days on which the school is in session. While viewing is thus effectively compulsory, the evidence on whether students actually pay attention to the show is somewhat more equivocal; and there is little indication that *Channel One News* is actively *used* by a significant number of teachers (see Buckingham, 1997).

Channel One has been extremely controversial. Originally produced by the Whittle Corporation, which specialized in wholly advertising-funded media, it has since been bought by the publishing company K–III, itself owned by RJR Nabisco. From its inception, the channel has been a significant money-spinner; it is currently estimated that its income from advertising is over $150 million each year. For its critics, Channel One has been seen as a symbol of the increasing commercialization of education; it is often described as a 'Faustian bargain', whereby schools have sold their educational souls to capital. While the majority of educational opinion and academic commentary has been opposed to it, the service has nevertheless been taken up in over 40 per cent of US middle and high schools, and the rate of contract renewal is extremely high.

While much of the debate around Channel One has focused on the issue of advertising, there has been comparatively little attention to its news content – although there have been some contradictory findings about its effectiveness in teaching current affairs (Buckingham, 1997). *Channel One News* itself is comparatively serious and even conventional. A typical bulletin contains three or four main stories, most of which would be categorized as 'hard' news: in my sample of programmes, there were several stories about national politics (events such as the US government shutdown in 1995) and international affairs (such as the war in Bosnia). In addition, there are 'specials', some based on investigative reports (for example, on the market in nuclear materials in the former Soviet Union) while others feature interviews with high-profile national political figures (such as the former Speaker of the House of Representatives, Newt Gingrich). The show is targeted at students from eleven upwards, and hence at an older age group than the other programmes considered here.

Constructing the Viewer: Content and Framing

Selections of Content

One obvious difference between these programmes is in terms of their relationship to conventional 'news values' – that is, the criteria that are used in selecting what *counts* as news in the first place. For example, research suggests that mainstream news typically privileges the doings of eminent people over those of ordinary people, the public over the private, and the novel event over the less spectacular, longer-term development (Galtung and Ruge, 1965). Each of these programmes diverges from these values to a greater or lesser degree, in ways which reflect their implicit assumptions about their audience.

Of the five, *Channel One News* and *First Edition* stay closest to the mainstream news agenda. *Channel One News* routinely features developments in national party politics, for example. Stories about the economy, crime and welfare are also prominent, and its coverage of foreign affairs is also more extensive and in-depth than the other programmes. The programme has its own foreign correspondents (covering issues such as the rise of Islamic fundamentalism), although it also uses footage and correspondents from the ABC network. *First Edition* also features stories about party politics, the environment and crime, and it occasionally covers major foreign stories such as the dispute over weapons inspections in Iraq. However, both programmes also feature stories that are seen to be of particular relevance to their audience. In the case of *Channel One News*, these included items on drug testing in schools, and extended investigative reports on gang violence and on tobacco companies' targeting of teenage smokers; while *First Edition* tends to focus more on school, with items about bullying, school funding and military cadets.

The comparison between these programmes and *Newsround* is particularly striking. While *Newsround* does cover some 'political' events, its coverage of broader social issues such as welfare, crime, social conflict and the economy is distinctly limited (with the possible exception of health). By contrast, the category which emerged as by far the largest was that of ecology: in my sample, one fifth of the stories were concerned with issues such as animal welfare, conservation, nuclear testing and pollution. Such stories were completely absent from my sample of *Channel One News* and featured only intermittently on *First Edition*. Also notable here is a high level of coverage of areas that correspond to subjects on the school curriculum, particularly science and history – for example, in stories about new discoveries or archaeological investigations. Finally, *Newsround* also places a significant emphasis on what are traditionally considered to be 'children's interests' (or, perhaps more accurately, *boys'* interests): in my sample of programmes, there were numerous stories on space exploration, volcanoes and earthquakes, and natural mysteries (such as the Bermuda Triangle or a Welsh version of the Loch Ness Monster). In these latter respects, *Newsround* appears to resemble those 'improving' publications often directed at the young in earlier decades, such as *The Boy's Own Paper* or *Look and Learn*.

As weekly magazine programmes, *Nick News* and *Wise Up* are predictably less concerned with topical events, and they also veer more towards 'softer' and more 'personal' news stories. While all the other programmes tend to follow the structure of conventional news bulletins, moving from serious to lighter items, and often ending on a humorous story, these programmes adopt a more mixed approach.

In the case of *Nick News*, this is fairly formulaic: two longer serious items are interspersed with lighter ones (and, of course, with advertising breaks). These lighter items include a short humorous feature entitled 'Who's in Charge Here?', which gently mocks the weird and wonderful behaviour of adults (a man who has a dog as best man at his wedding, a group of sky-diving Elvis Presley impersonators); and longer items, generally on sports, pop music or dance, which often focus on 'positive images' of African-Americans. In terms of the more serious items, ecology emerged as a significant theme, although nowhere near as prominently as in *Newsround*; there were also reports on domestic social issues (affirmative action, the debate over welfare, gun control, armed militias) and international politics (the Zapatistas in Mexico, the war in Bosnia). There were also several instances of what the show's producer, Mark Lyons (1995), referred to as 'empowerment' stories – that is, stories featuring young people actively tackling social problems: in my sample, these included stories about an organization for children who were not receiving adequate child support, and about children campaigning to prevent child labour.

Wise Up contains a broader range of items and is even further removed from the conventional news agenda. Like *Nick News*, it has regular lighter slots, such as 'Knowing me, knowing you', in which teenage couples undergo a test of how well they know each other, or 'Home truths', in which the young presenters complain about the embarrassing behaviour of friends or family members. Some of the more serious items also have a distinctly personal focus: two girls complain about the pressure on girls to wear 'training bras', while another argues in favour of virginity. Others are concerned with young people as consumers, as in items about 'rip off' sticker albums or school dinner prices. In some instances, these stories take on a more political inflection, as in the case of an item about the low wages paid to the workers who manufacture sports shoes. Even at its most serious, *Wise Up* is primarily concerned with political and social issues that directly pertain to young people, such as youth crime, police harassment and education funding. Among my sample, there are only a couple of items about events overseas, and only three which directly concern 'politics' as traditionally defined – that is, the actions of political parties or of government. (In these respects, the two items from *Wise Up* discussed in Chapter 7 are somewhat exceptional.)

Of course, these differences of emphasis – in effect, of 'news values' – are partly a reflection of generic differences, and of the context of production. *Wise Up* does not present itself as 'news', even if some of its content does relate to issues covered on mainstream news; and despite its title, *Nick News* is essentially a news magazine rather than a bulletin. As weekly shows, which are syndicated or repeated, these programmes are bound to be less immediately topical, and as longer programmes, they have to structure their material in a different way in order to retain their audience.

Yet these differences – both between the programmes themselves, and between them and the 'adult' news – also raise some significant questions about how news itself is conventionally defined. This is partly a matter of the relationship between the personal and the political. *Wise Up* in particular is much more concerned with the private sphere – with family life, relationships and personal problems. It largely neglects the public sphere of party politics and government. On the other hand, it is centrally concerned with the 'identity politics' of gender and ethnicity, both at the level of social relationships and in terms of cultural expression, and it also seeks to draw out the 'political' dimensions of the 'personal' – for example, in areas such as consumerism, fashion and music. As we shall see in more detail below, it also explicitly espouses a form of youth politics, focusing on issues that specifically affect young people, and taking their part in their encounters with adult authority. These dimensions are also present to a lesser degree in *First Edition* and *Nick News*.

In comparison, *Newsround* and *Channel One News* are much closer to mainstream news. For these programmes, and to a large extent for *First Edition* also, 'news' is effectively a given; their primary aim is simply to make it accessible. In the process, they do not radically depart from what is seen to *count* as news in the first place: at most, they seek to provide a young person's angle on the mainstream news agenda. Nevertheless, there are some significant differences of emphasis here, both in terms of *what* is covered and in terms of *how* it is covered; these too reflect some quite specific assumptions about young people's interests and concerns.

Episodic and Thematic Frames

The producers of children's news have to make some hazardous assumptions about the existing knowledge of their audience. Research on adult news suggests that producers typically overestimate what viewers already know about a given topic (Robinson and Levy, 1986), and that they often fail to provide adequate background in order to contextualize and explain news events (Iyengar, 1991). While this is certainly a problem with adult viewers, it requires particular care in relation to children.

Shanto Iyengar (1991) makes a useful distinction here between 'episodic' and 'thematic' frames. Episodic frames are oriented around specific events or individual case studies, often of a topical nature. By contrast, thematic frames 'place public issues in some more general or abstract context', providing more background information about general outcomes or conditions. Iyengar finds that mainstream TV news is heavily dominated by episodic frames: what we mostly see are reports of decontextualized, one-off events, with little attempt at background explanation. According to his research, this episodic approach leads viewers to make individualistic rather than societal attributions of responsibility for social problems.

By contrast, thematic framing is much more prominent in all the programmes analysed here. While this might be expected with a news magazine like *Nick News*, or an access programme like *Wise Up*, it is also the case with *Channel One News*, *First Edition* and (to a lesser extent) with *Newsround*. Statistical measures may be somewhat misleading with a comparatively small sample of programmes, but in the case of *Channel One News*, only one quarter of the stories could be categorized as mainly episodic, and of these half were shorter items. Likewise, in the case of the longer items on *Newsround* (as opposed to the one- or two-sentence stories in the Newswrap segment), only slightly more than half were mainly episodic; while only three stories on *First Edition* (two of which concerned the Louise Woodward case) could be described in this way.

One obvious problem here is that many news stories combine these two approaches; although what is particularly notable about these programmes is how they frequently move from an episodic introductory section to a more thematic explanation. For example, both *Newsround* and *Channel One News* covered the signing of the Israeli–PLO peace treaty in November 1995; but both used this as the introduction for an historical explanation of the background to the conflict, using archive footage going back to the foundation of the state of Israel – knowledge that most producers of 'adult' news would probably assume their viewers already possess (whether correctly or not).

Even in the case of some shorter and more episodic items in these programmes, coverage of broader thematic issues was often taken up in later programmes. Thus, *Channel One News* began its coverage of the US government shutdown in late 1995 with a (somewhat personalized) account of the conflict between the two parties, and followed up with stories focusing primarily on the *effects* of the shutdown, for example on government offices and tourist sites (cf. Glasgow University Media Group, 1976). Yet as the story developed, it increasingly focused on the underlying reasons for the dispute, eventually giving over a whole special edition to a discussion of welfare funding. In the case of *Newsround*, some of these more episodic stories implicitly fit into its dominant thematic frames (particularly that of ecology), even if this connection is not made explicit at the time. For example, *Newsround*'s Newswrap section frequently includes brief episodic items about events like chemical fires or the banning of mushroom picking in the New Forest or the return of rare species of birds – events that are probably unlikely to feature on mainstream 'adult' news; yet these are clearly intended to feed into its ongoing preoccupation with questions of pollution, animal conservation and so on.

This balance between thematic and episodic frames is likely to have major implications in terms of viewers' comprehension, and perhaps also in terms of their political attitudes. Iyengar (1991) finds that the dominance of episodic framing has a significant impact on viewers' willingness to subscribe to what he calls 'pro-establishment' positions – which might lead one to expect the opposite effect in this case. Ultimately, this remains an issue for further investigation; although research clearly needs to address the *content* of frames, not merely whether they are episodic or thematic.

The Definition of 'Children's Issues'

If the prominence of thematic frames is one area in which 'adult' news might have things to learn from young people's news programming, there are also some potential criticisms of the ways in which issues are selected and framed here. Defining an issue as a 'children's issue', or presenting it in ways which are seen to be comprehensible by children, sometimes results in a form of over-simplification or evasion, in which bigger thematic explanations are ignored.

To a greater or lesser extent, all these programmes emphasize stories that are seen to affect their target audience specifically – and this ranges from items about school dinners or bullying to more explicitly 'political' items about curfews and youth crime. However, certain issues that are of general relevance are implicitly seen to be more appropriate to young people – particularly when compared with their frequency in 'adult' news. For example, ecology is very often framed as a children's issue in the media generally; and, as I have noted, it is a central preoccupation for *Newsround*. A fuller analysis of this phenomenon remains to be undertaken, but I would argue that this kind of environmental discourse is one which largely avoids questions of economics and politics. This is particularly true of *Newsround*. The threat to the environment here is not seen as systemic but as a result of individual villainy: it is, at most, a result of the conflict between people and nature, and it can be solved by individual interventions, not least in the form of charity (cf. Gauntlett, 1997; Myers, 1995). Furthermore, it could be argued that framing ecology as a children's issue effectively removes the responsibility from adults; it is as though adults are passing on to a future generation a problem for which they themselves are largely responsible.

A rather different example of the problematic consequences of this framing of topics as children's issues arises in the treatment of gun control in *Nick News* (1 October 1995). The report begins with an account of a case in which police shot dead a teenager holding a toy gun, believing it to be real, and goes on to discuss whether toy guns should be banned, contrasting the views of children, parents, toy shop owners and manufacturers. In the process, more awkward issues (at least for many Americans) about whether the police should be armed in the first place, and about the wider availability of guns (which made the confusion possible to begin with), are effaced. While the framing of the report guarantees its relevance to children, this tends to foreclose the discussion of wider issues.

A further example here concerns the treatment of entertainment and popular culture in these programmes. As a schools programme, *First Edition* largely ignores this whole area; although pop music and television itself are a recurrent theme in both *Nick News* and *Newsround*, accounting for around 5 per cent of items in each case. The engagement of *Channel One News* with popular culture is rather more implicit (as we shall see), but it too occasionally includes interviews with pop artists and even invites them to act as guest presenters. My concern here is not that serious news is being corrupted with such apparent triviality. On the contrary, I would argue that these things – which are, after all, of central importance for most young people – are not taken seriously *enough*. By and large, these reports are little more than a form of promotion for the acts or programmes concerned – and, it must be said, they often focus on programmes that appear on the same channel as the news shows themselves. Ultimately, it is hard to avoid the impression that they have been included as a kind of sugar to accompany the pill.

Wise Up adopts a rather different stance here, although there are significant variations between items. In some cases, its treatment of issues such as fashion and style is decidedly celebratory: one item, for instance, featured a group of girls enthusing over the fashion for hairsprayed fringes, providing tips on how to achieve the best effect and confronting the producer of a popular children's drama programme on the need for more characters with this particular hairstyle. As I have noted, *Wise Up* also features young people creating music, albeit for only 29 seconds at a time; and the practice in earlier series of inviting adult musicians or DJs to offer a critical assessment of their work has now been dropped. In other instances, however, the stance is one of campaigning consumer journalism; a disabled girl questions TV producers about the lack of disabled characters in soap operas, or a boy confronts cinema managers about the mark-up on soft drinks. In some instances, this verges on a form of self-righteousness or political correctness, as in the case of the two boys who expose the low wages paid to the workers who produce sports shoes and then smugly point out that they do not wear such shoes themselves. In general, however, *Wise Up* strikes a difficult balance between celebration and criticism of young people's popular culture with some success.

The attempt to engage the younger audience inevitably entails assumptions about their existing knowledge, and about what will interest and entertain them. As I have shown, young people are defined – and indeed constructed – here as distinct from adults in quite consistent ways. While this process has certain gains, it also results in some losses, particularly in terms of developing political understanding. The attempt to make news accessible to young people can result in more thoughtful and informative styles of presentation, but it can also result in superficiality. More fundamentally, such attempts often appear to leave dominant definitions of 'news' – and indeed of 'politics' – unchallenged.

Addressing the Viewer

Establishing Authority

If the selection and framing of stories in news inevitably invokes assumptions about its audience, so too does its form. The central question here is to do with how the text positions the viewer. We need to consider how the viewer is positioned *epistemologically* – that is, in relation to the various sources of knowledge that are provided. In principle, there are various possibilities here: for example, the viewer can be positioned as a sceptic who needs to be convinced; as a participant in a debate, judging the contending arguments; as a witness, simply observing the unfolding of events; or as a deferential pupil, passively accepting the wisdom of revealed truth.

In the case of news, critics have typically argued that a limited range of positions is on offer. Robert Stam (1983), for example, suggests that news positions the viewer as 'the audio-visual master of the world', giving us the illusion that we are being granted unlimited and ubiquitous access to events through the power of technology. The viewer becomes the privileged witness, joined through identification with the news team to an illusory community, 'the regime of the fictive "we"'. By contrast, as we have seen, Fiske (1989, 1992) argues that the news attempts to foster a deferential stance. The discourse of news is, he asserts, 'literate, homogenising and textually authoritarian', and it seeks to establish 'subjected, believing, reading relations' – even if viewers do not necessarily adopt the positions it marks out for them.

As Bill Nichols (1981) demonstrates, different formats or modes of address typically embody different subject positions for the viewer. For example, on-screen presenters who directly address the camera possess a higher authority than interviewees whose gaze is directed off-camera. Likewise, 'experts', 'vox pops' and witness testimony all possess a different status depending upon how they are nominated by the presenter or the voice-over commentary. Through these kinds of devices, the news attempts to establish what Nichols calls a 'hierarchy of credibility'.

The programmes analysed here adopt rather different pedagogic strategies in this respect. *Newsround* and *First Edition* are the most hierarchically organized. Both rely centrally on a single authoritative studio anchor, who hands over to correspondents who present particular filmed stories. In *First Edition*, these are often identified as specialists, and hence endowed with additional authority (the 'Channel 4 science correspondent' or the 'environment correspondent'); while in *Newsround*, they are hardly ever seen on screen, allowing them to function in Nichols' (1981) terms as 'the voice of god'. Within the items themselves, 'experts' are typically nominated as unquestioned sources of truth ('scientists have discovered', 'a report today has shown'), while ordinary people (not least children) are typically heard only in brief 'vox pops'. In *First Edition*, the use of young people as interviewers barely upsets this hierarchy: they generally seem to stick closely to their prepared questions, and rarely challenge the authority of their inter-viewees, even where they are promoting controversial viewpoints. By contrast, the questions put by Jon Snow, the presenter, are occasionally more challenging.

Channel One News also appears to position the viewer as a pupil, who is in need of a simple explanation of events which (it implies) would other-wise appear incomprehensible. It asks questions, apparently on behalf of the viewer, but it always goes on to answer them: as Nichols (1981) puts it, it 'invokes and promises to gratify the desire to know'. There is a clear hierarchy of knowledge between presenters, correspondents and other partic-ipants, and the programme always returns to what Fiske (1989) calls the 'safe, socio-central sense of the studio'. However, *Channel One News* also makes much greater play of the personalities of its newsreaders and corre-spondents, and the process of 'on the spot' news gathering. In this way, it appears to take on a specific *institutional* voice – if not a 'personal view' – which is rather different from the almost sanitary air of objectivity of *Newsround* and *First Edition*.

By contrast, *Nick News* and *Wise Up* explicitly encourage the viewer to be sceptical and to challenge the points of view that are presented. Indeed, the voice-over on the opening sequence of *Nick News* describes it as 'the show that asks the questions'. Where the opening sequence of *Newsround* takes the conventional form of a series of 'bullet points', that of *Nick News* is in the form of questions, with question words (what, where, why, how) flashed up on screen in the form of headlines for a mock newspaper. While the programme does use a single presenter, her introductions to the items (which are much longer than those in the other programmes) often include questions or injunctions such as 'see what *you* think!' The film reports them-selves use a minimum of presenter voice-overs. On the contrary, they are narrated by a range of individuals (many of them children), who introduce themselves by name, and who offer a series of contrasting perspectives on the topic. The programme sets out to show that issues cannot easily be seen in terms of 'black and white'; and items are frequently structured in the form of a debate between two sides. Of course, this is not to suggest that the programme is therefore somehow absolved of the charge of bias. As I have implied (for instance in the case of the item on gun control), there is a limit to the questions that the viewer is invited to ask; and, as we shall see in Chapter 6, there are instances (not least, as with *Newsround*, in the case of environmental stories) where the programme clearly comes down on one side of a debate. Yet at least on the level of rhetoric, it is attempting to establish a rather less deferential subject position for the viewer.

Wise Up goes even further in this respect, in that it explicitly abandons the attempt at 'balance' in favour of a series of personal views. There is no studio and no adult presenter or voice-over. Where the young people featured on *Nick News* talk past the camera, those on *Wise Up* address it directly. Furthermore, they are rarely equivocal in their views. It almost appears to be a precondition for participation that one should have strong opinions; the dominant style is not that of witness testimony, but of impassioned harangue. In constructing their items, presenters will typically interview adults in authority, with some of whom they disagree, but they will end with a clear restatement of their own position, and often with a critique of the people they have interviewed. At times, this assumes self-parodic dimensions: some editions have featured an item called 'the rant', in which individuals let off steam about anything and everything that annoys or concerns them – which can range from clean socks to Turkish Delight to cat food advertisements to boys spitting. In general, however, the items do seek to provide information as well as opinions; in several instances, the young presenters emerge as much more knowledgeable than the supposedly 'expert' adults whom they interview.

Finally, while all these programmes have broadly 'educational' motivations, it is the two US programmes that adopt the most conventional forms of teaching, albeit in different ways. Every Friday, *Channel One News* runs a multiple-choice 'pop quiz' or test based on the week's broadcasts, leaving viewers time to debate their answers, then presenting the correct one. To a large extent, news is implicitly presented here as an inert body of 'facts' in the manner of a quiz show (cf. Tulloch, 1976). By contrast, *Nick News* concludes by attempting to draw out a common theme from the various items in the show – which, given their diversity, often appears quite strained. The presenter signs off with what can only be described as a moral homily on the chosen theme, for example 'creativity', 'stereotypes' or 'compassion' – an approach which (for this viewer at least) appears highly patronizing.

Addressing the Young Audience

As I have implied, there are several ways in which these programmes seek to address and position their viewers specifically as 'children' or 'young people'. This is a process that is, perhaps inevitably, fraught with difficulty. In her study of the classic children's book *Peter Pan*, Jacqueline Rose (1984) goes so far as to argue that the whole enterprise of children's literature is effectively 'impossible'. Adult writers, she suggests, have to construct a fictional position for the child in the text and then attempt to persuade the child to occupy that position – to want what is on offer. Of course, this is true of communication in general, but it is inevitably more fraught where adults are addressing children. As Rose argues, there is no form of communication that is so clearly premised on a distance – indeed, an unbridgeable gulf – between the writer and the addressee.

As I have suggested elsewhere (Buckingham, 1995a), this argument can be productively applied to children's television. Indeed, the historical evolution of children's television – and particularly of broadly educative programming – is marked by a growing anxiety about the risks of 'talking down' to children, and thereby generating resistance to its pedagogic mission. The fear that children will refuse the position of the pupil, that they will demand ever-increasing doses of 'fun' to help them swallow their 'facts', has led to the emergence of a distinctive form of 'edu-tainment'. This kind of material does not always escape the charge of being patronizing, however assiduously it may attempt to avoid it.

This approach is manifested partly in the *content* of programmes – most obviously in the 'sugaring of the pill' described above. But it is also apparent in their audio-visual style, and particularly in what might be termed their *studied informality*. For example, all these programmes employ stylistic devices and modes of address drawn from young people's popular culture. Their graphics and artwork are more reminiscent of music videos or teenage magazines than of mainstream adult news. Both *Nick News* and *Channel One News* use contemporary pop music, not just as a focus for news items (which is also the case with *Newsround*) but also to accompany film reports themselves, and (in the case of *Channel One News*) to introduce and close the show. By contrast with the relatively conventional studio set-up of *First Edition* and *Newsround*, the linking sequences of *Nick News* are filmed in a room that resembles a trendy office, while *Channel One News* is broadcast from 'the Hacienda', a space somewhere between a studio and a night-club.

This studied informality is also apparent in the mode of address and the body language of the presenters. With the exception of those on *First Edition* and *Nick News*, the presenters are all significantly younger than those on mainstream news. *First Edition*'s Jon Snow is the only presenter who sits behind a desk; and his dress is also relatively formal, with the exception of his trademark luminous ties. While *Nick News*'s Linda Ellerbee is in her fifties, her clothes and appearance (particularly her baseball boots) are significantly more casual than those of mainstream news readers; the same could be said of *Newsround*'s presenters, although they too would appear to be well into their twenties or thirties.

By contrast, *Channel One News* presenters are implicitly offered as identification figures. Only slightly older than the programme's target audience, and unfailingly stylish and good-looking, they represent what in the business is often termed 'news flesh'. As Stam (1983) remarks, the sexual attractiveness of the newsreaders and the 'scripted spontaneity' of the 'happy news team' are a significant part of the *pleasures* of news spectatorship. On *Channel One News*, the presenters do not say 'good evening and welcome' but 'yo! what's up?" As they hand over to each other or to the on-the-spot correspondent, or sign off at the end of the show, they often use the characteristic gestures of rappers or hip-hop artists. This self-consciously 'cool' style contrasts with the comparatively conventional approach of the news reports themselves. Here, as in the case of the *Channel One News* use of music and graphics, the adoption of contemporary 'youth' styles seems to be little more than a form of window dressing for a fairly traditional product.

Wise Up and *Nick News* are much further removed from the formal style of mainstream news. The film reports in *Nick News* often use the hand-held camera style, 'paintbox' video effects and rapid-fire editing of MTV. In addition to these techniques, *Wise Up* uses hand-written graphics and captions; it occasionally (and deliberately) shows the camera and the boom microphone, and displays a compulsive infatuation with jump-cuts. In these ways, both programmes attempt to convey an impression of being spontaneous and 'hand-made': they implicitly claim to initiate a dialogue in which viewers themselves can participate as equals, and hence to bridge the gulf between producer and audience.

Space for Debate

Finally, to what extent do these programmes attempt to engage their viewers as participants in a debate? How far do they offer alternative ways of framing or interpreting the events they depict? To what degree do they encourage and enable viewers to make up their own minds?

As I have implied, *Nick News* is by far the most self-conscious in this respect. Almost all of its 'serious' reports (as opposed to its cultural items) are framed as a debate between two participants (often children) or two points of view. Thus, for example, its report on proposals to build a paper mill in a rural area of West Virginia (12 November 1995) contrasted arguments about environmental damage with the view that the mill would bring much-needed employment. While other speakers were featured, including a representative of the company and a union organizer, the main arguments were presented (highly articulately) by two pre-teenage girls. As I shall indicate in Chapter 6, this item did have an implicitly pro-environmentalist bias, and the students whom I interviewed were not slow in recognizing this. Nevertheless, the debate is not explicitly resolved within the report itself; at least outwardly, it claims to be inviting you to 'see what you think'.

By contrast, *Newsround*'s coverage of environmental issues could be accused of a more explicit form of bias. Both in terms of the prominence of these stories in the first place, and in terms of the range of views represented, the programme's position is very clear. It provides extensive coverage of campaigning groups such as Greenpeace and Friends of the Earth, and regularly reports on the research undertaken by organizations such as the Worldwide Fund for Nature – although, as I have noted, some of the wider economic and political issues at stake here are frequently effaced. While it would be an exaggeration to accuse *Newsround* of being environmentalist propaganda, the extent to which it enables viewers to make up their own minds on these issues, or to criticize established sources of authority (on either side of the debate), is very limited.

Generally speaking, *Newsround*, *First Edition* and *Channel One News* are much less likely to present items in a debate format, and only do so when the grounds for debate have already been publicly well-established. Thus, for example, *Newsround*'s report on the death of a boxer as a result of injuries in the ring was followed by a brief studio debate between a representative of the British Medical Association (which has called for a ban on boxing) and a representative of the boxing industry. Likewise, *Channel One News*'s coverage of the US government shutdown (discussed in Chapter 6) outlined the differences between the two political parties, supported with relevant film footage, and its subsequent report on welfare legislation also laid out contrasting views. In both cases, such debates are almost wholly confined to representatives of established political parties or interest groups, and in no case are children themselves seen to participate in them, or even to be capable of doing so.

First Edition is moving warily towards a more debate-based approach, via its use of access reports; although significantly, it often chooses to balance these reports with opposing viewpoints. Thus, one programme treated the issue of young women boxing with an access item presented by two teenage girl boxers; this was followed with a studio interview with a boxing promoter who was opposed to this. Here, and in the case of its items about fox hunting or curfews, a debate format is seen to be more appropriate primarily in relation to issues that have already been established as controversial. A similar approach is not applied, for example, to discussing the legitimacy of US involvement in weapons inspections in Iraq.

Wise Up's wholehearted adoption of the access format again places it in a rather different position. There is no attempt to provide balance, either within or between items, although, as I have noted, many reports take the form of a series of confrontations between the presenter and a succession of opponents, who are given at least a limited opportunity to present alternative views. In general, however, debate is not so much something contained within the programme itself (as it is in *Nick News*) as something in which the viewer is encouraged to participate: presenting strongly-held opinions is implicitly seen as a way of inviting viewers themselves to form their own and to talk back. Of course, questions might be asked about the criteria that are used in selecting these reports. There is a general tendency towards political correctness here, although my sample of programmes does feature items by a boy who confronts what he sees as feminism, and another who extols the virtues of the royal family. Either way, however, the bias of these items is overt and open to challenge – even if (as we shall see in Chapter 7) this approach can generate unpredictable responses.

In all these respects, these programmes are walking a difficult line. On the one hand, they need to establish their authority and credibility, yet on the other, they need to avoid talking down to their audience. They have to teach, but without appearing unduly 'teacherly'. Here again, there is a kind of continuum, with the more conventional news programmes towards one end and *Wise Up* and *Nick News* towards the other. As a schools programme, *First Edition* is probably the most traditional in this respect; although the informality of *Channel One News* and *Newsround* is little more than super-ficial. All three essentially seek to encourage what Fiske (1989) terms 'deferential reading relations'. By contrast, both *Nick News* and *Wise Up* explicitly encourage viewers to question and challenge their authority, although *Nick News* is more inclined to package such debates *within* items, and on its own terms. As I shall indicate in Chapters 6 and 7, all these differ-ences have significant implications in terms of audience responses.

Access and Empowerment: Whose Voices?

This latter point leads on to my third major theme. To what extent do these kinds of programmes offer or promote more active forms of citizenship and political participation among young people? As I have implied, all these programmes make a significant effort to establish the *relevance* of the mate-rial they cover to the lives of individual young viewers. While this is less the case with *Channel One News* than with the programmes for younger chil-dren, all of them consistently attempt to provide a young person's perspective on wider national or world events. At least by implication – and in some cases more explicitly – they suggest that young people themselves might be able to intervene in these events, or somehow make a difference to them. Yet two significant questions arise here. First, whose voices are being heard here, and what status are they given? Who is representing the child? Second, to what extent are young people being empowered or enabled to act on their own behalf?

'Giving Young People a Voice'

Over the past couple of decades, the official rhetoric of children's television has become increasingly 'child-centred' (Buckingham *et al.*, 1999). Both commercial and public service providers have frequently claimed to be acting on behalf of children, to be representing the world from the child's point of view, and even to be 'giving children a voice' (see Home, 1993; Laybourne, 1993). In the case of the programmes analysed here, this attempt to 'give children a voice' functions on several levels.

In some cases, it is little more than a matter of self-promotion. *Channel One News*, for example, is particularly keen on self-promotion, perhaps as a result of the controversy that continues to surround it. It encourages viewers to contribute artwork, to send in sweatshirts for the presenters to wear, and it organizes inter-school competitions such as 'sports coach of the year'. It persistently refers to students whose work is featured, or who are inter-viewed in the film reports, as 'Channel One students' from 'Channel One schools', as though Channel One formed the beginning and end of their education. As I have noted, *Channel One News* also makes greater play of the personalities of its journalists, and investigative stories such as the reports on tobacco companies' targeting of teenage smokers or the smuggling of nuclear materials in Eastern Europe emphasize the dangers and the glamour of news-gathering.

In this case, the viewer is implicitly invited to join a kind of club, or at least to identify vicariously with the 'illusory community' of the news team (Stam, 1983). In other instances, however, viewers are invited to contribute to the actual content of the programme, or to interact with it in other ways. Again, in some cases, this is quite limited, and perhaps tokenistic. All these programmes operate web sites, and several of them invite feedback in the form of telephone calls, letters or e-mail; although only in the case of *Wise Up* are critical responses (in the form of extracts from telephone calls) actually included in the programmes themselves.

In many instances, children or young people are featured in the items, even where they concern issues that do not appear to affect them specifically. Thus, for example, *Newsround* covered President Clinton's 1995 visit to Northern Ireland by focusing on the welcome speech given by a 9-year-old girl; while *First Edition* covered the 1997 handover of Hong Kong through the eyes of two young residents. In many such instances, however, this amounts to little more than a 'vox pop' approach: *Channel One News*, for example, featured a series of interviews with schoolchildren in its report on the Million Man March in Washington, although its main focus was on the political controversy surrounding its organizer, Louis Farrakhan; *First Edition* frequently uses children's 'vox pops' in this way, for example in stories about the debate over replacing the Royal Yacht or the Northern Ireland peace talks.

Nevertheless, many of these programmes also include forms of 'access', in which viewers are given more substantial control over content. In addition to *Wise Up*, both *First Edition* and *Nick News* enable viewers to author their own reports, while *Newsround* runs a kind of junior journalists' club. Yet the extent to which any of these things really amounts to 'giving young people a voice' remains open to debate.

Aside from *Channel One News*, the most limited form of access is provided by *Newsround*. In fact, *Newsround* rarely includes children's voices at all; and when it does so, this is largely in the form of brief 'vox pops' or witness testimony. Only very occasionally are children given more extensive opportunities to speak, and these are largely in the context of 'special child' stories (a girl who suddenly started writing backwards, a boy who was charged a fare for bringing his hamster on a bus). Much more frequently heard are adults expressing their concerns or plans for children – soccer players calling on children to 'kick racism out of sport', or Prince Charles and newsreader Martyn Lewis announcing their plans for a children's Internet service. The dominant voice here remains that of the correspondent, the largely invisible 'voice of god' (Nichols, 1981) – a voice which, as I have noted, is almost wholly absent from *Nick News* and *Wise Up*.

The only significant exception to this in my sample – apart from a running story about an international children's conference on the environment (p. 56) – is *Newsround*'s Press Pack stories. The Press Pack is a kind of club that invites viewers to contribute stories, and regularly organizes competitions for viewers who want to present a report for the programme. 'Assignments' that were on offer in my sample of programmes included reporting on a trip on Concorde, visiting the US to cover Christmas festivities and travelling to Uganda to investigate attempts to prevent ivory poaching. *Newsround* also organizes annual Press Pack awards, in which the writer of the year's best story is rewarded with a further glamorous assignment. While this certainly makes for a more participatory and less narcissistic approach than that of *Channel One News*, it also tends to construct an *aspirational* position for the viewer – as somebody who just might, if they are very lucky and/or extremely talented, attain the position of those whose work is displayed before them.

On one level, *Nick News* seems to provide a direct contrast to this approach, although in some ways it is no less limited. As I have noted, children are regularly used as presenters in its film reports; and while they do not speak directly to camera (and hence do not attain the pinnacle of the 'hierarchy of credibility') they frequently take the burden of the voice-over commentary. The use of first person introductions ('my name is . . . and I'm eleven years old') appears to confirm the impression that these children are telling their own stories in their own voices. In many of these reports, the children are actively involved as participants, not merely as victims, recipients or onlookers.

To some extent, of course, this is a deceptive impression. These children do not have unlimited access to the airwaves, but are chosen by the programme's producers in order to fit into a news agenda that is at least partly pre-established. What they say is edited and selected, and then combined with visual material, music and other voices. These are processes over which they have little or no control; and they may well result in very different interpretations of their arguments from those which they themselves may have intended. In this sense the programme could be accused of creating an *illusion* of access, a pretence that children are somehow speaking directly to children (cf. Morse, 1985) – although the extent to which the illusion succeeds in deceiving viewers themselves remains debatable.

By contrast, *Wise Up* seems to provide a more wholehearted form of access. Viewers are explicitly invited to write in with suggestions for reports they would like to make, which is not the case in either *Nick News* or *First Edition* (which has recently added an access slot). Of course, the items are selected, shot and edited by the series producers, and they also provide assistance with research and scripting. Yet the bulk of the reports appear to derive from suggestions and initiatives by viewers, and the very diversity of the topics chosen would appear to confirm this. Unlike the reports in *Nick News*, they are presented by the young people themselves: they speak direct to camera, without being introduced or mediated by adults, and they conduct the interviews.

At the same time, the programme could be seen to work hard at constructing an *illusion* of access, not least through its 'hand-made' style. As I shall indicate in Chapter 7, several of the students whom I interviewed suspected that the programme had been 'made to look' as though it was produced by children, even though (according to them) it was not. Many of them pointed to its obsessive use of jump-cuts, which frequently appears quite unnecessary in terms of editing. Furthermore, as I have suggested, *Wise Up* implicitly confines itself to young people with strong opinions: there is little space for ambivalence, or indeed for showing both sides of an issue, as *Nick News* explicitly sets out to do. Here again, children are given a voice, but the terms on which they are allowed to use it are highly circumscribed.

The Limits of 'Empowerment'

'Empowerment' is a dangerously vague and inclusive term, both in theories of pedagogy and in media research. The notion that radical teachers can empower students, for example, has increasingly been seen to amount to little more than rhetoric (Ellsworth, 1989), while the idea that watching television (or consuming popular culture more broadly) can be construed as a form of ideological empowerment (Fiske, 1987) has been widely ridiculed in recent years. If empowerment means anything in this context, it must surely refer to something more than a purely psychological process – a matter, perhaps, of 'feeling good about yourself'. On the contrary, it must imply a relationship – however indirect – between watching television and some form of social or political *action*.

On British children's television, social action of this kind tends to be exclusively confined to charitable activities. The BBC's long-running magazine programme *Blue Peter* is well-known for this, and it has often been criticized for promoting a patronizing attitude towards developing countries (Ferguson, 1985). While there is some force in these criticisms, they do seem strangely utopian – as though the only valid response to starvation in developing countries is to work for global revolution. As I have argued elsewhere, such charitable responses may well have greater potential in terms of developing political awareness (see Buckingham, 1996: Chapter 6). Nevertheless, perhaps the only area in which *Newsround* shows children engaged in more strictly 'political' activity – as opposed simply to charitable good work – is (predictably) in relation to the environment. Thus, its running story on the international children's conference on the environment emphasized the global scale of the problem and the need for governmental collaboration. While some of the television celebrities who represent the children's environmental industry were shown in attendance, the reports were almost unique for *Newsround* in their focus on children as autonomous political agents.

By contrast, *Nick News* and *Wise Up* explicitly promote forms of political empowerment for young people, albeit in different ways. In the case of *Nick News*, this is partly a matter of self-conscious rhetoric; and to a British viewer, it carries more than a hint of the morale-boosting discourse of American self-help manuals. Thus, for example, the presenter Linda Ellerbee sometimes ends one of her closing homilies with an assertion like 'kids really do have a lot of power'. Nevertheless, *Nick News* repeatedly features children acting to improve their environment, their personal situation or that of others. Thus, there are items in my sample about a group of US children campaigning to stop child labour in developing countries, a group attempting to persuade their senators to officially recognize a female 'hero' for their state, and a group agitating for stricter enforcement of the laws on child support. Of course, in such cases, there is the risk of children being used as stooges or surrogates for adult campaigns – a danger of which the show's producer, Mark Lyons (1995) was well aware; and needless to say, such activity can hardly be seen to be representative of young people in general.

Wise Up is much less precious in this respect. Indeed, of all the programmes considered here, it is the only one that successfully manages to be funny – not least by occasionally satirizing its own pretensions. At the same time, its stance towards adult authority is often more explicitly confrontational. Many of the more serious reports involve the presenters challenging authority figures – police officers, politicians, company representatives – using distinctly hostile questioning. In several instances, the presenters are shown attempting and failing to gain interviews with such individuals, while in other cases, adults are shown asking for the interview to be stopped, or for certain sections to be edited out. Captions are also sometimes used to undermine adult speakers, or to provide conflicting information, and adults interviewed over the telephone are sometimes represented through satirical animations (a representative from Reebok, for example, becomes a talking sports shoe). As I have noted, the young presenters also have the last word, and they frequently criticize the inconsistencies and weak excuses with which they have been presented.

This approach could be seen to represent a form of 'youth politics': it enables young people to express their views on issues that directly or indirectly concern them, yet on which they are rarely consulted. On the other hand, it clearly plays into a certain adult fantasy about young people, an image of them as somehow automatically rebellious and able to see through adult hypocrisy. Ultimately, there is a tension here that often characterizes debates about representation. One might wish that these programmes would feature children in more active or powerful roles, yet if they were to do so, one might well accuse them of being unrealistic, or engaging in a form of empty optimism. If the reality is that most children are largely powerless, then should we not show this as it is – or should we show them as powerful, in the hope that they might learn to become so? In this respect, the argument for positive images can conflict with the requirement for realism – although both are capable of a variety of definitions.

Conclusion

Television news programmes for young people can serve a variety of functions, and it is important to be realistic about what they can achieve. Despite the arguments of some journalists and critics, television news will not in itself bring about a healthy democracy, much less a participatory one – whatever we might take those terms to mean. As I have noted, research on the audience for television news suggests that it is, in fact, a comparatively ineffective means of informing people; even adult viewers frequently misunderstand, ignore or forget what they see (see Robinson and Levy, 1986). It would perhaps be a mistake to expect children's television news to act as a significant means of political education, although it clearly does have a role to play.

Nevertheless, what remains striking about these programmes – and particularly about *Newsround*, *First Edition* and *Channel One News* – is how conventional they are, both in terms of content and in terms of form. In an age when audiences' interest in news media is steadily declining, particularly among the young, it is surprising that these programmes adopt such conventional definitions of news and such traditional formats. While there are some valid and important attempts to make complex ideas accessible to young people – attempts from which the producers of 'adult' news could certainly learn – much of the address to young people here amounts to little more than a form of window dressing.

While they have undeniable limitations, *Nick News* and *Wise Up* do offer some indications of a more innovative approach, both in terms of their formal strategies and in terms of their representation of young people themselves. Of course, neither programme could really be described as 'news', in the sense of providing immediate reports of topical current events, but they do cover political and social issues that are conventionally seen as the main preoccupation of news. In different ways, these programmes push at the boundaries of what *counts* as news – and indeed as politics. At the same time, they adopt less conventional forms of pedagogy that address and position their audience in quite different ways from mainstream news.

Despite recent moves towards popularization, news remains one of the most conservative media genres, and as the official voice of the network or station, there may be reasons why it will remain so. Nevertheless, children's news programming could be an arena in which more exciting and innovative approaches to news journalism could begin to be developed. As we move into a more competitive, multi-channel era, in which television will have to struggle against less linear, more interactive media forms, innovation of this kind may be not only desirable but unavoidable.

Chapter Five

Talking News, Talking Politics

All forms of communication define and position their audiences in particular ways. While it may implicitly claim merely to be opening a window onto the world, television news is no exception to this. It inevitably addresses and seeks to construct an 'ideal reader' who will be entertained and informed by what it has to offer. Yet the extent to which the 'ideal reader' coincides with the real reader is something that cannot be deduced simply from the text alone.

In Chapter 4, I analysed how television news programmes aimed at young people attempt to define their target audience. Such programmes inevitably embody implicit assumptions about what will interest and entertain their viewers, and about their existing relationship with the broader sphere of social and political debate. We might say that such programmes construct young people as citizens-in-the-making – and simultaneously as news-viewers-in-the-making. My analysis pointed to some fundamental constraints and limitations here. With some significant exceptions, young people are defined as onlookers rather than participants in the processes of political debate and political action. Despite the rhetoric of empowerment and the promise that children's voices will be heard, young people are largely constructed here in adult terms, rather than as political actors in their own right.

Textual analysis of this kind provides a set of hypotheses, but it obviously cannot predict how audiences will interpret and respond to what they watch. To what extent are producers' assumptions and expectations about their audience accurate? Do viewers themselves recognize and occupy the positions that are marked out for them? In this chapter and the two that follow, I will be considering in some detail the ways in which young people made sense of these programmes, and (by extension) of news and political communication in general.

Context and Method

During 1996 and 1997, I conducted a series of small-group interviews with young people in two schools, one in Philadelphia, Pennsylvania, one in

London. I interviewed young people aged 11 (12 in the case of the London group), 14 and 17. There were three groups of three children in each age group, and each group was interviewed on two occasions. In addition, I conducted a pilot study and subsequent parallel interviews with young people aged between 11 and 14 in another Philadelphia school. Each interview lasted around 55 minutes, including some time for the screening of extracts from the programmes, although some were significantly longer. In total, 42 such interviews were conducted, generating more than 35 hours of discussion. This material was subsequently transcribed in full.

The first interview began with a warm-up discussion of the participants' favourite television programmes. It then moved on to consider news in particular. I asked the young people about whether they watched the news on television, whom they watched with, which programmes they preferred and what they liked or disliked about them. I also asked about whether they read a newspaper; about any recent news stories they were able to recall; and specifically about their responses to 'politics' in the news. The discussion then moved on to focus on two extracts from the programmes analysed in the previous chapter. Prior to viewing, the participants were asked about their existing knowledge of the issues covered. After watching the extract, I asked about their responses to the people featured in the item and to the views expressed and asked whether the people who made the item had a particular point of view about the issue. In the second interview with each group, this approach was repeated with two further extracts, although obviously the initial discussion was omitted. The extracts used, and the students' responses to them, are discussed in the following two chapters. The focus here is primarily on the initial discussions of news, particularly political news, in the first interviews.

Despite the growing importance of media education, young people rarely discuss their leisure uses of media in the context of school – at least with teachers. Popular culture is typically regarded by teachers as irrelevant to the serious 'work' of schooling, if not as positively anti-educational. Much of its significance for young people themselves also derives from the fact that it is set apart from the official business transacted in classrooms. This is not to suggest that popular culture is simply or automatically subversive of the official culture of schooling. Nevertheless, discussing a medium such as television in this context often seems to involve a crossing of boundaries – between leisure and education, between home and school, and to some extent between adult and child. I have considered this uneasy status of 'television talk' in some detail elsewhere (see Buckingham, 1993a, 1993b, 1996).

News is a significant exception to this overall picture, however. As several of the young people here acknowledged, it is a form of television that many teachers – and some parents, particularly fathers – actively encourage them to watch. News is strongly identified with the official culture of the school; it is generally defined as something young people *should* watch if they want to inform themselves about the world, and hence succeed in their academic studies. On the other hand, of course, this kind of official endorsement may prove counter-productive, if news viewing is perceived merely as a kind of pedagogical duty.

As a result, talking with children about news in this context feels very different from talking about soap opera or horror movies or sitcoms (which is the kind of material I have focused on in my previous research). In all the initial interviews, there was a significant shift in tone as we moved off the discussion of favourite programmes and on to the topic of news. The focus on news effectively positioned me as a kind of teacher and the young people as students. In writing the account that follows, I hesitated for some time between the terms 'children' and 'young people' – which both carry connotations of their own, of course – before settling on the term 'students' as a way of describing my interviewees. This term serves as a deliberate reminder of the institutionally situated nature of our encounters.

At the same time, young people may be positioned in quite different ways in relation to the official culture of the school, and hence to the category 'student'. The sociology of education amply demonstrates that students of different social classes possess very different orientations to schooling, and that schools systematically refuse to grant legitimacy to the forms of knowledge and cultural capital that are valued by disadvantaged groups. On the other hand, students themselves may also actively resist or seek to reposition themselves in relation to their official identity as students.

This created some significant dilemmas in constructing my sample, particularly in the US. The logistics of obtaining access to public (i.e. state) schools were difficult enough, but this was complicated further by the need for a sample that was socially and ethnically mixed. As in many US cities, Philadelphia schools have suffered from a process of 'white flight': crudely, inner city schools tend to be predominantly working-class and non-white, while suburban schools tend to be predominantly middle-class and white. My pilot interviews were arranged via a personal contact, a British teacher who was working on an exchange in a Philadelphia middle school. The school was located in a mainly white working-class neighbourhood, although students were bussed in from all over the city in an attempt to ensure a social and ethnic mix – although comparatively few could be described as middle-class.

These interviews were somewhat disconcerting, although in retrospect the students' responses were hardly surprising. The students expressed a clear sense of alienation, both from news and (particularly) from politics. In some cases, they were quite forceful and bitter; in many others, they were merely low-key and apathetic. More to the point, there were comparatively few students who appeared to watch the news with any enthusiasm, or who seemed to be interested in talking about it with me. Their responses to my questions were frequently monosyllabic.

In arranging to conduct the main US study, I needed to find a school with a broader age range, but with a similar social and ethnic mix. This did not prove easy, and I ended up (somewhat arbitrarily) with an inner-city public school that selected students on the grounds of academic ability. This has several implications in terms of the representativeness of my data. It may well mean that these young people are more likely to be interested in news and in politics than their peers who are judged to be 'less able' – although that is not to say that they did not share the expressions of alienation and mistrust that were so apparent among my pilot group. Indeed, it could be argued that such expressions of alienation are much *more* disturbing coming from young people who might reasonably expect to have more of a stake in social power, and in the political system, at some point in their future lives. Nevertheless, this particular sample was also more likely to play the game – or at least the game they might have expected I wanted them to play. They were much more likely to assume the position of the 'good student' in the context of our interviews, largely because of their broadly positive relationship with the official culture of the school. Indeed, some of the older students explicitly told me that they were unrepresentative of their age group: they knew they were 'special', and they tried in several ways to impress me of this fact. It was for this reason that I subsequently returned to the pilot school to conduct further interviews; although the extent to which the students there might be seen as representative – and of what – also remains open to question.

The situation in London was rather different, in that I was able to rely on personal contacts, and had a much wider choice of schools. The school I selected is one whose results are slightly above average in terms of national league tables – although, like most British educationists, I am extremely sceptical about the value of such comparisons. These students were rather less likely to adopt the 'good student' persona than those in the main Philadelphia school, and in some cases (as we shall see below) consciously subverted it. Even here, however, I was dependent on the class teachers to select students to participate; and beyond my general stipulations that I wanted a 'mixed' and 'talkative' group of students, it is impossible for me to judge how representative these students are. Within the limited terms of my sample, I can make generalizations in terms of age and gender; and 'race' becomes a significant issue in some of these discussions, albeit in complex ways. Nevertheless, my conclusions about differences of social class and educational attainment will necessarily be limited and tentative, and I can only surmise about other factors such as the role of parents or siblings on the basis of what the students themselves chose to tell me.

For all these reasons, then, I would not claim that this study is a representative survey. Neither is it an ethnography. Both would require different methods, and would almost certainly address different questions. My central focus here is on discourse about television – specifically on talk. This is not a study of how young people interpret what they watch, but of how they *talk* about it. As I have argued elsewhere (Buckingham, 1993a: Chapter 3), talk of this kind should not be taken at face value. It is not a neutral reflection of what really goes on at the point of viewing, or indeed in individuals' heads. It cannot be taken as straightforward evidence of individuals' competence as television viewers – or indeed, in this case, of their understanding of 'politics'. On the contrary, talk is a form of social action, a way of defining ourselves and of negotiating our relationships with others. 'Being interviewed' in this kind of context tends to generate a particular form of public discourse; the talk is addressed not merely to the others present (the other students and the interviewer), but also to a broader public audience, whether or not one knows who they are, or indeed whether or not one believes they might listen to what one has to say. (Printing such talk in the context of a book such as this, of course, confirms this 'public-ness', even though few if any of those whose words are quoted will actually read it.)

As discourse analysts have shown, talk is an exceptionally slippery medium. In interviews such as these, individual speakers will often prove to be incoherent, inconsistent or downright contradictory. They will proclaim one thing at one moment, only to deny it at another; they will make state-ments that are effectively undermined by their own qualifications and uncer-tainties; they will collectively talk themselves around to a given position, despite their disagreements; they will invent evidence, or wilfully misinterpret what others have said; they will make generalized statements that conflict with their judgements about specific cases or examples, and so on. Group talk of this kind is very far from the utopia of rational communication imagined by Habermas (1962/1989) and his followers, discussed in Chapter 3.

For many researchers, this alone is sufficient to render talk unreliable as a form of data – the implication being that one should adopt supposedly more neutral forms of investigation such as questionnaires or passive obser-vation, in which people will honestly reveal themselves as they really are. While recognizing the limitations of my chosen method, this is an implica-tion I would refute. The search for 'honest souls' or for transparent self-revelation is an impossible fantasy.

I would argue that analysing discourse in this way can provide insights into social processes that are characteristic of *all* forms of communication. Thus, in talking about television, these young people were not only providing interpretations of, and judgements about, what they had seen. They were simultaneously defining themselves as particular kinds of people, or claiming particular social identities; and they were also negotiating their relationships with others – and not only those who happened to be present. In earlier work, I have followed Norman Fairclough (1989) in terming these three processes *contents*, *subjects* and *relations*, and I am continuing to use this loose framework here, even if some of the complexities and contradictions are somewhat ironed out in the two chapters that follow (see Buckingham, 1993a: Chapter 4).

The key emphasis in this approach is that all these dimensions are inherently *social*. In talking about television, individuals construct – or at least make claims about – their own identities and their relations with others; but they do so using resources that are not of their own choosing. These resources are partly in the form of the texts they discuss, which constrain the potential diversity of meanings and pleasures; they also take the form of wider social definitions and discourses, which texts may invoke, and which individuals bring with them to any particular encounter with the medium.

In my view, this approach takes us beyond the rather pointless conflicts that tend to characterize contemporary debates about media audiences in Media and Cultural Studies. It does not represent viewers of television as wholly autonomous 'meaning makers', able to create any and every interpretation of the text according to their individual whim. Nor, on the other hand, does it attribute all-determining power to texts or the institutions that produce them. As I have argued elsewhere, the question here is not so much to do with how we *balance* the power of the audience against the power of the text, as how we *theorize* the relationship between them (see Buckingham, 1993a: Chapter 11).

Talking News

Despite the differences between the various groups of students whom I interviewed, few expressed great enthusiasm for television news. The programmes nominated as favourites in our warm-up discussions were almost exclusively comedies, soaps, movies and sport. Some students appeared to believe that news might be a required answer here, and claimed that it was among their favourites, although when asked to recall news stories they had seen recently, they were often unable to do so. With a few exceptions, expressions of even moderate interest in news were only to be found among the oldest age group. More frequently, news was rejected as simply 'boring', and in several cases exaggerated groans greeted my introduction of the topic.

In fact, it was clear from their subsequent discussions that most of the students did watch news, in several cases on a regular basis, but that in itself does not suggest that they necessarily enjoyed it. In some instances, they argued, they had no option but to do so, simply because there was 'nothing else on', or because their parents insisted on watching it. Nevertheless, this rejection of news also seemed to be a kind of expected ritual, which was partly to do with the students' collective construction of themselves as 'young people'. From this perspective, anything associated with 'adults' is automatically condemned as boring and irrelevant, unless it has the kudos of being explicitly forbidden to children.

The more working-class students in the Philadelphia pilot school were most explicit – or perhaps least polite – about this. Tom (13), for example, repeatedly assured me that 'news sucks': 'it's all the same thing . . . it comes on, like, six times a day." Dana (14) and Rosa (13) likewise claimed that the news was boring and that it 'put them to sleep'. Nevertheless, similar complaints were made in both the other schools, in Philadelphia and in London. In general, news was perceived as repetitive and lacking in entertainment value. Several students observed that, while the characters might change, the basic stories remained the same (cf. Graber, 1988). This seemed to be particularly the case in US coverage of crime: as Tom (13) put it, 'like a murder, it might be different people, but it's the same thing." Several US students also complained about the fact that 'breaking' news stories were allowed to interrupt regular programmes, as in the case of O. J. Simpson's notorious car 'chase'.

Somewhat facetiously perhaps, several students suggested that news might be made more entertaining, not only by incorporating more entertainment news in the content, but also by changing the format. Candace (12) argued that "[news] should be made into a TV show'; while Diana and Walida (14) suggested that they should incorporate stories that were not real, and call it 'Fakes' instead.

On the other hand, there were several students, particularly among the older age group, who rejected what they saw as a drift towards sensationalism and triviality in news. As we shall see in Chapter 7, the UK students were highly critical of the publicity stunts being used in the 1997 election campaign, and argued that the media played a part in encouraging this. In general, however, these charges of sensationalism and triviality were mainly directed at the tabloid press, and at the local news programme *London Tonight*, which was comprehensively demolished by one group. These students were also well aware of the political bias of the popular press. By contrast, the main evening news seemed to possess greater authority. As Chris (17) put it, albeit with some irony, 'when you think of the [evening] news, it's the Almighty, the Great English News – anything they tell you is right, it's the truth." Perhaps surprisingly, such complaints were less prevalent in the Philadelphia schools, although (as we shall see below) some students did criticize what they saw as the media's preoccupation with trivial political scandals.

These criticisms were to some extent supported by the evidence of what the students were able to recall from recent news broadcasts. Crime, entertainment and sport were far and away the leading categories here. In the Philadelphia schools, the kinds of stories most frequently mentioned included local murders and fires, as well as national stories such as the Unabomber and (inevitably) the O. J. Simpson case. In the London school, sport and entertainment were even more prominent, along with several bizarre 'human interest' stories. On the other hand, most students had seen coverage of the forthcoming elections – even if they typically dismissed such material as boring or trivial. Furthermore, many of the apparently 'non-political' stories that were recalled had implicit 'political' dimensions – and these were directly referred to by some of the students themselves. Thus, for example, some UK students recalled stories about Tiger Woods' victory in the US

Open, noting that he was the first Black player to win, while others referred to the racially-motivated murder of the London teenager Stephen Lawrence.

However, several students rejected the news on the grounds that it was emotionally upsetting. This was more strongly the case in the US, where local news in particular is much more graphic in its coverage of crimes and disasters than in the UK. Noah (11, US), for example, said he was 'disgusted' by much of what he saw on the news: 'like murder and child abuse and fire and stuff . . . sometimes I don't watch the news because some days it can be just plain depressing." Likewise, Suzanna (17, UK) said that she was inclined to avoid news stories like those about the Dunblane primary school massacre on the grounds that 'it just makes you upset': 'there's things going on in the world that you need to know, [but] sometimes you just don't want to hear those things." We will consider a more sustained example of this complaint later in this chapter.

On the other hand, there were some who saw this kind of material as interesting and as necessary to know about (cf. Buckingham, 1996: Chapter 6). One UK group of 14-year-old girls complained that the news was sometimes 'too horrible to watch', citing the coverage of wars in Rwanda; although they also acknowledged that, as Nisha put it, 'if you watch it right, it gives the idea of other people, the way they live, their feelings, it makes our feelings stronger towards them." One US group of 14-year-old boys engaged in an extended condemnation of the V-chip legislation on precisely these grounds:

Michael: It's like the parents can block out what the kid is going to see, but that's like trying to protect the kids from what they're going to see [anyway]. I mean, the news is more violent than most shows on TV . . . They are acting like people don't know what's going on anyway. 'Cause everybody knows what's happening, but the people in government don't seem to realize that we do . . . A good person should be educated about that stuff. They should not be protected from it.

Michael's assertion of his right to know was echoed by some other students, particularly among the oldest age group. While there were certainly elements of duty here – as in Michael's comment about becoming 'a good person' – many students expressed a strong personal motivation to 'know what's going on'. The availability of news was seen both as an opportunity to satisfy a personal compulsion, and almost as a privilege:

Olivia (17, UK): I don't know about you, but I have this need, I need to know what's going on. I don't know why. I have to know what's going on, and [in the news] I find out what's going on in other countries that I wouldn't have the opportunity otherwise.

Chris: Yeah, not everyone has this opportunity to find out what's going on in the world around them at any time . . . So as we've got it, we might as well take advantage of it.

Others saw this more in terms of social interaction. While some implied that their viewing of news was a result of pressure from parents or teachers, others actively sought to 'keep up' with the news in order to be able to converse with adults:

Joel (13, US): My grandmother and I like to watch [the news] 'cause we don't feel like fools when we're talking to somebody. 'Cause there's always something you can learn from it.

These general discussions of news thus revealed some typically contradictory and ambivalent responses. On the one hand, the large majority of students asserted that news was 'boring'; and much of what they remembered having seen of it might broadly be described as 'entertainment' rather than 'hard news'. Yet on the other hand, many of them condemned attempts to make the news more entertaining: if the news was bad, it seemed that 'light news' was even worse. There was equal ambivalence about the serious content of news – for example, its coverage of crime and disasters. On the one hand, it was argued that such material was often too upsetting to watch; yet on the other, it was argued that viewers (including young people) had a right to know about it.

In general, the older students displayed greater interest in news, although they were also more inclined to criticize it, on the grounds of its sensationalism or its potential bias. As I shall indicate, these differences can partly be understood in developmental terms; yet they also reflect the ways in which speakers actively position themselves in talk, and thereby claim particular social identities. Critical judgements about bias or sensationalism in the news, assertions of one's need to know, ritualized rejections of news as 'boring' – all need to be understood as social acts, not merely as reflections of how individuals really think and behave.

Talking Politics

Given the fact that the interviews in both countries were conducted in the run-up to an election (in 1996 in the US, 1997 in the UK), one might have expected the students to be more aware of politics – and perhaps to be more interested in it – than they might have been at any other time. Yet of all the issues covered in news, politics was the one most consistently singled out for rejection and condemnation. The picture of young people's alienation from politics described in Chapter 1 was, on one level, very much confirmed in these discussions. Politics was seen by the large majority as simply irrelevant to their lives.

> *Michael (14, US)*: If it affects me particularly, like my family, then I will pay attention to it. But if it's like something that's not really all that important, but they just did to make it look like they are doing something in Congress, I don't really watch that, 'cause that's really boring.

As Michael's comment illustrates, 'politics' was defined here primarily in terms of the actions of politicians and elected representatives. As I have noted, several of the news stories that were discussed – from the O. J. Simpson case to Tiger Woods – clearly had broader 'political' dimensions and resonances, even if these were not always made explicit by the students themselves. But only a small minority of students expressed any interest in 'politics' as conventionally defined, and those who did appeared to do so more out of politeness towards the interviewer than from any great enthusiasm. For most, politics was simply 'boring', not least because it was 'hard to understand'.

This sense of the irrelevance of politics was partly seen as a structural consequence of the students' position as 'children'. Many argued that political changes did not directly affect them as much as they did adults; but they also pointed out that they did not have any stake in bringing about those changes. They did not pay taxes and they were not allowed to vote, so what difference did it make what they thought? As Liam (14) argued, 'I'd rather take an interest when I can change [things], but not when I can't."

However, this sense of alienation was also fuelled by a profound – albeit quite generalized – cynicism about the motivations of politicians. For many students, the word 'politician' was effectively a term of abuse. Politicians were routinely condemned as untrustworthy, insincere, inconsistent and incompetent. They were simply 'playing games', trying to maintain their own popularity at any cost, and they could be counted upon to break their own promises or otherwise 'mess things up'. While some students claimed to be interested in keeping up with the electoral race, there was considerable criticism of the tactics used in the campaigns, and particularly of the emphasis on negative campaigning. As we shall see, politicians were also criticized for their neglect of issues specifically relating to children and for what were seen as authoritarian policies in areas such as education and youth crime.

Here again, there were differences in terms of age and social class. While the older children were generally more aware of politics, they were also the ones who condemned politicians most strongly. Even among the older middle-class children, some of whose parents were active in party politics, there was considerable cynicism and disaffection. Significantly, this also extended to the minority of students who were more enthusiastic about news: the desire to 'know what's going on in the world' rarely seemed to encompass the desire to know about politics. One group of 17-year-old girls in the London school debated this issue at some length:

Siobhan: [Politics] doesn't really affect our lives that much, so you don't notice it.

Nandi: I don't think people realize that it will affect their lives, and so there's no point [being interested in it] . . . I think it has a lot to do with class and school, so it's not just young people . . . the more middle-class people are more interested in it than working-class people . . . I just think that most people don't care, because even though they're more likely to be affected by it than us, they just don't care, they're not aware, they don't have the information that would say this could really . . . who wins this election could change my job or my education or what have you.

Suzanna: We've had a Conservative Party for so long, nothing's gonna change. It's like, what's the point voting if nothing's gonna change . . .

Siobhan: We've all had Conservative for our entire lives, so we can't think back and think 'oh yeah, Labour did that then." And now, because Labour have switched, it makes it even less important.

These students provide some very cogent reasons for their own alienation from politics. These are partly to do with their position as young people, and partly with what they perceive as a lack of information. Class and education are also seen as important, although it is difficult to identify how Nandi classifies herself in these terms. Interestingly, they also situate this historically, effectively defining themselves as 'Thatcher's children'. Siobhan clearly knows enough about contemporary politics to assert that 'Labour have switched'; although this also confirms the view that voting – and, by extension, informing oneself about politics – is fairly pointless. This extract makes particularly interesting reading in the light of Labour's subsequent election victory – although of course these students were just too young to be first-time voters. It might perhaps qualify the triumphalist assertion that this victory reflected a more fundamental change of political mood or orientation.

   Despite this general alienation from the world of national politics, many students clearly had very strong feelings about more 'local' political issues. In this, I am not referring to the rather generalized 'politics of everyday life' identified by Fiske (1989: see Chapter 3), as much as to issues that arose in the students' experiences of *institutions* – not least school itself – and in their experiences of their local *neighbourhood* and *community*. Thus, for example, one group of Philadelphia students engaged in an extended discussion of proposals to introduce school uniform. This is an issue that might be seen by some as merely a matter of personal preference, but the students' discussion explicitly drew out the broader political dimensions. For example, they pointed out that uniforms were being promoted as a solution to the problem of violence, and argued that this was a distraction from its real causes; they also saw it as a civil rights issue, which applied specifically to students in public rather than private schools.

This dimension was very apparent in the UK students' discussions of *Wise Up*. At the end of the second interview, I asked them if they would like to make their own report for the programme, and if so what topic they would choose. Some of the topics suggested here were more obviously 'political', at least in a somewhat broader sense, such as racism in the police or environmental pollution. Others were seemingly 'non-political', although on further discussion it became apparent that the students perceived them to have a clear political dimension. Thus, for example, one group suggested a report about the poor quality of school dinners, and they went on to blame this on the fact that the school meals service had been privatized. Likewise, another group said they would like to produce an item about sport on TV, but here again, their concerns were motivated by the fact that major sporting events have been bought up by subscription channels, thus preventing the students from watching them. Several of the issues identified here could be seen to derive from a kind of 'youth politics', which was most explicit in the case of the group who proposed an item about the contradictions in the laws relating to the age of majority. In almost every case, these suggestions were based on the students' direct personal experiences, yet they displayed a striking ability to think through the implications of those experiences in broader social and political terms. In some respects, this supports the more general need for 'relevance', discussed in Chapter 3; although it also implies that relevance is not so much inherent in a given topic as a matter of how the connections between the 'personal' and the 'political' are forged.

Here again, it is important not to take these observations at face value. Expressions of distrust in politicians have become almost ritualistic conversational clichés, not just among the young. As I shall argue, they may reflect little more than a superficial form of cynicism, which derives from a sense of individual powerlessness – although ultimately they may also serve to reinforce it. In this respect, perhaps, the students were merely saying what they thought they were expected to say. Yet when it came to political issues that were closer to their own experience, which they might have some power to influence, and they were much more engaged. To this extent, their sense of alienation from politics, as conventionally defined, cannot be seen to derive simply from a kind of laziness or ignorance. On the contrary, it could be seen as a logical response to the constraints of their own social position.

Defining Differences, Claiming Identities

As I have indicated, there were some systematic differences within the sample in terms of the students' orientations towards both news and politics. These were very far from absolute, and there were several notable exceptions.

Nevertheless, some broad generalizations are possible here, particularly in terms of age, social class and (to a lesser extent) gender.

In general, it was the older students who were more likely to express an interest in news and (to a lesser extent) in politics. The same was true of boys as compared with girls, although this difference was much less marked; and of middle-class as compared with working-class students. By the same token, however, students who were more interested in news and politics were also more likely to be sceptical or critical about them.

For the younger students, news was essentially about sports, human interest stories, crime and weather. Boys were predictably more likely to express an interest in sports, although several girls did so too; girls were more interested in stories about animals, medicine and the environment. Particularly in the US, the younger students were also more interested in local rather than national or international news. In general, the older students were more inclined to project themselves in the role of 'citizens' or 'serious viewers of news'; and simultaneously more keen to display their own critical expertise in identifying biases or other shortcomings in what they watched.

This research was obviously not intended to provide a statistical survey in which demographic variables could be systematically isolated, and these tentative generalizations are only valid in terms of my small and unrepresentative sample. Nevertheless, the differences identified in this and the following two chapters largely coincide with those found in more broad-ranging surveys.

For example, Piagetian stage theories have been used in attempting to relate the development of political understanding to more general developments in formal reasoning – although in the process it has been suggested that children's abilities may have been underestimated (see Connell, 1971; Moore *et al.*, 1985; Stevens, 1982). The two younger age groups in this study are situated at either end of what Connell (1971) calls 'the period of the construction of the political order', while the oldest age group has moved towards what he terms 'ideological thinking'. In general terms, older children are seen here as progressively more able to 'decentre', to take account of alternative perspectives and to reflect self-consciously on their own biases.

Likewise, attitude surveys have discovered differences between girls' and boys' orientations towards politics and political media, although again these differences can be overestimated (Furnham and Gunter, 1983; Moore *et al.*, 1985; Stevens, 1982; Wober, 1980). Middle-class children have been found to employ more complex and differentiated language in their discussions of politics than working-class children, and hence to display more critical and reflexive patterns of political thought (Connell, 1971). Broadly speaking, these different orientations towards politics appear to be sustained into adulthood. Working-class people and women are less likely to be involved or interested in conventional politics (Wilkinson and Mulgan, 1995), while the audience for television news is skewed towards men and towards middle-class viewers – albeit not dramatically so (Gunter, 1987).

I will return to some of these broader generalizations in my concluding chapter, though I would emphasize that my theoretical approach to these issues is rather different. Without necessarily denying that such differences exist, I would seek to avoid the more deterministic implications of such an approach – not only because it fails to account for the many exceptions and anomalies, but also because it appears to rest on a rather mechanistic account of the relationship between social being and individual consciousness or subjectivity. People do not have particular orientations towards television news or towards politics, for example, simply *because* they are male or female. At the very least, what politics or news mean to them will depend on how they define and live out their own gendered identities; and such processes and meanings are crucially dependent upon the discourses in which they are manifested.

The qualitative, discursive approach adopted here implicitly presumes a more dynamic and contested model of this relationship. The emphasis here is on the diverse and sometimes contradictory ways in which individuals *lay claim to* and *construct* particular social identities in the process of talk. In expressing feelings and making judgements about what we watch, we are inevitably and simultaneously defining ourselves as particular kinds of people. From this perspective, the meaning of categories of age or gender ('child' or 'adult', 'male' or 'female') is not given or predetermined, but constructed in and through social interaction. We may attempt to lay claim to an 'adult' identity, for example; but that identity is not simply given – it is something we have to construct and define, not least in relation to its opposite, the 'child'.

This is not to imply that individuals are wholly autonomous in this respect; they cannot simply assume any identity that happens to appeal to them, or which they find metaphorically lying around in discourse. Individuals are positioned socially in all sorts of ways, both in interpersonal interactions and in their encounters with institutions and representations of many kinds. They come to any particular discursive encounter – any conversation or interview, for example – with a history of such prior positionings with which they may feel more or less comfortable; and these prior positionings may be mobilized or cued in particular ways by virtue of the particular characteristics of that encounter.

Furthermore, such identity claims are often inherently contradictory and open to challenge. Claims to identity are essentially claims to social power. But social power is not a possession that can simply be held; on the contrary, it is always a matter of relationships. Bids for power depend upon a degree of consent, and they may have to be justified through argument. Furthermore, while individuals may lay claim to a particular identity on the grounds that it appears to guarantee prestige and social power, such claims can sometimes prove to be quite double-edged.

In the context of these interviews, for example, the students might well have sought to lay claim to an 'adult' position, on the grounds that this would align them with the authority of the school, and perhaps of the interviewer also. Displays of 'critical' acumen or world-weary sophistication might appear to promise this kind of authority, not least by demonstrating one's superiority to other, less mature audiences, who are presumed to be more gullible or vulnerable to the effects of the media. On the other hand, such displays might well be undermined by other students in the group, particularly those who chose to adopt the more subversive position of the rebellious child or adolescent. In this situation, refusing to 'take it seriously' – or indeed to play what might be perceived to be the interviewer's game – offers a different kind of power. Yet there is no position here – be it that of the mature adult or the subversive child – which necessarily *guarantees* uncontested power.

Thus, several of the students who strongly rejected the whole area of politics and news explicitly claimed to be doing so from the position of 'kids' or 'young people'. This was particularly notable among the more working-class students in the Philadelphia pilot school. Tom (13) argued that politics was 'for older people'. 'Kids our age, they don't care what the President has to say, 'cause it doesn't interest us.' Likewise, Dana (14) asserted that 'old people watch the news'. 'Adults just sit there and watch the whole show, I don't know how.' Eric, Terry and Candace (14) argued that the newscasters were always making jokes that 'kids wouldn't understand':

Eric: If they have, like, younger people on it, then we might like it better.

Terry: Instead of speaking Morse code.

Eric: And the guys that announce it are, like, 70 years old.

Candace: I know, they all have grey hair. Say they found a cure for men's baldness. They'll be sitting there making jokes about it, 'I guess I can get some hair now.' And you're sitting there and looking at that, boy, like they're crazy, and they'll be sitting there laughing and giggling.

On the one hand, these students perceive themselves to be excluded from the world of television news, yet they also actively exclude themselves, by exaggerating their own distance from it, for example in claiming that the newscasters are '70 years old'. While there may be aspects of adulthood to which they aspire, grey hair and baldness are clearly not among them; mocking the news becomes a way of mocking 'old people' generally, and hence of asserting a positive youthful identity.

However, news viewing was seen by some as a kind of guarantee of maturity (cf. Gillespie, 1995). Anna (12, UK), for example, claimed that she had not watched the news when she was younger, partly because she did not understand it, but that she did so now. 'Now I would choose to watch it, because I know a bit more ... I'm trying harder to learn." As with several other students, Anna's implicit assertion of her own maturity was framed in terms of a desire to know. 'There's something about the whole world, what's happening, that you need to know." In general, this kind of self-positioning was more common among older students, although it was rarely as explicit. In some senses, the younger students had more options here. Displaying interest in news could be seen as a bid for an older, more mature identity, while expressing dislike was equally safe, since the news could justifiably be characterized as an embodiment of everything that was boring about adults. For the older students, who might justifiably expect to be seen as young adults, rejecting news could lay them open to charges of ignorance or immaturity, or of failing to exercise their proper duty as citizens.

As this implies, this process of self-positioning is often ambivalent and contested. Another example, relating in this case to gender, demonstrates this clearly. Birgit, Christine and Monica (US, 11) argued that boys were much more interested both in politics and in news. Birgit and Monica criticized the emphasis on politics in *Channel One News*, and the neglect of issues relating to nature and the environment. They asserted that the latter were issues that particularly interested girls, and that the boys in their class at school did not really 'care' about them. As Birgit baldly asserted: 'politics is boys' stuff – boys are boring – politics is boring." On one level, these girls were collectively constructing a gendered identity, both by asserting their own unique concerns and by differentiating them from those of their opposites, who are accused of being uncaring. At the same time, Christine stood out against this, asserting that she had been interested in following the news stories about the 1996 Republican primaries, and she subsequently countered the others' generalizations by asking rhetorically, 'Do I look like a boy?'

This collective assertion of a gendered identity came up against further contradictions. Despite their earlier claims, all the girls refuted my summarizing suggestion that news was 'a boys' thing', noting that there were several women news presenters; although their own preferences were for human interest news magazine programmes like *20–20*. However, their rejection of politics on behalf of women in general left them with some explaining to do, if it was not to be seen as a symptom or ignorance or laziness:

> *Birgit*: Maybe [boys are more interested in politics] because they know more about politics than girls and women, because earlier, women and girls had nothing to do with politics and all the men did the politics. Now women are getting into it.

As with the students quoted above, this rejection of politics is defined in terms of broader social identifications. Yet the girls have to do a certain amount of self-justification (or 'identity work') if this rejection is not to be seen as a failing on their part, but on the contrary as a matter of active exclusion.

As these examples suggest, this process of self-positioning is complex and variable, yet it is far from wholly individualistic. The power relationships enacted in such talk are often defined in terms of broader social differences – even if the *meanings* of those differences are subject to negotiation. Definitions of gender, age, social class and ethnicity were significant resources in this respect; the students' talk implicitly and explicitly drew upon discourses and assumptions about what was appropriate or typical for boys or for girls, for children or for adults (or indeed for children of a particular age), and so on. I have focused here on age and gender, since these were the most explicit dimensions of this process. By contrast, social class was almost wholly implicit, even though there were clear differences between the working-class and the middle-class children in the sample. Meanwhile, as we shall see in the following chapters, ethnicity became a very significant – and indeed quite fraught – dimension of some of the discussions of specific news items.

Reading Political Discourse

One further dimension of this process is that language itself offers particular repertoires or routines that become familiarized over time. Individuals do not simply invent language afresh each time they speak: on the contrary, they adopt particular styles of talk whose implicit rules they have learned in the past, and which they know they can use as vehicles for social action. Mikhail Bakhtin (1986) refers to these styles of discourse as 'speech genres'. Speech genres embody particular subject positions, or constructions of identity, from which the individual learns to speak.

Kum-Kum Bhavnani's (1991) analysis of young people's talk about politics, discussed in Chapter 3, makes some important moves in this direction. Bhavnani's central concern is with how 'politics' is constructed in discourse, and within everyday relationships – and with how, simultaneously, relations of power are reproduced, negotiated and contested. In the process, she places a central emphasis on the social context of research and the relations between the researcher and the researched. Discursive protestations of ignorance or cynicism about politics are, she argues, strategic responses to a sense of disenfranchisement. Cynicism should not be confused with simple apathy; on the contrary, it may be a self-conscious way of dealing with powerlessness, and even a precondition for certain kinds of political action.

Two further studies of individuals' talk about politics have addressed this discursive dimension in more detail. Nina Eliasoph (1990) conducted interviews in the street, on the pretence that she was gathering 'vox pops' on political issues for a television programme. Her emphasis is not on individuals' opinions or knowledge about politics, but on 'how people think they are supposed to sound talking about political things in public'. She identifies three ways in which people chose to present themselves in this situation. First, there are speakers who approach the whole issue with irreverence, adopting forms of cynicism, exaggeration or disinterest. Secondly, there are those who are so intimidated and lacking in confidence about political matters that they are able only to resort to clichés or expressions of their own ignorance. Finally, there are the speakers who project themselves as 'concerned citizens', who actively participate in debates about politics, and who believe that what they have to say actually matters.

Each of these positions can be detected in the material analysed here, although the irreverent stance Eliasoph describes is particularly apparent. Eliasoph argues that this stance is essentially a defensive response against a sense of one's own powerlessness – a position that applies particularly to young people. As she argues:

> Such people used their words as a wedge between themselves and the world of politics. They were more interested in showing distance between themselves and politics; in saving face as individuals; in absolving themselves of responsibility for what they saw as the absurdity and corruption of political life (1990: 466).

By rejecting, or positioning oneself as superior to, the whole domain of politics, one is effectively justifying one's own lack of involvement and defending oneself against accusations of ignorance or laziness.

Eliasoph identifies two variants of this irreverent stance that are particularly applicable here. First, there are speakers who adopt what she calls 'cynical chic':

> Cynical chic speakers capitalize on ignorance and powerlessness, making them seem intentional, even exaggerating them. They strenuously, though sometimes with subtlety, assert that they do not care, that they have not been fooled into wasting their time on something they cannot influence, and cannot be held responsible for whatever happens. Perversely, by making lack of power and knowledge seem intentional, the chic cynic can gain an appearance of control (1990: 473).

Secondly, there are those who adopt the position of 'literary critics', condemning the media's coverage of political issues and thereby distancing themselves from what they perceive to be the errors and delusions of the average audience member:

> ... the literary critic analyzes the political performance disinterestedly, cuts through the moral or political content of the show and

'penetrates' right to the aesthetic core of the matter. Sitting in an armchair, observing, the literary critic does not pass judgment. Their key phrase is a passive, 'it appears . . .' (1990: 478).

William Gamson's *Talking Politics* (1992) shares Eliasoph's emphasis on self-presentation in talk. Gamson acknowledges that his data – drawn, like those here, from focus group discussions among friends or acquaintances – cannot be seen as a neutral reflection of people's real opinions and beliefs. In this kind of sociable public setting, people inevitably 'talk to the gallery' – they adjust their contributions not merely to what they perceive as the requirements of the interviewer, but also to a wider audience whom they imagine will read the results of the research. Gamson argues that such talk is often a hybrid of two kinds of talk, or speech genres. On the one hand, there is 'serious public discourse', oriented towards logical argument, accuracy and objectivity, while on the other, there is social talk, which is often playful and not always intended to be taken literally. In combining these two speech genres, the sociable public talk of these interview groups often takes on a 'legendary' form. According to Eisenstadt (1984), this 'legendary' style is one in which

> . . . facts and interpretations of facts were blended to give a pattern of belief which was dramatic, satisfying, consistent with other legends, and more or less true; but truth was not particularly relevant. The power of a legend depended not upon its referential accuracy, but upon the extent to which it could generate consensus and enlist the imaginative energies of participants (quoted in Gamson, 1992: 21).

Gamson also draws on Eliasoph's analysis of the phenomenon of 'cynical chic', which was equally apparent in his interview groups. As Gamson argues, this position is an expression of the speaker's powerlessness and lack of political agency, yet it also serves to confirm it. The cynical chic view leads to 'the expectation that greed and the pursuit of narrow self-interest are typical and, perhaps, even part of human nature' (1992: 36). Political action, Gamson argues, is unlikely to proceed from this kind of boredom and apathy – it needs what he calls the 'hot cognition' of injustice, a sense of righteous indignation rather than weary resignation.

In the two chapters that follow, I present an analysis of the students' discussions of eight specific news items. In summarizing and comparing the responses of different groups, much of the complexity of this negotiation and self-presentation is bound to be lost. In the remainder of this chapter, therefore, I want to present a reading of some more sustained extracts from these discussions, in order to illustrate the process in more detail. The styles of discourse identified above – and particularly the more irreverent stance described by Eliasoph – are readily apparent here, though, as I shall indicate, speakers will often shift – however confidently or uneasily – between these different styles of discourse and the positions they provide.

Cynical Chic?

This group was interviewed at the pilot school in Philadelphia, and consisted of three 13-year-olds: Joel (white), Jeff (African-American) and Winnie (Asian-American). The following extracts come from a point early in the discussion before any of the news items had been screened; although the students were familiar with *Channel One News* because it was used (somewhat intermittently) in their school. In the previous part of the discussion, they had claimed to watch the news only for weather, sports and local stories, particularly those relating to crime. Broadly speaking, it was the two boys who competed with each other to dominate the discussion: Winnie was somewhat marginalized, although her contributions (particularly in the latter part of this extract) are significant.

1 *Joel*: [*Channel One News*] talk most about politics, I noticed that, all the time.

    Jeff: Presidential, nobody really cares about the Presidents.

    Winnie: They talk about the elections and stuff.

5 *DB*: What do you mean ... you said they talk about POLITICS, like this is something nasty in your mouth. What do you mean by 'politics' like that?

    Joel: They talk about Bill Clinton, yeah, what the people expect and then, you know. They're backstabbers anyway, so what's the difference. They say they're going to lower taxes, they raised them. It's not –

10 *Jeff*: I know, who cares about the President? I don't care about the President. 'Cause they're not doing nothing anyway. 'Cause they say they're gonna do something the next time, they don't do it and then – just like Bill Clinton. He said a lot of things, but he don't do it. Every President did that, said a lot of things, but they don't do it.

15 *Winnie*: They make all these promises, and when they are elected President, they don't even care. They don't keep their promises.

    DB: Can you think of an example of that?

    Jeff: I think mostly all the Presidents are bad.

    DB: So they're all the same, pretty much, yeah?

20 *Joel*: With the exception of Carter.

    Jeff: But when they get signed, they think they're more powerful than everybody else just because they're President. I don't know, I think all of them bad, 'cause just like Whitewater and all of that, I think all of them was bad, like George Bush and all of them, Richard Nixon.

Joel: With the exception of Carter, I think that all of them, once they're   25
up there, they lose all sense of who they are, where they came from, and who helped them along the way.

Jeff: They think they're powerful now. They think they can do anything.

Winnie: If it wasn't for us, then they wouldn't be President.

DB: Now this is interesting, can you think of an example, where, you   30
know, they've said they'll do something, and they didn't do it?

Joel: Clinton said he would lower taxes.

Jeff: I know, Bush said he would do the same thing.

Joel: In fact, he raised them.

DB: . . . But don't you think it's important to know about?   35

Jeff: No!

Joel: For us it's not, we don't pay the taxes.

Jeff: Why should we learn about Presidents? We don't pay taxes and my parents don't real care to pay taxes 'cause they're getting cheated out of their taxes too. They've got to pay all these taxes and they're get-   40
ting cheated in them, too. A lot of people get cheated in their taxes.

DB: Yeah?

Joel: Yeah, I don't need to know it, I'm not the one paying taxes.

Winnie: Yeah, that's what I'm saying . . .

Joel: I don't care about politics. I don't need it. It's not going to help me   45
along the way of my life at all.

Jeff: Unless I want to be President.

DB: Yeah? So don't you think if you did pay taxes, then it would make a difference?

Joel: I mean I'd pay attention, or if I had to vote, I mean I'd pay atten-   50
tion, but I wouldn't really care. I mean I'd vote because it's my duty as a citizen, but other than that I don't care.

Jeff: I know, I don't care either.

DB: Yeah, so you don't think it makes a difference who you vote for in the end?   55

Joel: No, there's too much politics, that's the problem.

Jeff: No.

DB: So, if you were going to vote now, who would you vote for?

Jeff: Nobody.

60 *Winnie*: None, I wish we didn't have a President. I wish we could be ourselves.

Jeff: I wish the people could be their own President.

Winnie: Yeah, I mean, I wish we didn't have a President, who cares? I
mean there's always a leader always in this world, like a ruler or a
65   leader, and I don't like that. I wish we could be ourselves, like free.

Joel: I honestly haven't heard the debates on what they're planning to do,
so I wouldn't know.

Jeff: Basically, we have our own choices about what we want to do.
Everybody should be a President and say if they want to cut taxes and
70   everybody would have to agree with it. Like everybody has to make a
choice about who wants taxes and what we should do about crime and
all that, instead of just one person making bad decisions . . .

Joel: And with the two parties, it's even worse. For instance, with the budget . . . the Republicans want to cut Medicare, they want to cut welfare,
75   and the Democrats don't and the Republicans even want to cut Social
Security, but when people are relying on the Social Security and when
people are honestly using welfare to get back on their feet, it's going
to put them back down in the gutter. It's not helping them at all.

Jeff: They don't, I think they should have welfare because some people
80   do need it 'cause some people don't have the chances. But they should
have tests for people on welfare to see if people are on drugs or not
'cause they're probably using it to get drugs. And take the story about
the budget and all that – I think we have the most baddest cops in the
world. We have some real bad cops. They're arresting for nothing . . .

85 *Joel*: They're corrupt, that's what it is.

Jeff: Yeah, corrupt cops . . . I don't like cops. All I like [is] the good ones.
'Cause my uncle was a cop and now he's retired. He's been retired for
a long time, I like good cops but –

DB: Yeah? Let's just go back to the welfare thing. Do you think there
90   should be more welfare, yeah, or they shouldn't cut it?

Joel: I think they shouldn't cut it. They should honestly work harder at
not letting people misuse it because, when they do that, they might pay
somebody five dollars an hour, minimum wage, to do testing to make

sure that these people aren't coming back and back to get all this
money.   95

Jeff: But there aren't a lot of good jobs out here right now. People got to
work at McDonald's, they don't have a lot of chances to get a lot of
money. See they have to go through college, like say 20 years ago, a lot
of people couldn't go through college because they didn't have the
money, the Moms were working two jobs and they have to stay home   100
with the kids and all that. Like my Grandma, she didn't make it past
ninth grade because she had to watch her little sisters and brothers and
all that 'cause it's hard. It's harder for older people to get jobs now,
they really can't 'cause they all have degrees and college degrees, 'cause
they can't get it if they don't have good jobs.   105

DB: So you think if they made it easier for people to get jobs, then they
wouldn't have to spend so much on welfare? What do you think about
that Winnie, do you think that's right or do you think they should cut
welfare or have more welfare?

Joel: Exactly.   110

Winnie: I mean, I'm sure, even if you hadn't gone to school, you still could
start a home business and stuff. My Dad doesn't go to school, he never
went to school before except kindergarten or something. He can still
start his own business like we did last year.

Jeff: Yeah, well how does he get the money?   115

Winnie: He earned it himself as hard work. You just don't get on
welfare.

Jeff: How did he get a job if he never went to school?

Winnie: He never did. I don't know, he told me, when he was younger he
tried to read the newspaper and tried to learn the words and every-   120
thing so then, I don't know.

Jeff: If you never went to school, if you don't have the knowledge that
people – 'cause when they go to school, they tell you different things
that a lot of people don't know, then they know more, they get a
better job.   125

DB: See, the point is, all the debate you're having here, you're talking
about, you know, should there be more welfare or less welfare or
should they create jobs for people and whatever. Now isn't that
what politicians are debating about all the time? Isn't that what they're
talking about in Washington?   130

Jeff: No, they talking about welfare, but they're trying to cut welfare.

Joel: Yeah, but a lot of it's just a lot of BS too.

DB: So they're talking about it, but you don't believe what they say?

Joel: Talking about it, but there are two different parties, they don't
135   believe in the same things and so they're going to argue about it for
the next year or so.

Jeff: Yeah, a lot of what they're saying, they don't really care about.

The early stages of this extract could be read as a symptomatic example
of 'cynical chic'. The students adopt a principled rejection of politicians as
dishonest, unprincipled and self-interested. There is a strong sense of collaboration here, as though they are rehearsing a familiar litany of complaints
in a way they have done several times before. Thus, there is a lot of repetition, particularly of key phrases ('I don't care'), and several contributions
complement and build upon the ones that precede them. On one level, the
arguments appear relatively superficial. Much of the criticism is very generalized (lines 10–16), and the students are unable to provide an example when
asked on the first occasion (line 18). Nevertheless, they do manage this on
the second invitation (lines 32–4), and they also refer to Whitewater as a
contemporary example of political corruption (line 23). Joel, who appeared
to be marginally better informed than the others – he had talked earlier
about watching the news with his grandmother in order that he would not
'feel like a fool' when talking to people – also makes an exception for
Jimmy Carter, although the grounds for this are not explained (lines 20,
25–7). In this case, and perhaps in general, it might not be unreasonable to
conclude that at this stage the students are simply rehearsing arguments
derived from their parents or other family members. Why, one might ask,
do they seem to be so concerned about taxes when (as they subsequently
point out, lines 37–42, 44) they do not have to pay them?

However, there is a considerable amount of anger and bitterness here,
which is more than merely 'chic'. The tone is quite forcefully dismissive, as
is some of the vocabulary ('backstabbers', line 8; 'cheated', line 39).
Nevertheless, the problem, as far as they are concerned, is not so much the
system as a whole as the weaknesses and inconsistencies of individuals.
Thus, the students attempt to place personal blame on individual presidents
(lines 21–40) just as they later distinguish between 'good cops' and 'bad
cops' (lines 84–9). The offending presidents are described rather in the way
one might describe a bully in school: 'They think they can do anything'
(line 28). Significantly, however, Winnie poses the issue in more explicitly
political terms, as a matter of the relationship between the people and their
elected representatives – 'if it wasn't for us, then they wouldn't be President'
(line 29) – and this prefigures her later comment (lines 60–1, 63–5),
which almost anarchistically proposes that the people should become their
own leaders.

As in some of the comments discussed earlier in the chapter, the students
explain their alienation from politics in terms of their structural position as

children: they do not pay taxes (line 37–44), nor do they have the right to vote (line 51–4). As such, their views are simply irrelevant; there is no point in them bothering to develop any, or in informing themselves about politics. Joel's 'us' (line 37) clearly refers to young people, as compared with Winnie's more inclusive 'us' (line 29), which refers to people in general (although the fact that young people cannot vote might seem to exclude them from this). However, Joel argues that even as a voter or a taxpayer, he would not necessarily become more interested in politics. The tax system is also condemned as unjust (lines 38–40), and it would seem that voting is merely a matter of one's mechanical 'duty as a citizen' (lines 50–2) – a formulation Joel used again in a later interview. At this stage, the rejection of politics is comprehensive and absolute (lines 54–9), and this leads inevitably to the anarchistic individualism initiated by Winnie (lines 60–5) and taken up by Jeff (lines 68–72) – although its rather self-consciously fanciful status is clearly indicated by Winnie's repeated use of the word 'wish'.

At this point in the discussion, however, an interesting shift occurs. Joel's response to the question about voting (lines 66–7) is noticeably less absolutist than the other students'; and there are indications in his next contribution (and perhaps also in his earlier reference to Carter) that he does in fact have some understanding of the differences between the parties. In this relatively substantial contribution (lines 73–8), Joel steps down from his principled rejection of politics *per se*, to make a point that is both politically partisan (in this case, pro-Democrat) and concerned with a specific area of policy (in this case, welfare) – even though he appears to be rejecting the two-party system (lines 73–8), as he does again towards the end of this extract (lines 73, 134). Joel's point here builds on the other students' earlier comments about the relations between politicians and the people – he voices his concern on behalf of 'people' who are 'honest' and in need of 'help' – but it also moves the discussion into a different register.

Significantly, this new direction is primarily taken up by Jeff and Winnie. The topics covered in the discussion that follows include drugs, police corruption and harassment, alternatives to welfare, unemployment and under-employment, poverty, the problems faced by the elderly and by immigrants, and the need for education (lines 79–125). Although I do attempt to steer the discussion back towards the debate about welfare (lines 89–90, 106–9), the students all volunteer substantial contributions without prompting from me.

What is most obvious about this part of the discussion is the way it is anchored in personal experience, or at least the experience of the students' families (Jeff's grandmother, line 101–3; Winnie's father, lines 111–14). These are experiences of the struggle with poverty that run across several generations, and they implicitly represent the experiences of the ethnic minority groups to which Jeff and Winnie belong. Yet while Jeff argues that education is the means to advancement (lines 122–5), Winnie's position is even more voluntaristic: she argues that advancement can come about through 'hard work' and self-education, rather than by looking to the state (lines 111–21). Interestingly, Joel takes a back seat at this stage; his contribution to the welfare discussion does not refer to personal experience (lines 91–5), and arises in response to my attempt to pull the discussion back to a more conventional political agenda. He does not re-enter the discussion until it returns to the topic of party politics (line 132), which may suggest that, for all his overt cynicism, his engagement with such issues is more conventionally political than he might care to admit.

As I point out (lines 127–30), the issues being discussed here are clearly 'political', and they have direct resonances with contemporary debates in Washington – for example, the debate around the government shutdown, discussed in the following chapter. However, even here, the students directly refute the suggestion that politics as conventionally defined has anything to do with their experience; they reassert the 'cynical chic' position that politics is a pointless series of arguments (lines 132–7), and that politicians simply do not care about the people whom they represent. A clear distinction is drawn between the 'BS' of conventional politics and the more broadly political issues that relate to their everyday lives.

This discussion indicates some of the dimensions of 'cynical chic', but also some of its limitations. On the one hand, there is a fairly generalized distrust of conventional politics, as both corrupt and irrelevant, yet on the other, there is a deeply-felt engagement with more local political issues, that emerges from personal experience and family history. The crucial point is that the students perceive there to be no connection between the two – and indeed, deliberately refute this connection when it is proposed to them. These students' critical rejection of conventional politics could certainly be seen as an expression of the resistance of the powerless, but there is also a sense in which it undermines the possibility of them developing political agency. Indeed, in some ways it could be seen to reinforce the voluntaristic individualism that Winnie adopts here, and which could be seen as characteristic of American political culture.

The Media Critics

This group, recorded at the Philadelphia school, consisted of three 17-year-old African-American students, Dartagnan, Acacia and Patrick: all were high academic achievers, and claimed to be regular viewers of news and news magazine programmes like *Dateline* and *20/20*. Acacia was employed by the school to do secretarial work for an hour each day before lessons began, and she said that one significant motivation for her to watch the news was in order to keep up with the conversations of the 'three men' she worked with. This discussion turned quite quickly towards criticisms of the emphasis on 'bad news', particularly in local news programmes:

1   *Dartagnan*: ... the news that you hear, [it's all] like violence and
    everything, you know that stuff is going on. They constantly keep
    telling you about the violence and the killings, I mean, it's OK
    to know about it, but you know about it to a point where they're
5   telling you OK somebody else got shot, you know? Another
    building burned down.

    DB: So you feel there's too much coverage of that?

    Dartagnan: There's not too much coverage of it, but, I mean, if it
    goes on and it happens, it should be news that the people should
10 be aware about, I mean, you should be aware about what's going
    on around you.

    DB: But there kind of comes a point where you're not so inter-
    ested in hearing anymore about it?

    Dartagnan: Right.

15 *DB*: OK, alright, Patrick, how about you – is there a particular
    news show that you choose to watch?

    Patrick: Usually, I just watch Channel 6, because I think their
    ratings are the best, they're just professional, better than – But
    what I don't like about the news, all the time, is it's just so nega-
20 tive, that you don't want to watch it, it's like – Or they put all
    the negative stuff in the front and then at the very end there's
    a million positive things that are happening, but it doesn't make
    the news because, I don't know, I guess it's not good for the
    ratings or something. But I'd rather watch it and listen to good
25 news rather than, 'cause you know, when someone says like three
    people got shot in a subway, it doesn't affect me, I don't really
    care, it's like, all right I've heard it 20 million times, just get
    over it. But, you know, when like we protested against the school
    board, against the city for more funding, then I wanted to hear
30 that 'cause it was something that we did and it was positive and
    I think we should have gotten more coverage.

    DB: Did that get on the news, I mean, I heard about it on the
    radio actually?

    Patrick: Yeah, for like 15 seconds, but see someone that ran in a
35 market and shot 20 people gets on the news for like an hour.

    DB: Yeah, so you think, particularly the crime news, you think
    there's too much of it now, or the balance is wrong, yeah?

    Patrick: Yeah, I don't like the crime news. They make it just seem
    like it's like nothing though, you know? I mean they make it
40 seem like people are just gonna do it so, why don't they just

cover it and then, you know, I mean that's what people want to see and that's what people want to hear all the time and I think sometimes it plays a role in how people actually think about the way it is here.

45　*DB*: Yeah, you mean they get more fearful?

Patrick: Yeah, and then they, you know, they just get more paranoid about things and then the next thing you know they're carrying a gun and they shoot someone, they're on the news.

DB: Yeah, so it kind of escalates?

50　*Patrick*: Yeah.

Dartagnan: It needs to give a more balanced [view of] society than we actually [get]. I mean, I'm not saying we're living in a bad society or anything, but I mean, you know, things are not perfect, so we know there's that. There's gonna be violence, there's gonna
55　be killings. But it takes you to the point where you think every time you go outside, you're gonna see someone get shot or you're gonna see someone get murdered, or you're gonna see a fire. They do, like you say, escalate to that point. Every time you turn on the news, it's just like –

60　*DB*: Yeah, you don't agree, Acacia?

Acacia: Well, yeah I agree in a little bit, but I mean, I'm not saying I like to hear stuff like that, but I'd rather know where the most killings and the most stabbing and the most robbing and raping and fires are, so I could know, not necessarily go to that
65　particular place at nine o'clock at night.

DB: Right.

Acacia: I mean, keep me informed, I don't want to be left in the dark about someone getting brutally murdered around a corner from me, you know ... I don't know, maybe I'm just negative
70　thinking, but I figure, these journalists want to keep people informed and that's what they love to do, but over all the people that are in charge, I really don't think they care what they put on there. I mean, news stations get ratings just as well as sitcoms and everything else, so I mean the more ratings they get,
75　I guess, the more money maybe, they're making more money, so they're going for better ratings and if they see that people watch blood and want to know until they're scared and they watch more news and maybe, you know, then they just keep on putting it on.

80 *DB*: So you think that's true. I mean, do you think people really want to watch that kind of stuff?

Acacia: Well, I don't think they want to watch it, I think more people do watch it so they can be informed as, you know, it's like, if it's happy stuff, well, then OK, it's happy, you know, I
85 don't need to hear anything, but if my children are getting, going to a school where there's murder and stuff, I'm gonna want to watch the news to find out what's going on – my children are gonna need to move them out to find a better place and they tend to watch it for the safety . . .

90 *DB*: OK, we talked a bit about crime news. One other big kind of news is about politics, yeah? Is that something that interests you, or bores you, or –

Acacia: Well, I'm just really tired about . . . hearing about Whitewater and I mean, I know it's stuff you have to keep
95 current with, but gosh, it's just like the O. J. trial! I'm just tired of it. I mean, it's been like a year and a half.

Patrick: Yeah, let's not get into that please.

Dartagnan: Politics!

Acacia: Talk about writing something into a hole.

100 *Dartagnan*: It's like I wrote in my English paper, I said politics is like they're playing a game. I'm not saying it is a game-game, but I'm putting in an analogy, they're playing a game and just because they're not playing by the rules, that they're giving, could be like the coaches, the politicians are like the coaches,
105 and they're playing a game, just because they're not playing by the correct rules, people that can't nag them and talk to them about and like bench them all the time because we're the one who put them in there. We're the ones that voted them in there and I mean –

110 *Patrick*: I didn't.

Dartagnan: Well, the people who are 18 and over voted them in there. But once they get in office, there's not too much we can do until election time comes around and I mean, if we're not informed about what's going on, we don't like really know who
115 to vote for. Like if we didn't know that David Duke was a racist, we probably would have voted wrong and we would have had a racist person as President. It's OK that we know some stuff, but other stuff that is important – Hillary Clinton, so what if she had fingers on the document? It's not important that her finger-
120 prints were on the document.

Acacia: Yeah, but I get really tired of the mudslinging ... during Election time. I mean, I don't care who slept with who ten years ago, if they're not that type of person now, I mean, what's the purpose in telling me?

[Section omitted: dismissive discussion of the Republican primaries.]

125 *Patrick*: All we want is one decent president – one who didn't do anything, a Boy Scout, that's all we ever want.

DB: You don't think that's going to happen?

Patrick: Nope.

Acacia: You're going to get a Boy Scout that slept with a Girl
130 Scout Leader that robbed a bank when she was 13.

Dartagnan: I mean all this really started with Nixon and Watergate, that's why they started like getting the scoops out on all the presidents and before everybody thought that the presidents were like the best people in the world.

135 *Patrick*: Untouched.

Dartagnan: I mean, but I don't see why the journalists have to like dig back into someone's lives –

Acacia: 'Cause they're nosy.

Dartagnan: So what if Bill Clinton smoked marijuana when he was
140 in high school? I mean so why dig them up, when he is trying to like be the better President? He won't be the better President if you keep mentioning his mistakes ...

Acacia: Keep messing with him.

Patrick: But the ideal we have about these people is all made by
145 the media, so you don't really know that.

Acacia: Yeah, like other persons are made into saints. Like Teddy Roosevelt was about as dumb as an ox, but you know, I mean they didn't have media coverage, so he wasn't seen on TV, he wasn't publicized, the media wasn't as –

150 *DB*: I mean, some people would say it's legitimate for the media to discover all of these things, you know, to tell us if they're hypocrites.

Dartagnan: But like I said, it's freedom of the press, but the press should be limited to a certain amount of freedom ...

[Section omitted: discussion of invasions of privacy, comparing media coverage of the Dunblane families with coverage of the 1995 Pan-Am disaster.]

155 Dartagnan: ... they want those ratings, they want to be the first people to get it out there, so they can say well, I found it, I discovered it first, and they get more ratings – that's what it all comes down to: money and ratings, and it's a shame.

   Patrick: Just money, just money.

160 *Acacia*: The American economy.

These students claimed to be regular viewers, both of nightly news bulletins and of news magazine programmes such as *20–20* and *Dateline*. Nevertheless, the bulk of their comments on news were extremely critical. Of course, given their age and their status as high academic achievers, they might well have seen this as an implicit requirement of the situation: despite our initial discussion of their favourite television programmes, a research interview about their responses to news was implicitly an invitation to engage in rational critique rather than playful celebration. In Gamson's terms, their talk is closer to 'serious public discourse' than 'sociable interaction' (Gamson, 1992: 20–1). They 'talk to the gallery', in the expectation that their views will be taken seriously.

Their complaint about the dominance of 'bad news' is, on one level, a familiar one in public debates about news. Indeed, it is a complaint that has led some US television stations to provide 'happy news' or 'family-friendly' news, which avoids the kind of material mentioned here. Nevertheless, as the students acknowledge, this is a double-edged debate. Dartagnan's second contribution here (lines 4–5) emphasizes the 'need to know', almost as a kind of moral duty ('the people should be aware'); while Acacia's later contribution to this debate (lines 61–89) sees it in much more personal terms. On the one hand, Dartagnan is keen to present himself as a 'media critic'; but on the other, he does not want to relinquish the equally powerful position of the 'concerned citizen' (cf. Eliasoph, 1990).

Patrick's initial observation about news is a positive one, although it is significant that he quickly abandons this in order to pursue Dartagnan's critique. His long contribution (lines 17–31) extends this critique in two ways. First, even in his initial observation, he emphasizes the status of news as a *product*, as something that is more or less 'professionally' produced, and which is primarily motivated by the drive for 'ratings'. Secondly, he implies that this emphasis on 'bad news' can lead to a form of bias – although he does not directly suggest that this is politically motivated. His mention of the students' protest against the school board – in a dispute over inequalities of funding – also serves to position him as a political actor in his own right.

As I have argued elsewhere (Buckingham, 1993c), this 'media literate' discourse implicitly assumes the existence of an 'other' – the mass audience of viewers who are gullible enough to believe and be influenced by what they watch. This dimension becomes explicit in Patrick's contribution on lines 38–44. The media are condemned, perhaps in a somewhat contradictory way, both for encouraging violence and for making it appear less serious than it actually is. However, this is not a simplistic 'effects' theory; Patrick's argument is not that media violence simply triggers real-life violence, but that it creates a climate of opinion, which then justifies particular kinds of behaviour (cf. Gerbner and Gross, 1976). At the same time, Patrick's account clearly does distance him, as the media critic, from the 'people' (line 41) who are prone to such delusions: the third-person pronoun 'they' is repeated five times in lines 46–9.

Dartagnan's contribution here (lines 47–54) develops Patrick's earlier observation about bias (lines 25–8), implying that it is the media's responsibility to provide a 'balanced', accurate representation of the world. This call for accuracy derives from what Corner *et al.* (1990: 50) term the 'civic frame': that is, it is implicitly concerned with 'propriety in addressing a national audience on a controversial topic'. This concern with accuracy (and related notions of bias, objectivity and balance) plays a major role in the discussions of specific items analysed in the following chapters.

By contrast, Acacia's contribution to this debate adopts a much more personal stance. She positions herself – and her future children (lines 82–9) – as potential victims of crime. Unlike Dartagnan's rather generalized assertion of the need to 'be aware' (line 10), she asserts that there are very specific reasons for this, to do with her own safety. The potential of such material to generate an unrealistic fear of crime is set against the need for self-protection and crime prevention (cf. Buckingham, 1996: Chapter 6). At the same time, Acacia extends Dartagnan's earlier emphasis on news as a product. She distinguishes between the motivations of journalists, which are implicitly seen as honourable, and those of the 'people in charge', which are condemned as merely commercial. Significantly, news is compared with a form that is seen as trivial, the sit-com. Here again, there is an implicit condemnation of the mass audience, the 'people' who want to 'watch blood' (line 77) – although Acacia is somewhat equivocal in her response to my question on this (lines 82–4), implying that her motivations are identical with those of people in general.

The students' discussion of political news, while possibly somewhat more articulate, is initially very close to that of the previous group. They are critical both of the amount and repetitiveness of media coverage of politics, and of the behaviour of politicians (for example, the 'mudslinging': line 121). There is a generalized cynicism about politics, which Dartagnan encapsulates in his rather self-consciously clever analogy with a game (lines 100–8). The media are accused of failing to distinguish between what is 'important' and what is not (lines 113–19).

On the other hand, the students do recognize some sense of duty to 'keep current' (line 94) and to inform themselves sufficiently in order to make sensible decisions about voting in the future (lines 110–13). However, the fact that they are unable to vote now inevitably means that they have less of a stake in this process (lines 110–19).

In the discussion that follows, there is a genuine ambivalence about the students' criticisms of the media. On the one hand, they condemn the media's invasions of privacy, particularly in the case of incidents that occurred in the distant past (lines 120–1, 136–7); and in the section omitted here, they are highly critical of interviews with the relatives of those killed in the 1995 Pan-Am disaster. On the other hand, they imply that their ideals about politicians are merely illusory: they will never be 'Boy Scouts' or 'saints', however much one might fantasize about this (lines 125–30, 146). In this respect, the role of the media is seen as extremely powerful but also as quite double-edged. The media both create these ideals and destroy them; they can make it difficult for the president to do his job (in the case of Clinton: line 139–41), but they can also misrepresent the President and hence mislead the public (in the case of Roosevelt: lines 146–9).

While they continue to imply that these media-created ideas are merely illusory, they also position themselves in a rather different way from their earlier discussion of crime news. Patrick in particular talks about 'we' (lines 126, 144), implicitly aligning himself with the mass audience who share this media fantasy of 'untouched' decency; although the others situate such beliefs historically, and in terms of what 'everybody' (line 133) used to think. Arguably, however, Patrick's 'we' is an extremely distanced one – it represents the American people in general, rather than a group with which he personally is strongly identified. The discussion here is effectively about 'mass psychology'. Like Eliasoph's 'literary critics', Patrick implies that one cannot look beyond the media – that the show is everything, and that one will never know what these people are really like (line 144–5) (cf. Eliasoph, 1990: 479–80).

Ultimately, however, they return to what seems to be a more comfortable position, namely the condemnation of the commercial motivations of broadcasters. Nevertheless, 'ratings' seem to exist here as a kind of abstraction: they are not related to real audiences – or at least to any audience which these students seem to be willing to admit to joining.

This extract provides a clear instance of another of Eliasoph's 'irreverent' presentations of self, namely that of the 'literary critics' (Eliasoph, 1990: 478–80). These students position themselves at some distance from the news and from the public performance of politics. They condemn the media for their sensationalism, their violation of privacy, and their ultimately commercial motivations. They present their own stance as rational and dispassionate. This 'media literate' discourse thus offers a considerable degree of power and security. In distancing themselves from the media, the students also distance themselves from what they perceive to be the average audience member. By virtue of their superior critical powers, they are able to 'see through' phenomena that delude or mislead lesser mortals.

This presentation of self is perhaps partly a consequence of selective schooling (cf. Buckingham, 1993a: Chapter 4). Towards the end of our interview, these students directly pointed out to me that they were unrepresentative of their age group; their selective school had given them a training in critical awareness which they suggested was denied to students who attended 'neighbourhood schools'. This critical stance is thus not so much a matter of the resentment of the powerless, as it is to some extent in the case of the previous group. On the contrary, it would appear to represent a typically 'educated' discourse about the media.

Nevertheless, as an elite group in the making, the students appear equally keen to present themselves as 'concerned citizens'. Like Eliasoph's respondents in this category, they refer to past conversations (or in this case, school assignments) on these issues, and draw on relevant facts; and they clearly assume that what they have to say really matters. Their perspective on the media is not merely that of frustrated consumers who want to be entertained. While they may be somewhat pessimistic about it, they do hold out a possible role for the media in encouraging citizenship and bringing about an informed democracy, in terms that come close to those of Habermas (1962/1989). Likewise, while they are dismissive of politicians – particularly Republicans – they do implicitly support the notion that Clinton might be a 'better President', and that their vote might make a difference.

The relationship between these presentations of self and the students' potential for political agency remains an open question. As Eliasoph (1990) remarks, the literary critics are metaphorically 'trapped in their armchairs', observing the spectacle and the show without feeling obliged to take it seriously. And yet, as 'concerned citizens', and as members of an educated elite, these students are precisely those who are more likely to engage in political action – as they have already done in relation to their own school funding. In this case, perhaps, irreverence may be only skin-deep.

The Disrespectful Readers

This group was interviewed at the London school, and consisted of three 12-year-olds: Imran (British-Asian), Matt and Keirra (both white). This interview took place at the end of a fairly intensive week of fieldwork, and it was also disrupted at an early stage by a fire alarm, which meant that we all had to pile out into the playground. As a result, the tone of the interview was comparatively informal and distracted; there was a great deal of laughter, shouting and generally riotous behaviour.

Unlike their peers in this age group, the students clearly set out to have a good time: 'serious public discourse' was conspicuous by its relative absence. There was also a good deal of competition for the floor, particularly between Matt and Keirra: in our initial discussion of favourite programmes, each frequently dismissed the other's choices in quite absolutist terms. Imran was effectively marginalized, although (as we shall see) he did achieve some limited success in buying into their dynamic.

DB: Let's just talk a bit about news, yes? [General groans] News is boring?

Keirra: News is crap.

DB: OK. Tell us why it's boring.

5　*Keirra*: It's not a good idea if the man's doing this [imitates] – just sitting there going blah, blah, the news tonight is lah, lah, lah, and it's boring, isn't it?

Matt: Lah, lah, lah.

Keirra: Depends if you're listening to it or not.

10　*Matt*: The news tonight. There's been an IRA bomb in Liverpool. Lots and lots of people were killed.

Keirra: It's a bit stupid to say 'lots and lots of people were killed – and now to the next news'.

Matt: Yeah. 'Cause he's looking at the camera.

15　*Keirra*: [Shouting] People were killed and it was very, very funny. [Noises] They're boring.

Matt: And the Channel 5 News is just stupid, because they're trying to make it appeal to the [parodic voice:] 'younger generation'. And it's just shitty. It doesn't appeal to me. They're walking

20　round the newsroom to make it interesting. It's not. It just makes it that you can't hear them.

DB: All right. Are you at all interested in news then?

Matt: Well, if it's on, then I'll probably watch it.

Keirra: I like the lead story, but not the presenters.

25　*Matt*: If I've got nothing better to do then I'll watch the news. Sometimes it's completely boring and other times it's just quite interesting, like the time they cloned the sheep or something like that. And like all that stuff on the planets and that. But when it comes to there's a war still going on there – we all know that.

30　*Keirra*: Like it's stopped?! [Laughs] ... And they say, and there is still a war in Bosnia. Well, we know this day, and it's not going to stop the next day, is it, it's obviously still going to be going on. Why don't they just tell us when it does stop?

Matt: Yes.

35　*Keirra*: It's all about dead bodies – it's not interesting. It's just – yuk. It's all horrible.

DB: Do you ever find the news is quite upsetting like that, when it shows you horrible –

Keirra: Well, it doesn't seem upsetting any more once you've seen
40   – you see it on the news . . .

DB: So Imran, do you like the news?

Imran: No, I hate it.

DB: You hate it. So why? Tell me.

Imran: I dunno. It's just – I keep wondering if they wear shorts
45   under their – [much laughter]. It hacks me off. Because I'm
       thinking if they do and I don't pay attention to it –

Keirra: They should have glass under the desk, so you could see
       what they're wearing. Then they would resolve the question . . .

Matt: And what's on the papers that they always shuffle at the end
50   of the news?

DB: You mean, what are they for?

Matt: They just have these papers and shuffle them.

Keirra: They've finished the news, yeah, and then all the lot –
       they're all shuffling and looking at each other and [imitates news
55   readers' banter].

Matt: It's like people expect that they've forgotten their screens.
       [Laughter]

Imran: They're bumping into their desks and they're going like
       that when the lights go dim.

60 *Matt*: It's like a load of madmen in the dark. Going around shuf-
       fling papers.

Keirra: They probably can't even see the letters on the keyboard.

Matt: You can't see to shuffle the papers. I mean, they shuffle them
       and sit there shuffling them. They definitely shuffle – for five
65   minutes . . . And what do they do after they've shuffled them?
       They just re-shuffle them.

Keirra: It's like one of those surveys; the newsreaders spend 50
       per cent of their time shuffling papers.

Matt: They shuffle them, and get them into order, then they put
70   them down and they just walk away, and leave them to the next
       newsreader to come on and shuffle them again [laughter] . . .

Keirra: And the other thing is that all the good stuff on the News at 10 it goes – BONG! [imitates Big Ben sound from the *News at Ten* headlines].

75   There is a war in Bosnia. BONG! There is a war in France. BONG! There is a curfew in New Zealand – and the interesting stories – they always have stories put in the middle and sport, and then at the end it does a five second feature of an unbelievable story.

80   *DB*: All right. So what would be a really interesting story then?

Keirra: There's this little one about –

Matt: Show off!

Keirra: This teacher who made this owl to get the class to keep quiet. It was a little electric owl and it just sat there and flapped
85   its wings and it goes 'you are being too noisy'. Like a robot.

I thought that was very funny . . .

Matt: They have those little diagrams, those little animated diagrams, it's like – 'and the tax is' – and the bar goes up – it's like Wow! I don't usually know what they're about, but they're
90   fun, the way these little things go up.

[*Extract omitted: Keirra praises* Newsround *because it only features wars 'once in a while".*]

Keirra: [*Newsround*] is like for 7-year-olds and they don't want to put them off their food. It's like they're thinking of someone rushing round and that –

Matt: A land mine. [Laughter]

95   *Keirra*: When you see a picture of, like, a headless, armless, yuk, you don't – that's the problem with the news, they tell you all about bodies, they say 'oh, his head was chopped off, was in this –". They always say stuff, like to build up pressure.

Matt: And they show the grave.

100   *Keirra*: Oh, he was a lovely person, and –

Matt: A lovely person and he was killed in this way. They make it sound really interesting, like he was a serial killer or some-thing. And I want to see that body – it sounds really interesting, but all they show you is this little body bag.

105   *Keirra*: Or a table with this white sheet over it. A few blood stains, and you like go – [sarcastically] 'that's interesting'.

Matt: Or they show you the grave . . .

DB: So you'd like more killing of animals and dead bodies?

Matt: I just want to see what they're talking about and have inter-
110   esting stuff – so that you can actually see the interesting stuff.

Within this discussion as a whole, the means for achieving status are quite straightforward, and are established very quickly. Power is gained through subverting the 'serious' intent, both of television news and of the interview itself. As in the groups discussed above, there is a clear 'speech genre' with which the students are evidently familiar, and within which they are able confidently to improvise.

Condemnation of the news is at a premium here, although this condemnation itself has to take a subversive form. There are no elaborate complaints here about bias in the news, or its inadequacy as a source of information: to speak in such terms would be to take it – and the interview itself – much too seriously. On the contrary, news is judged as though it were a failed type of entertainment: mockery, parody and exaggeration are the order of the day. There is a great deal of acting out, complete with appropriate gestures, facial expressions and tones of voice – much of which is obviously lost in the transcript. Crucially, much of this debunking of the pomposity of news is directed at its *form*, as though too much would be lost by appearing to take its content too seriously. To use another Bakhtinian concept, this is a case of interview as carnival (Bakhtin, 1968).

Keirra's first contribution here very much sets the tone, using a word I suspect she would be unlikely to use in front of her teacher (line 3). Matt's choice of the bomb incident as the basis for parody (line 10–11) reinforces this; laughing at death and human suffering, as the students go on to do repeatedly, is clearly intended as an affront to 'good taste'. At the same time, the students are implying that the news itself does not take such material sufficiently seriously (lines 12–13) – reflecting a degree of ambivalence on this issue which is developed later in the discussion.

Matt's comment about 'looking at the camera' (line 14) is hard to interpret at this point, but it clearly implies that news is a constructed artefact, and this is strongly developed in his subsequent criticism of Channel 5 News (lines 17–19). Matt effectively refuses to be constructed here in terms of adults' patronizing conceptions of the 'younger generation'; and he too uses a taboo word, signalling that this situation is one in which conventional school decorum has been temporarily abandoned.

At this point, and at my instigation, there is a slight break in the proceedings as both Matt and Keirra somewhat grudgingly acknowledge that they do watch the news (lines 23–4). Even here, however, Matt argues that the news is only acceptable if he has 'nothing better to do', and the news stories he mentions are concerned with scientific discoveries rather than domestic or international politics. Significantly, the discussion quickly returns to the condemnation of news coverage of war. Here again, my attempt to introduce a more 'serious' tone (lines 37–8) is effectively shrugged off; for Keirra to admit that she found such material upsetting would result in a loss of face, partly because it would be an admission of weakness, but also perhaps because it would undermine her subversive stance. Nevertheless, she does again implicitly blame the news for not taking this kind of material seriously enough – hence for bringing about a kind of desensitization (lines 39–40) – although this more serious criticism is not pursued.

My question to Imran, who had hitherto been rather marginalized by the competitive banter of the others, seems to pose him with a dilemma. His eventual response (lines 44–6) rather calculatedly sustains the air of carnival, even if the question it poses has been stock-in-trade for generations of satirists. This leads on to some further parodies of the routine mannerisms of news presentation – the obsessive shuffling of papers, the pointless typing on keyboards once the lights have gone out, and so forth (lines 49–71). There is a great deal of hilarity and exaggerated parody here, which cannot be conveyed in the transcript.

Although some of this debunking is far from original, it does nevertheless require a certain degree of familiarity with news conventions, which somewhat contradicts the students' overt rejection of the genre. Keirra's subsequent parody of the introductory headlines of the ITN *News at Ten* (lines 72–9) is quite perceptive in this respect; she displays a clear understanding of the typical sequence both of the headlines and of the programme itself.

While Keirra's response to my invitation to describe an 'interesting' story is fairly facetious (lines 83–6), she does eventually return to the topic of media coverage of wars. This would suggest that, despite distancing herself from the '7-year-olds' who watch *Newsround* (lines 91–3), she herself is occasionally upset by such material.

Given the overall tone of the discussion, however, the students' account of this more serious topic is inevitably somewhat uneasy. Some of the comments and responses here sustain the subversive stance established in earlier parts of the discussion (see lines 10–14): the laughter that follows Matt's mention of land mines (line 95), for example, is self-consciously 'sick'. Matt also adopts a 'hard', almost bloodthirsty, stance akin to that of a horror fan (cf. Buckingham, 1996: Chapter 4), particularly through his mention of a potential 'serial killer' (lines 101–4). Keirra's stance is rather more ambivalent, however. On the one hand, she represents such material as disgusting (lines 96–8), in line with her earlier comments (lines 36–7), while on the other she complains that the news does not show enough of it. She accuses the news of using verbal description to 'build up pressure', leading viewers to expect explicit images that are eventually denied to them (lines 95–9, 106–7). Both Matt and Keirra repeatedly use the word 'interesting' here (lines 103–4, 106, 109–10) to apply to such apparently forbidden material. Here again, their stance may be partly subversive for its own sake; it also reflects a refusal to accept the kinds of protection which they suggest are seen as necessary for younger children (lines 91–3).

In some respects, these students could be seen to represent John Fiske's 'ideal reader' of television news, discussed in Chapter 3 (Fiske, 1989). They display scant respect for conventional forms of 'seriousness' or 'good taste', and attempt to subvert the logocentric, consensual world of news at every turn. As I have implied, this response is partly cued by the context of the interview itself: in refusing to take the topic seriously, they are also seeking to challenge my authority – and perhaps, beyond that, the authority of the school. These students are flagrantly refusing to play the part of 'good students' – or indeed of 'good little citizens'.

In this respect, this extract is untypical of these discussions; and I have included it partly as a kind of antidote to some of the more intense seriousness that follows. This is not to say that there were not elements of this in other discussions, but in general most students were more willing to play what they perceived to be the game. While I suspect many of them might have relished this kind of playful subversion, they clearly felt it to be inappropriate in the context.

Ultimately, however, this subversion is comparatively superficial. Keirra in particular hints towards some more serious criticisms of television news, particularly in terms of its coverage of wars and disasters. She is clearly upset by such material, and returns to it on several occasions. She argues that it is not treated sufficiently seriously (lines 12–13); that it has a desensitizing effect (lines 40–1); that it is held out as a kind of 'teaser' to attract viewers (lines 98–9); and, perhaps inconsistently, that it should be shown in more detail (lines 105–6). Nevertheless, these more serious criticisms cannot be sustained or developed in this context; to do so would be to take both news and the interview itself much too seriously, and hence to abandon the security and power which seem to be promised by subversion.

Conclusion

In several respects, the data presented in this chapter appear to provide strong support for the concerns discussed in Chapter 1. The overall picture is one of alienation, indifference and cynicism. On the face of it, it would be tempting to conclude that young people today could not care less about politics, at least as conventionally defined. They seem to perceive little motivation to become 'informed citizens' or active participants in civil society. On this basis, there is indeed significant cause for concern about the future of democracy.

However, it is vital to take account of the social contexts in which such statements are made. Whether they are giving voice to alienation and apathy or engaging in detailed critical discussions of political issues, we cannot take what individuals say at face value. Talk needs to be interpreted, not as a straightforward reflection of what individuals really think or believe, but as a form of social action.

In this respect, there is a significant difference between the material presented here and that which is to follow. The data analysed in this chapter have largely been taken from the students' general discussions, both of politics and of television news. By contrast, the two following chapters focus in some detail on their readings of specific news items. In the process, several of the themes introduced here are explored in more detail, though this more focused material also raises rather different questions. The activity of talking about specific items makes it much harder for the students to sustain the generalized positions and orientations analysed here. 'Cynical chic', for example, can be maintained in the context of a general discussion, where there is no explicit requirement to be accurate or to appeal to the evidence. It is much harder to sustain when one is required to account for one's views on a specific topic, or to provide an interpretation of a text that everyone present has seen – unless, of course, one simply refuses to participate.

In some ways, therefore, the following chapters should prove more reassuring. They show that, beyond the superficial cynicism discussed in this chapter, young people can display a high degree of commitment and critical sophistication in their responses to television – even to a genre such as news, of which they may have relatively little experience. On the other hand, they also point to the influence of specific news texts – a factor that has been largely ignored thus far. As I shall indicate, texts do exert considerable constraints on how they can be read, not least by virtue of what they include and exclude, and how they frame and define the issues with which they are concerned. In the case of television news, visual evidence can often play a particularly powerful role.

The generalized responses presented here are an important part of the overall picture, yet they do not tell the whole story. In the following analysis of their responses to specific news items, these young people will emerge both as less cynical and as less autonomous in their relations with television news than the analysis thus far would appear to suggest.

Chapter Six

Reading Interpretations: The US Study

This chapter and the next present findings from the focus group discussions of specific news items. As I have described, each group was shown four items, two from each programme. Prior to the screening, questions were asked to probe the students' views and knowledge of the issue addressed in the item. Depending upon the topic, this initial discussion was sometimes quite specific, although in other cases it was rather less direct. The item was then screened, and students were asked further questions designed to elicit their responses to the issues and opinions featured, and subsequently their perceptions of the item's style and 'point of view'. These questions did not follow a fixed script, and different questions were asked in each case depending upon the topic, and in order to allow for clarification and further explanation. Nevertheless, there was a broad agenda of issues which was covered in each case.

In presenting my analysis of these data, I have chosen to take each item in turn. Each section begins with a detailed summary of the item, followed by an analysis of the students' discussions. As will quickly become apparent, there are several broader themes which cut across these items; but to have organized my account conceptually in this way would, I suspect, have resulted in considerable confusion. As such, therefore, these chapters provide something of a mosaic. The focus in relation to each item is rather different; but, taken together, they may just add up to a coherent picture.

This chapter presents material from the US discussion groups. In the first interview, the students watched two items from *Channel One News*, concerned with the US government shutdown and with the Million Man March, both of which had taken place a few months previously in late 1995. In the second interview, they watched two items from *Nick News*, one on the militia movement and the other on the proposal to build a paper mill in a remote rural community.

These items were selected in order to cover a range of different *types* of 'political' issue. Thus, the government shutdown item is concerned with politics as conventionally defined – that is, with the actions of politicians, of political parties and of government, in this case in relation to the economy and to welfare. The Million Man March item broadens this focus somewhat, in that it is concerned with a social movement, and specifically with the politics of race – although it also features the views of elected representatives. The item on militias is concerned with a rather different kind of social movement, which explicitly raises questions about the relationship between the government and the individual citizen, and about freedom of speech and behaviour. Finally, the paper mill item addresses a less conventionally 'political' issue, that of the environment, and focuses on the relationship between individual and community interests and those of corporate capital.

In addition to investigating the students' interpretations of the issues themselves, I was also interested in their perceptions of how they were represented. By specifically asking them to consider the 'point of view' of the items, I was explicitly raising the issue of *media bias*. The notion of bias is often seen by media researchers to imply a naive belief in objectivity. Yet bias remains a crucial conceptual category in ordinary viewers' interpretations of television – although they may define what they mean by bias in several different ways. As I shall argue, it is important to distinguish here between apparently related notions such as 'objectivity', 'fairness' and 'balance' (cf. Corner, 1995; Lichtenberg, 1991).

My central concern here is to explore how these judgements are made, what motivates them, and what functions they serve. In particular, I am concerned with the relationships between viewers' existing biases and their perceptions of bias in television. In the process, I cannot avoid invoking my own judgements about bias – and, more generally, about the meanings of the texts concerned – even though these do not always coincide with those of the students. Ultimately, it is impossible to make judgements about viewers' interpretations without distinguishing between 'correct' and 'incorrect' readings. All readings are not, in this respect, equally valid; and ordinary viewers do not behave as though they are. The account in the chapters that follow is thus implicitly based upon a dialogue between my own readings and those of the young people whom I analyse – and it is a dialogue in which my readings are unavoidably privileged.

In the course of this analysis, different themes and variables relating to the audience (notably age, gender and ethnicity) come into the foreground at different times. Responses to the government shutdown item, for example, raise questions about how young people position themselves in relation to the domain of 'politics'; and ultimately, about the nature of 'political thinking'. The Million Man March item brings into focus the complexities and tensions of contemporary discourse about race, and how young people (both black and white) negotiate these. My analysis of the students' discussions of the militias item takes a more developmental perspective, focusing on the evolution both of political reasoning and of perceptions of media bias. This issue of bias comes to the fore in relation to the final item, on the paper mill, where I concentrate on the relation between students' existing commitments and understandings and their readings of the item itself.

Across these items, there are several grounds for comparison. Thus, the contrast between students' responses to *Channel One* and to *Nick News* raises significant questions about how these programmes position and address their viewers. Meanwhile, one can trace different orientations towards 'politics' among different groups, and in relation to different issues; and one can also perceive different orientations towards television news. The relationships between what might be termed 'political literacy' and 'television literacy' are also diverse and far from straightforward. These broader comparisons will be addressed more explicitly in my final chapter.

Channel One: The US Government Shutdown

Summary

Note: Unlike the other companies we approached, Channel One refused to grant permission to reproduce extracts from transcripts of their programmes. Here and elsewhere in this and the following chapters, material in italics is my own summary.

Newsreader [to camera: graphic in background 'Budget Compromise']: Recaps on the previous week's story: the government had been partially shut down and 800,000 workers sent home, following the failure of the President and the Republicans to agree on a budget.

[Graphic of Gingrich and Dole. Captions: 'REPUBLICAN POSITION.' 'Interest on the debt threatens the future of the nation.' 'Budget should be balanced by the year 2002.']
Newsreader: Summarizes the opposing positions: the Republicans argue that government spending is out of control and that the interest on the national debt is threatening the future of young people. They argue that the budget must be balanced by the year 2002. Clinton argues that the Republican plan to balance the budget will mean cutting programmes such as Medicare, the health insurance plan for the elderly.

[Graphic of Clinton. Caption: 'PRESIDENT CLINTON. Republican plan goes too far.']
Newsreader: However, the President and the Republicans have now reached a compromise, which means the government will resume.

[Over computer graphics of government bills, the newsreader explains that the federal budget is a combination of 13 separate spending bills, known as appropriation bills. An appropriation bill creates an operational budget for specific government functions, such as the Department of Energy or Transportation. Only six of these bills have so far been signed into law.]

If Congress and the President can't agree, they can enact a continuing resolution.

Graphic: 'CONTINUING RESOLUTION. Allows the government to continue operating until all appropriation bills are passed.' This is 'kind of like a student asking a teacher for an extension on her term paper that they both know will eventually have to be handed in.' However, the President and Congress cannot agree on the terms of this resolution, and so the federal government has ground to a halt.]

[Slow-motion impressionistic film sequence: tilting camera shows scales appearing to unbalance. The scales contain dollar bills, coins, medicine bottles and tablets.]

Newsreader: The President and the Republicans disagreed about when the budget should be balanced. The Republicans in Congress wanted to do this in seven years, but the President argued that this would result in cuts in Medicare, the federal programme that pays for healthcare for the elderly.

[Footage of elderly people undergoing medical checks, helped by nurses: 12 seconds.]

Newsreader: Republicans point out that the Medicare budget is growing by 10 per cent each year: they want to slow the rate of increase, rather than make a cut in real terms.

[Extract from Republican Congressional leader Bob Dole's announcement of the compromise to Congress: 'a very satisfactory solution to what has been a rather tense situation, the last several days'.

Extract from Clinton's press conference. He is described as 'upbeat about the compromise'. 'The real winners tonight are the American people . . . the people who put us here.']

Newsreader: The President will sign a continuing resolution, to keep the government funded until December 15th – by which time he will have to agree a plan with Congress to balance the budget by 2002. In the President's words, this new budget should 'protect future generations, ensure Medicare solvency, reform welfare, and provide adequate funding for Medicaid, education, agriculture, national defense, veterans, and the environment'. [This quotation is shown on a graphic, above a photograph of shaking hands.]

[Shots of government workers leaving their offices.]

Newsreader: The continuing resolution will allow government workers to be paid until December 15th, when the deal expires. The government could be shut down again if another deal is not agreed by that time.

Duration: 3 minutes 50 seconds.

Readings

[Note: This item was used only with Grade 5, Grade 8 and Pilot groups.]

Of all the items screened to the Philadelphia groups, this was the most explicitly 'political', in the sense that it was centrally concerned with the operations of government and of political parties. It also met with the most overt expressions of confusion, boredom and indifference, particularly among the working-class students, the younger students and the girls. While some of these latter groups were prepared to admit, albeit without much enthusiasm, that the item was 'kind of informative', it was frequently judged to be 'boring'. In comparison with the other items, the discussions here were shorter and much less animated.

These responses were partly motivated by a genuine confusion about the issues, which the item itself did little to dispel. While some of the students claimed to know very little about the shutdown (which had happened some three or four months previously, and had been very widely reported), those who had heard about it spoke mainly in terms of its *effects* rather than its *causes*. The emphasis here was on the government employees who had been locked out of their places of work, or the visitors who had been prevented from gaining admission to federal tourist sites such as Philadelphia's Liberty Bell. One group related the story of a group of tourists who had apparently journeyed all the way 'from the other side of the world' to see the Grand Canyon, only to find the site closed. By contrast, many explanations of the causes of the shutdown were much more vague: it was about 'the economy' or 'money', 'a budget problem'.

In this respect, such responses appeared to confirm the accusation, made by two of the Grade 8 (14-year-old) boys' groups, that the media were largely responsible for this focus on effects at the expense of causes (cf. Glasgow University Media Group, 1976). Ed, for example, argued as follows:

> *Ed*: Some of the stories, they don't give you the facts, they just . . . I really didn't know that much about it, and at one time I thought it was saving money, shutting down earlier. But they really didn't tell exactly what it was about, they just told the fluff, so –
>
> *DB*: What was the fluff?
>
> *Ed*: Well, just that there was arguments in the government . . . [It was] basically about how it's affecting the people, not what it was about.

However, there was a clear gender difference in terms of the students' existing knowledge. In both age groups, the boys were able to give much more coherent accounts of the party political arguments between the President and the Republican representatives which formed the immediate background to the shutdown, and of the fact that the disagreement hinged on the issue of welfare.

While the item itself did seem to explain the basic terms of this debate clearly enough for most, the underlying economic principles remained fairly opaque, even for most of the Grade 8 students. Thus, there was considerable confusion about the meaning of the term 'debt' in this context. While most agreed that the government owed money, it was far from clear to whom they owed it, or why. Some groups argued that money was owed to other countries, although it was also suggested that other countries were in debt to 'us'. Others argued that the government had borrowed money from 'people' or 'citizens', and was having to pay it back; while others suggested that it had incurred significant debts as a result of involvement in overseas wars in the Gulf or in the former Yugoslavia. Molly (14) was not untypical in her inability to understand why, as she put it, 'we owe money to ourselves'.

Likewise, there was some uncertainty about what it might mean to 'balance the budget'. This was not explained in the item itself, and was conveyed only by means of some highly abstract, impressionistic sequences of balancing scales. Several groups argued that balancing the budget meant allocating the same amount of money to various categories of expenditure: as Monica (11) put it, 'they don't want to spend too much on one thing and then too little on another thing'. By contrast, two Grade 5 (11-year-old) girls, Shawn and Bediah, who described themselves as 'activists', seemed to define this lack of 'balance' in more political terms, as a matter of inequalities between rich and poor: if Bob Dole was elected, Shawn argued, 'they will have a tough time balancing the budget – if people are down here and he is all the way up there to the ceiling . . .'

Of course, there are many adults who might find it difficult to understand or explain such issues. Nevertheless, the item itself seemed to have done little to clarify them. Several students found the section on 'appropriation bills' particularly confusing; there were some suggestions that the government might be giving money to the appropriation bills, or that 'the appropriations were borrowing money'. One group of Grade 5 girls complained that the presenter 'talked too fast' and (quite justifiably, in my view) that the programme failed to explain key terms such as 'debt' and 'interest':

> *Monica*: They really didn't explain each thing. So you would have had to know what they owe the debt to, to understand the programme.

Taking Positions

Like most of the other items, this report was structured in terms of a debate between two contrasting positions, although in this case these positions were already well established in the political domain. More than many of the other stories, therefore, it evoked explicit statements of political affiliation. Most of the young people here were fairly clear about which 'side' they were on (and all of those were pro-Clinton), even if they were confused or indifferent about the actual issues. Particularly in the case of the younger children, these affiliations were avowedly derived from their parents, without necessarily involving much conscious reflection. Molly (14), for example, asserted that her parents were Democrats, and so she would 'automatically agree with the President'. In some cases, there was very little understanding of the differences between the parties: Birgit (11), for example, described how her mother supported the Democrats on the grounds that they were in favour of women's right to abortion, although she claimed to be uncertain about whether Clinton was a Democrat or a Republican.

Insofar as there was a rationale for favouring Clinton's position, this was defined primarily in terms of a view of him as 'caring', or as in some way principled. Justin (11), for example, argued that Clinton had 'feelings' for other people that somehow transcended self-interest, and that this was a requirement of his position that went beyond that of other politicians:

> *Justin*: I think, like, the President has to have more feelings 'cause he has to control the entire country and he has to keep everyone safe and secure and the Representatives don't have to do this. They just have to make bills. They don't care about anyone else. But once, like say Bob Dole, he has to get more feelings if he wants to become President, because he was a Representative.

This argument was partly reinforced by the extract from Clinton's press conference, in which he appears to claim a solidarity with 'the American people', and to present himself as merely a servant of 'the people who put us here' (that is, in Washington). For many of these students, it would seem, Clinton appears to occupy a space which is somehow beyond politics.

Even Joel, whose generalized cynicism about politicians was discussed in the previous chapter, seemed to make some exception for Clinton in this respect. On the one hand, he again asserted that politicians were 'stupid' and had 'screwed up' over the national debt. He claimed that the shutdown was 'just another political argument – and they're going to destroy everyone's lives "cause they're arguing!' Yet on the other hand, he professed indifference to the whole affair: 'I could care less when the government shuts down.' Nevertheless, Joel rejected his friend Jeff's assertion that Clinton too was a 'bum': 'at least he's not trying to backstab all the senior citizens'. However, he also implied that Clinton's stance here may have been dictated by political expediency, and that senior citizens would now be more likely to vote for the Democrats. This argument was carried further by a group of Grade 8 boys, who also suggested that Clinton's position was dependent upon such pragmatic considerations, particularly in the run-up to the election: his argument for not cutting Medicare, they suggested, sounded like a 'campaign promise'. Clinton was thus only partially exempted from the category of 'untrustworthy politicians'.

By contrast, several students argued that the Republicans were wholly motivated by self-interest. Decisions over welfare, it was argued, made no difference to Republicans (or, some argued, to the 'upper class', with which they were seen as synonymous) because they could rely on their own personal wealth. While none of the students questioned the wisdom of 'balancing the budget' or 'paying off the debt' – although, as have seen, there were some conflicting interpretations of what this actually meant – several of them saw the Republicans as motivated simply by self-interest and greed:

> *Shawn*: I think the Republicans care about themselves more, and I think they really like to get the money when they are in Congress and stuff. They like the term 'money' [*laughter*]. Their first word was 'money' or something, so ... Medicaid is like for people all around the country, the elderly people that might have had strokes or heart attacks or had to have something amputated or have Parkinson's disease have to get treated and stuff, so they have to go to hospital. So it's not right. I think that's why we agree with Clinton.

Shawn was one of the students who repeatedly proclaimed her support for Clinton, and in this respect her argument here – and her reinforcement of it by the rhetorical listing of illnesses not actually referred to in the item – is not particularly surprising. Nevertheless, the inclusion of footage (however brief) of elderly people in hospital was referred to by several students, and seems to have prompted this kind of reaction – not least in comparison with the highly abstract representation of the notion of 'balancing the budget'. As I shall indicate, visual evidence of this kind does appear to carry substantial weight, although it can also be more ambiguous in this respect than verbal evidence.

The Personal and the Political

While these statements of position were often fairly forcefully expressed, the highest degrees of investment were apparent when the discussion veered somewhat away from the topic at hand. In some cases, this was simply a reflection of the fact that the students were more interested in talking about quite different issues: one group of Grade 8 girls, for example, span off into a discussion of the merits of school uniforms, which was a topic of discussion both in the school itself and in the news at the time. Yet even in relation to the issues raised in the item itself, the 'personal' politics were of much greater interest than the conflicts between political parties.

Thus, several students discussed the potential implications of cuts in Medicare for their own elderly relatives. Likewise, in their attempts to interpret or explain more abstract debates about 'the economy', several of them drew on evidence from their own experience. For example, Bediah (11) asserted that, if the Republicans were elected, 'the economy would be bad', and explained this as follows:

> *Bediah*: In order to pay your bills, you have to have a certain amount of money, so you can pay it all off. And with the economy being bad, you won't be paid as much money, so you can pay your bills off. And especially if you have children . . . You know, you need your food and everything else. But luckily I have two parents in the home, so it's a little bit better than just having one parent on welfare.

Here, the abstractions of 'the economy' and 'balanced budgets' are defined in terms of household finances. Significantly, the position of children is central to Bediah's account; and she is very much aware of the difficulties faced by children whom she sees as less fortunate then herself.

Likewise, several groups discussed the issue of entitlement to welfare, even though this was not explicitly raised in the item itself. On one level, this could be seen as evidence of the influence of a dominant news agenda. The question of what should be done about the 'scroungers' who are allegedly living off the honest toil of the majority is a key issue in most media discussions of welfare, both in the US and the UK (see Glasgow University Media Group, 1982; Golding and Middleton, 1982). Several students condemned welfare recipients who 'just sit there and do nothing', yet it was also acknowledged that some people were in genuine need. Most of the older students argued that welfare should serve as a means of helping the unemployed back into work – as Molly (14) put it, 'it should be like training wheels on a bike, you know, to start them off, and then they will be OK by themselves'.

Jumatatu (14) argued that it was unfair to 'stereotype' all welfare recipients as abusers of the system:

> *Jumatatu*: The federal officers who give out welfare or whatever, they need to check into people's lives and try to find some way to help them . . . They are saying that all people are a certain way, like all people are abusing welfare, instead of like saying that each person is an individual. And sometimes they have to do some research on these people to see what kind of way they can help them. They do need help.

Such observations could, of course, be accused of 'personalizing' structural or political issues. Sorting out the 'work-shy' from the genuine cases merely deflects attention away from the broader reasons for unemployment, and indeed its functions within capitalist economies. Despite the prevalence of Democratic sympathizers, the students were by no means universally liberal on this issue. On one level, Jumatatu's argument moves beyond the binary logic of the item itself – 'more welfare' or 'less welfare' – and suggests that there may be alternative approaches to the issue of government 'over-spending', for example through supporting such people's attempts to get back into employment. Yet it fails to engage with the more fundamental issue of whether satisfying jobs are actually available in the first place – and why, in many instances, they are not. Nevertheless, this kind of argument significantly shifts the debate away from the abstractions of 'the economy' to questions that are much closer to the lived realities of many of these students' neighbourhoods and family lives.

Making Connections

In fact, there were a number of students in both age groups who sought to draw connections between this issue and broader political debates. Thus, some groups argued that there were other forms of excess spending by governments: Ed (14), for example, argued that 'government officials have too many luxuries, little sports cars, pools, mansions . . .', while his friend Brandon pointed out (without explicitly criticizing it) that US involvement in 'other people's business, like in Bosnia' also 'cost a lot of money'. The Grade 5 'activists', who were keen to proclaim their support for Clinton's position, broadened out from the issue of Medicare into a kind of shopping list of social issues:

> *Shawn*: [Clinton] was afraid that things like Medicaid and stuff for elderly people and welfare and like housing projects and stuff like that – well, not necessarily that, but insurance and welfare and stuff would be cut and money would be taken from that . . .
>
> *Bediah*: [The Republicans were saying] that they were going in debt . . . and they still had to pay Medicaid and everything, so like elderly people could be healthy and everything, and education, like the books, and welfare . . .

One group of Grade 8 boys went much further in situating this issue within a broader set of political concerns – although here again, their arguments were far from wholly liberal. This group understood most about the reasons for the shutdown to begin with, and their discussion ranged widely across a whole series of issues which were, for them, clearly related. Thus, they argued that involvement in overseas wars had been a major cause of debt; and that there had been a rise in population owing to increasing immigration, which (according to them) would mean 'less jobs for Americans'. Interestingly, they detected a kind of generational politics in the debate about Medicare:

Seth: They are always saying about protecting the future generations and stuff, when they blame us for a lot of their problems at the same time. It doesn't make sense ... They blame, like, some of the people in the next generation for most of the crime that is going on and stuff.

On one level, these arguments clearly distinguish between 'us' ('Americans', the young) and 'them' (immigrants, the older generation) in ways that verge on xenophobia. Yet Michael in particular argued that the Republicans were simply playing political games with the issue of welfare, and that they could afford to do so because it was unlikely to affect them:

Michael: From a political manoeuvring point of view, it was good for the Republicans because they didn't need the vote for presidency like Clinton did. And shutting down the government is really bad for his political image, which is, like, it is good for the Republicans 'cause they want Dole to win ... The political manoeuvring is kind of a cheap shot, but the fact that balancing the budget being the only thing they are concerned about is also kind of selfish. Because they don't have to worry about Medicaid and Medicare, because they will never be on it. They kind of afford to pay for private health plans all their lives. Those people are loaded ... If they got laid off, they still have like 3 million in the bank somewhere in Switzerland.

Michael clearly comes to this issue as a confirmed Clinton supporter, and part of his argument rests on representing the opposition (in somewhat exaggerated terms) as cynical, corrupt and uncaring. However, he makes an interesting distinction here between 'political manoeuvring' – which is about things like 'image' and the struggle for electoral advantage – and the actual issues at stake. While he is less overtly cynical than Joel (whose dismissal of this as 'just another political argument' was quoted above), he appears to share a view of 'politics' as essentially a kind of game, which is only partly about broader issues of principle.

Reading Bias

Discussions of potential bias in this item were somewhat uncertain, and it is hard to detect any consistent pattern. Nevertheless, these discussions do begin to point to the different *definitions* of 'bias' which were employed here, and the kinds of evidence which were used in support of such judgements. The Grade 8 boys just discussed argued that the item was biased against Clinton, although this view seemed to derive as much from a principled critique of news in general as it did from an analysis of this specific item:

> *Michael*: They missed a lot of stuff. Like Clinton did actually have a plan to balance the budget, but the Republicans thought it would take too long. But they didn't put that in. And they didn't put all the other stuff the government was planning on doing. There was some stuff that I heard about off the regular news that probably was shorter than this and I actually heard more from it. So I don't know they brought out everything that was there.
>
> *Seth*: . . . They put more emphasis on the Republicans. And Clinton's idea, Clinton, nobody, people were still not quite clear what Clinton was thinking. Because not a lot of people, the media and stuff, they don't talk about his side as much as the Republican side.
>
> *Michael*: But that's the same with a lot of news . . . They just talk about the Republicans' plans and the fact that Bill Clinton doesn't agree with them.

In this case, the boys use evidence from beyond the text, derived from 'the regular news', which Michael suggests is both more efficient in delivering information and more even-handed. At the same time, they also take a more generalized stance of suspicion, characteristically indicated by their use of the word 'media'. As Seth's comment indicates, this position also implies a belief that 'people' (other than themselves, of course) are somehow misinformed or negatively influenced.

Whether or not Clinton did have a 'plan', it could certainly be argued that the item presents him as merely reacting to the Republican position (compare the captions early in the item, which give no indication that he has any positive stance). Furthermore, to argue that the Republicans want to 'slow the growth' of Medicare spending rather than 'cut the budget' could be seen as a somewhat favourable representation of their position. (The question of why Medicare spending might be rising – which is as much to do with the fact that private healthcare corporations are charging vastly inflated rates as it is with the increase in the population of elderly people – is not addressed at all in the item.)

On the other hand, one Grade 5 group argued, with some validity, that the weight of the visual evidence supported Clinton:

> *Justin*: They were talking about how the President was talking about the bills for Medicare and how the Representatives didn't want Medicare and they showed pictures of these elderly people who looked really sick. So I think they were more for the President because of the Medicare bill.

One of the year 8 groups also suggested that the presenter might have had a pro-Clinton bias, claiming to detect a shift in her tone of voice when she talked about Medicare. Whatever validity these arguments may have, the fact that they were made at all is striking – particularly given that the item generated so little interest, and that it was presented in such a bland and abstract way. As these extracts suggest, several students were very aware of the potential influence of how news stories were selected, edited and constructed.

Nevertheless, other groups argued that the item did not have a particular 'point of view'. Some argued that it was evenly balanced between 'both sides', suggesting a definition of bias in terms of opposing 'sides' which reflects how the debate was defined in this case. Others argued that it was simply 'informative' and 'didn't really show that many opinions' – which reflects an implicit opposition between *fact* and *opinion*, although it may also reflect the relative lack of quotations from key participants in the item itself. The Grade 5 pro-Clinton 'activists' argued from a more principled position (as they did in relation to many other items) that bias would be somehow inappropriate, if not dangerous:

> *Bediah*: I think they were showing both sides, because they weren't really saying that Bill Clinton is right and the Republicans were wrong. Because I don't think you can really say just what you want on television unless you are interviewed, you know, like us, like you are just speaking your mind or just saying your opinion. But as a person who is talking on the news, like a newscaster and everything, I don't think it would be appropriate to say who is right, who is wrong.

> *Shawn*: . . . If they were to show their point of view on things, that they did not agree and other people did, there would be a whole big fiasco about who agreed with what and things people want to see weren't seen because of the newscaster's or crew's point of view.

This is, on the one hand, a clear instance of what Corner, Richardson and Fenton (1990) term a 'civic frame' – that is, an argument that the duty of the media is to report objectively. On the other hand, 'bias' is clearly defined here as a matter of the opinions of individual reporters or newscasters, rather than as a broader structural issue, as it is to some degree by the Grade 8 boys quoted above. Interestingly, however, this group was also one of the most passionate in their discussion of the issues, and they repeatedly elaborated upon them, or drew in additional evidence, in support of their arguments. In a sense, they were themselves very 'biased', and the vehemence of their opinions suggests that they were also aware of this fact – as when they acknowledge here that they are 'speaking their minds'. And yet they seem unwilling to address the question about whether the news item they have seen is biased also. They can certainly hypothesize a situation in which news *might* be biased, but they somehow trust that the ethics of producers – or at least their desire to avoid public 'fiasco' – is strong enough to prevent this.

Channel One: The Million Man March

Summary

Newsreader [African-American male, to camera]: Introduces the item. The Million Man March was a rally, rather than a march. It was organized by Louis Farrakhan, the 'controversial' leader of the Nation of Islam; and it 'brought to mind' the march for civil rights organized by Martin Luther King in summer 1963.

[Black-and-white footage of 1963 Washington March. Martin Luther King speaking, brief applause.]

King's march was a demand for equal rights, directed at the government. The Million Man March was directed at African-Americans themselves: it was a call to address their own problems such as poverty and crime.

[Description with map of the location of the March, the National Mall in Washington DC.]
Reporter [Asian-American female, on location in Washington, to camera]: The March was described by its organizers as 'a day of atonement' for African-American men. It was the largest ever demonstration by African-Americans.

[Footage of people arriving at the Mall, with Nation of Islam members in suits clapping and chanting 'Black man! Black man!']

[Sequence showing the reporter travelling to the Mall with a group of African-American students from a middle school in Washington. The reporter interviews them on the Metro. The students are 'excited'. One 11-year-old says that the March is 'a time when I can go and witness history and I can have fun at the same time'.

The students and reporter are shown arriving at the Mall. They are 'shocked by how many people they saw'. One 12-year-old, interviewed as they walk, is 'looking for a role model': 'When I was five years old, my father died. So I'm marching so I can look at these men, they can teach me some things my father never taught to me.']
Reporter [on location]: While those attending are enthusiastic, there has been criticism of its two main organizers. The Reverend Benjamin Chavis, former leader of the NAACP, was expelled for using its funds to defend a sexual harassment claim. [Footage of Chavis addressing a rally.] Louis Farrakhan, the Nation of Islam leader, is even more controversial. [Footage of Farrakhan arriving at and addressing a rally.] He is more well-known for 'hateful rhetoric' than inspiration. President Clinton recently praised the March, but implicitly attacked Farrakhan.
Clinton [addressing university in Texas]: One million men are right to be standing up for personal responsibility. But one million men do not make

right one man's message of malice and division. No good house was ever built on a bad foundation. Nothing good ever came of hate.

Reporter: Some Black leaders also opposed the March.

Gary Franks [Republican representative, Connecticut, talking to reporters]: The nation of Islam is an organization that would talk about hating whites, Jews and Catholics. They are an organization that would believe that we should have a separate America.

Reporter: Some women also criticized the March for excluding them.

[*Interview with a teenager attending the March: 'it's about time the Black community pulled together and did something as a whole instead of doing things separate'.*

Reporter (on location) contrasts this with the 250,000 who attended Martin Luther King's rally: the March 'certainly outdrew Dr. King's crowd'. A brief discussion of contrasting estimates of attendance by organizers and police.]

[*18-year-old from a Mississippi High School describes how people in his home town are just 'getting high, shooting and gang banging'. He says that the March carried a message of hope.*]

Reporter [over shots of Farrakhan speaking]: When it came to Farrakhan's speech, 'the crowd was all ears'. [*Shots of crowd, then Farrakhan speaking.*]

Farrakhan: But every time we drive-by shoot, every time we car-jack, every time we use foul, filthy language, every time we do things like this, we are feeding the degenerate mind of white supremacy. And I want us to stop feeding that mind, and let that mind die a natural death.

Reporter [to camera]: Those attending the March promised 'to improve themselves spiritually and economically', and not to abuse women or children. The organizers also urged people to encourage others in their communities to register to vote. [Hands back to newsreader, with brief musical link.]

Duration: 4 minutes 40 seconds.

Readings

Compared with the discussions of the government shutdown item, these were generally much more animated. Only the most consistently alienated working-class group expressed a lack of interest in the item. Many students already possessed a considerable degree of prior knowledge, derived from other media coverage, from discussions at home or in school, or (in a couple of cases) from having attended the event themselves. While the younger groups were predictably less well-informed, most were able to identify the fact that the march was for black men, and that it was intended to counteract crime and violence, and to generate 'unity' and 'pride' in the black community. Nearly all the groups identified Farrakhan, and many knew that he was a controversial figure; most of these put this down to him being 'racist', 'prejudiced' or 'anti-Semitic', or to his 'preaching hate'.

However, discussions of this item were bound to be sensitive. As in many arenas of civil society, both in the Unites States and in Britain, the very *naming* of racial difference in schools is surrounded with taboos and tensions (cf. Buckingham and Sefton-Green, 1994: Ch. 6). This is partly a matter of the direct influence of teachers: students are typically schooled in an official discourse of multiculturalism, in which the emphasis on 'positive images' of cultural diversity and equality is sustained by the repression of any more positive assertions of difference or identity which might disrupt it. Furthermore, in the context of ethnically mixed interview groups, the naming of race as an issue could create all sorts of potential for disagreement among peers (cf. Buckingham, 1993a: Ch. 3). In fact, many of these groups of students were ethnically homogeneous (although I was not responsible for selecting them); and yet my own presence as a white interviewer meant that none of them was homogeneously black.

In this context, introducing a topic like the Million Man March was potentially fraught with difficulty; although in fact these discussions were rarely awkward. It may have been that I had a kind of advantage as an 'outsider' (a 'teacherly' adult, and a Brit), which might have led the students to feel they should play along. There was a moment in one of these inter-views, with an all-black group, which epitomized some of these tensions: Naisha (14) mentioned Farrakhan's reference to 'a white person', and promptly excused herself, saying 'no offence' – apparently in deference to me. Nevertheless, black and white students were in very different positions here; and what they said needs to be interpreted in the light of the social context of the interview, and of their social purposes at the time.

Negotiating Positions: White Perspectives

If the shutdown item encouraged students to take up positions on party-political lines, albeit somewhat ritualistically, there was a more complex process of negotiation to be undertaken here. Broadly speaking, all groups began from a position that distinguished between Farrakhan and the March itself. This position was, I would argue, clearly signalled by the item itself. It is evident, for example, in its persistent description of Farrakhan (and not the March) as 'controversial', and in the ways in which it shifts from one topic to the other, for instance in using words like 'but' or 'despite'. Nevertheless, those students who knew more than the most basic facts about the March also seemed to *begin* from this position, rather than appearing to take it up following their viewing of the item.

For the white students, this separation appeared to hinge upon a desire to see the March as a call for 'civil rights', addressed to the white majority, rather than solely to blacks. Justin and Mark (11), for example, expressed their dislike of Farrakhan on the grounds that he somehow disturbed this view. Like the item itself, Mark compared Farrakhan to Martin Luther King, arguing that Farrakhan had been 'different than what I thought'. Justin went further:

> *Justin*: I think they don't march for Louis Farrakhan. I think they march because they want to get equality for Black Americans. And I think that most of the people who were there didn't really want to hear speeches, they wanted to march. It's a trademark that they are getting hired. Society and people are trusting them more. They are becoming – people are accepting them more.

Justin's implicit distinction here between 'them' (black people) and 'people' (that is, white people) is symptomatic; although Mark's assertion, earlier in the same discussion, that 'the Negroes [*sic*] are finally getting some equality' was even more revealing. These comments were made before the boys had seen the item, although they seemed to be reinforced by the item itself. Asked whether the producers had a particular point of view, Justin replied:

> *Justin*: I think they had the point of view that Louis Farrakhan was more hateful than a leader should be, and that it showed how proud the blacks were for being part of the Million Man March.
>
> *DB*: . . . So what makes you say that?
>
> *Justin*: Well because they showed that speech made by the President in Texas and they commented on it a lot and said that it was very true. And they made sure that everyone knew how hateful [Farrakhan] can be by comparing [Farrakhan's speech] to Martin Luther King's speech. How people will listen to anything, since there were 1.5 million here and only a couple of hundred thousand in King's.

Interestingly, Justin perceives a distinct bias in the item, for example in the privileging of Clinton's speech (although he exaggerates in claiming that 'they . . . said it was very true') and in the pointed comparison between Farrakhan and King. It is also worth noting that the word 'hate' or 'hateful' is repeated three times in the item. Yet while Justin claims to approve of the March, he can only explain Farrakhan's apparent popularity with the Marchers by asserting that 'people will listen to anything'. Nevertheless, the item has effectively provided him with the ammunition he is looking for to support his own position.

Michael (14) made a similar separation between Farrakhan and the March itself, and for similar reasons. Significantly, his description of the aims of the March appeared to want to deny the racial dimension – 'it was a bunch of people, like, coming together, and they just happened to be black males, trying to build up their image'. At the same time, he too sought to distinguish between the aims of the marchers and those of Farrakhan:

> *Michael*: I saw it on the news, there were a lot of people talking about it, saying how they wanted to march for themselves, not for Farrakhan. They didn't really talk about that on the news, which I think they should have, because that was one of the better messages from the March. Because I personally don't really like Farrakhan, but I have no problem with the March.

Interestingly, Michael emphasizes the individual nature of his judgement – 'I personally' – which might also appear to disavow any racial dimension: it is, perhaps, something he just 'happens' to think. Here again, the argument is framed in terms of critical assertions about media bias – even if Michael is adducing evidence from his viewing of the news to criticize the news itself. Michael and his friends went on to attack the item on the grounds that it over-emphasized Farrakhan (although, it should be acknowledged, this argument was made by several other students, both black and white). Michael asserted that 'a lot of people who went there, they weren't going for Farrakhan, they were going there for the other guy, I can't remember his name'; while Seth (in the same group) argued that 'there were other speakers besides Farrakhan, and some even spoke more than him' (a dubious assertion, in the light of Farrakhan's marathon speech). The boys then went on to widen the debate, criticizing the media's tendency to 'puff stuff up' and to focus on the private lives of celebrities – a change of direction which enables them to side-step the sense of unease Farrakhan provokes. This is not to say that their critique of the item is therefore illegitimate – one could well argue that it does unfairly personalize the issues – but that it clearly serves particular purposes within the context of the discussion. The problem with Farrakhan, for these boys, is evidently not that he is misrepresented by the media, but that, as Michael very clearly put it, 'he calls *us* racist'.

The two all-white groups discussed here made explicit a tension which may have been implicit for the other white students: understandably, the white students in ethnically mixed groups were much more non-committal. Interestingly, it was also in these two groups that the question of the numbers attending the March seemed to be important. Justin's opening comment was that 'maybe it wasn't a million men there' – although, as we saw above, he later went on to quote the figure of 1.5 million. Likewise, Michael claimed that Farrakhan had been 'freaking out' because only 600,000 people had attended. Here again, the discussion of this issue in the item itself provided useful ammunition for the attempt to undermine Farrakhan's position.

Black Perspectives

However, it was not only white students who made this distinction between the March and its principal organizer. All the black students were very positive about the March itself, although a couple were doubtful about whether the initiative would be sustained, and whether the people who were responsible for crime had actually been reached. Unlike most of the white students, who perceived the March as a call for 'equal rights' or as a challenge to 'racism', the black students recognized that the March was primarily directed at African-Americans. However, there was an underlying doubt about how the March – and particularly the figure of Farrakhan – would be interpreted *by whites*.

In this context, several of the black students felt called upon, or were directly challenged by others, to defend Farrakhan. Thus, some suggested that his message was basically good, but that he was not his own best advocate, or that he had been misinterpreted:

> *Shawn* (11): I thought that most of the things he said about, like, different cultures and stuff, he could have just kept that to himself. But I think he was trying to make a point, and he thought that was the only way he could get the point across was to say what he was thinking. And that didn't appeal to everyone.

There was particular criticism here of the black Republican representative quoted in the programme, Gary Franks. Jumatatu (14) argued that Franks was focusing on 'the little slips that Farrakhan makes ... the small points he makes up in his conversations', rather than 'all the good that he is trying to do for the black community'. Likewise, Bediah (11), pursuing the political line she had proclaimed in her discussion of the shutdown item, also questioned Franks's position on the grounds of his unrepresentativeness:

> *Bediah*: Most black people are Democrats. I know most of them are. And the man who was a Republican said that they [the Nation of Islam] were trying to talk in a bad way about – sort of like in a condescending way about white people and everything, and Jews and Catholics. And I think it was not the point. But somewhere when Farrakhan was talking about how bad language and everything about the white man, I don't really think he had to say all of that. But I don't really think he was talking about how Jews are wrong and bad and Catholics and everything.

Bediah's position here is typically ambivalent. On the one hand, she argues that Farrakhan has been misinterpreted, and that his aim is basically 'to build self-esteem' (as she subsequently put it); but on the other, she also challenges his judgement in saying the things he does. The problem here, as Careema (14) put it, is that Farrakhan is bound to be 'misinterpreted' if he fails to give a 'thorough explanation of what he's saying'. Yet implicitly, the people who will be most likely to 'misinterpret' him in this way will be whites.

Nevertheless, other black students were much more comprehensively critical of Farrakhan. In one Grade 11 group, Patrick and Dartagnan condemned him in the strongest terms, leaving Acacia to defend him. The following is only a short extract from a much more extended debate:

Patrick: . . . to me, he just stands for, you know, hate. And in a way, I compare himself to Hitler. I mean, Hitler did build Germany up pretty nicely, but I think it's very scary if this man ever comes to power of any sort, and I mean he has power right now, but if he really gets into power, I think it could be very scary. 'Cause he's a very powerful speaker and he can really do some damage, but on the other hand he can really help, lots.

Acacia: Well, maybe you have to understand where he came from. I mean, Louis Farrakhan wasn't always this great speaker, he used to be a Caribbean singer . . .

Dartagnan: That fits the perfect description of what you just said, I mean Hitler and Farrakhan. Hitler was a nobody, I mean, he was an artist on the streets, he wanted to go to a university, but he couldn't get into the university and so he became a street bum, he was a nobody, then he became a somebody.

Acacia: I wouldn't necessarily –

Dartagnan: But look, that's because Hitler hated us. But this is Farrakhan hating the people who hated us.

Acacia: Hitler hated and persecuted.

Patrick: He hasn't the power to do it yet. He needs the power.

Acacia: True, but I can't sit here and say that if this man had the power, he would tell all black people in America to go around and kill all the white people, I really doubt. He is, maybe he is like Hitler in that he hates an entire race of people, which is, in our views wrong, but he is telling us – but I'm no follower of Louis Farrakhan, believe me – he's trying to voice his opinion. Maybe, it's not right, I mean, everyone has an opinion.

Dartagnan: We'd all be just like him if we had an opinion?

Acacia: I mean, no one likes the KKK, but they voice their opinion,
    they're marching.

All these students were clearly well-informed about Farrakhan, and drew
extensively on evidence from beyond the item itself (as Acacia does here).
Much of the debate here proceeds through analogy, for example with Hitler
and with the Ku Klux Klan. The students use these analogies both to reinforce their own positions and to challenge those of others; and yet they also
consciously use them to think through weaknesses and inconsistencies in
their own arguments. The ambivalence surrounding Farrakhan is partly a
result of their attempts to 'decentre' and to take account of opposing points
of view. Yet it also arises because the debate invokes two central themes in
US political debate: the theme of the self-made man, and the theme of
freedom of speech.

   Thus, Acacia says that she admires Farrakhan on the grounds that he has
apparently risen from a lowly position – although this argument is clearly
undermined by Dartagnan's pursuit of the analogy with Hitler, another self-
made man. Acacia goes on to disclaim her support for Farrakhan, as she does
at several points during this debate; although at other points she also expresses
admiration for his work on education and housing projects, and (as we shall
see below) is highly critical of what she sees as the media's bias against him –
not least in the item itself. However, her subsequent argument here for
Farrakhan's right to freedom of speech is (perhaps self-consciously) undermined through her own analogy with the Ku Klux Klan. Patrick is more
consistently opposed to Farrakhan, yet he too is bound to acknowledge opposing points of view. Thus, he argues that Farrakhan can 'really do some
damage', and yet he also accepts that he 'can really help'; and he later accepts
the freedom-of-speech argument, while simultaneously expressing some doubt
about whether he 'really believes' the positions he assumes (thus perhaps
implying that he is doing so merely in order to gain popularity). Interestingly,
however, Patrick agreed that the item was 'very biased against Farrakhan',
and his own bias did not seem to prevent him from perceiving this.

   This outwardly logical mode of argument – using analogies, seeking out
inconsistencies, weighing opposing positions – characterized several of these
discussions, despite the considerable personal and emotional investments
which were at stake. The central question here, perhaps, is whether it is
rational (in Dartagnan's terms) to 'hate the people who hated us'. Thus, one
group of Grade 6 girls argued that Farrakhan's message was at least inconsistent: he was arguing that people should not commit crimes, but he was
also inciting them to hate other races. This was wrong, Dana argued, because
'all races are the same'; and because, according to Walida, race was an acci-
dent of birth – 'ain't nobody choose, when they was inside, they reported
and say "I want to be born in a white person's body"'.

   As this implies, it was not only white students who attempted to deny
the significance of race, while simultaneously retaining it as the central term

in the debate. Thus, one group of Grade 7 girls broadly supported the aims of the March, although they argued that Farrakhan was wrong to emphasize the racial dimension:

> *Latoya*: You can't blame what people do on anybody but themselves, because everybody has a mind of their own. And [Farrakhan] blaming cursing and drugs on Caucasian people is not right, because I mean black people have minds of their own and nobody can tell them what to do unless they want to do it themselves.

Ultimately, they argued the March 'was giving an example for the children', showing them that 'we are all humans made of one colour, we are all the same'; and that the next March should be 'a Million Man, not just black or white'.

These were not the only criticisms of Farrakhan. Two groups of girls – one black, one white – also criticized the absence of women on the March, and the Muslim beliefs on which this was based. Walida (12) argued that this view was at least old-fashioned: 'I'm sorry?! Women will stay home and cook and clean like the olden days and listen to their husbands all day?' Likewise, Molly (14) argued that, if the aim of the March was to 'improve the community', women should have been included.

For both black and white students, the figure of Bill Clinton again appeared to occupy a kind of fantasy position which was somehow beyond politics. Clinton's argument – in favour of the March (representing 'personal responsibility'), but against Farrakhan (representing 'hate') – was clearly shared by most. And yet (unlike Franks, the other critic of Farrakhan quoted in the item), Clinton seemed to possess the ability to 'speak for us all'. Walida, who is black, said that she agreed with Clinton for this reason:

> *Walida*: I agree with him more than I agree with Farrakhan ... Because Clinton wasn't just talking for the white people, he was talking mainly for everybody. Because Farrakhan was only talking to the black people.

Meanwhile, others suggested that Clinton may have been motivated by a desire for popularity. This criticism of Clinton as a *politician* – and, implicitly, of the ambivalence which many of the other students adopted – was most directly stated by Kyle (17), a white student:

> *Kyle*: He looked like he was trying to double-think – hold two contradictory statements in your mind and believe them both – which is said of a lot of politicians. It was both condemning Farrakhan and applauding the March, which of course came through Farrakhan.

As I have implied, these discussions are symptomatic of the conflicts and contradictions that surround discussions of race in contemporary multi-cultural societies – and perhaps particularly in the United States. On the one hand, there is the undeniable historical fact of racial inequality; while on the other there is the attempt to deny difference and to assert that 'we are all the same'. On the one hand, there is the need to protect freedom of speech; while on the other there are the problems which arise when people incite others to hate those who are different from themselves. On the one hand, there are the merits of self-reliance and personal responsibility; while on the other there is the danger of excessive individualism and the desire for political power. And finally, for black people in particular, there is the desire for assimilation and equality on the one hand; and the attractions of separatism and racial pride on the other. For both black and white students – albeit in different ways – the figure of Farrakhan clearly served as an important focus for these tensions and contradictions.

Reading Bias

As I have indicated, the discussion of media bias served some complex functions in these discussions. Irrespective of how strongly they disagreed with his position, several students drew attention to what they saw as the negative way in which Farrakhan was represented in the item. A broad range of different types of evidence was drawn upon in support of this view. Thus, there were comments about the relative amounts of time given over to Farrakhan, as compared with his critics; the lack of interviews with people explicitly supporting Farrakhan (as opposed to just the March); the fact that the critics were featured before Farrakhan himself (which Ed (14) described as 'telling the final score before the game was played'); the prominence given to Clinton in particular; the selection of the quotation from Farrakhan's speech, featuring his linking of 'white supremacy' and 'death' in the same sentence; and the comparison with Martin Luther King, which was felt to be potentially misleading, as well as damaging to Farrakhan. Acacia (17), who was Farrakhan's most vocal defender, argued that the item was typical of media treatment of him, citing what she saw as similar mis-representation of his 'World Peace Tour' which had happened more recently. On the other hand, it was generally felt that the March itself was presented positively in the item, particularly through the use of the young participants – although the inclusion of this material was also seen to reflect Channel One's attempts to appeal to its young audience. All these are, in my view, justified observations.

Of course, not all students perceived bias in the item; and indeed some explicitly said that it was merely 'telling what happened' or that it 'showed both sides'. Yet whether or not it was perceived, different *definitions* of bias were employed. Some implicitly perceived bias as a matter of the individual reporter's opinions – as, for example, in Careema's view that 'they just kept their opinions about Farrakhan to themselves'. Others perceived bias more in terms of balance, or the lack of it – as, for example, in Diana's view that 'they were trying to balance it out evenly, seeing both sides, why people were going there and why people disagreed'. Paul (17) argued that they were merely presenting Farrakhan as 'controversial', rather than directly condemning him – thus acknowledging that a diversity of views existed, without taking a particular stance themselves. Others were able to detect bias more in terms of the construction and selection of the item, rather than in terms of the opinions that were (or were not) overtly expressed.

A further conception of bias that emerged in several groups here is one which might be termed 'audience-oriented'. This overlaps to some extent with Corner *et al.*'s (1990) 'civic frame', discussed above, in that it entails a view that bias is in some ways *inappropriate* in forms of public communication such as news, and that balance and objectivity are almost moral necessities. However, several groups also saw this as a matter of reflecting (what they chose to define as) majority public opinion, or what 'a lot of people thought'. More cynically perhaps, some saw it as a matter of not offending the audience, or certain sections of it – and discussed what might have happened if this had occurred. Jumatatu (14), for example, argued that the programme-makers would not want to offend Jewish viewers by appearing sympathetic to Farrakhan. Molly and Nicole (14) argued that if the programme had done more than simply 'show what was going on', schools might have boycotted it, and the journalists might have 'gotten fired'. More cynically, Kyle (17) argued that the programme-makers may have tried to disguise their own views and adopted a stance in favour of the March in an attempt to appeal to their target audience:

> *Kyle*: You find your typical teenager as being more liberal than his adult counterpart, and that's what they're trying to appeal to. So they're going to work with a more liberal perspective.

Interestingly, this attempt to avoid offending the audience was defined by some as a matter of 'political correctness':

> *Patrick*: They were trying to be politically correct, they were trying to tip-toe on both sides and they were trying to balance it out.

> *Acacia*: I should hope they would, because this basically goes into every school, or every high school across the nation. I mean people tend to believe what they hear on the news, what they hear on TV and in the media and what have you. But if you tell a whole bunch of school kids with their young minds to hate Farrakhan or to like Farrakhan, you're going to get a lot of [trouble].

As Acacia's argument shows, this view also appears to entail a belief in the potential influence of the media on audiences – particularly in this instance, young audiences. Just as Kyle implicitly distances himself from (and presents himself as superior to) 'your typical teenager', so Acacia defines herself as very different from the 'people' – and even the 'school kids' – who are foolish enough to believe what they watch.

However, these arguments did not necessarily entail a *disagreement* with this perceived bias – or even, in some cases, an ability to avoid apparently being influenced by it. There was no simple correlation between the students' existing beliefs, or their existing levels of knowledge or interest in the issues, and their perceptions of bias in the item. Some of the complexity of these relationships is revealed by comparing the three Grade 5 groups. The first group, consisting of three white girls, pointed out a number of the ways in which the item was biased, for example, in the selection of the quotation about 'killing' from Farrakhan's speech, and in the prominence given to his critics, particularly Clinton. Nevertheless, the item still seemed to have influenced their views of Farrakhan:

Monica: I didn't know he was so much into hate and everything. I thought he was like a better person . . .

Molly: Like they talk about how he talked about hate of Caucasian people and how he thought like there should be a separate America. And I didn't think he thought about that.

Birgit: I thought he was more like Martin Luther King.

The second group, which consisted of two white boys and one (symptomatically very reticent) black boy, was discussed above. The white boys, Justin and Mark, were very aware of the bias of the item, drawing attention to the damaging comparison between Farrakhan and King, and the emphasis on Clinton's criticisms. Yet this bias effectively confirmed their own views: the programme-makers, they argued, simply 'made sure that everyone knew how hateful he can be'.

The third group, consisting of the two 'activist' black girls and one (somewhat silent and intimidated) black boy, was the most enthusiastically engaged with the issues, and talked more volubly and at greater length. The two girls were aware of criticisms of Farrakhan, but frequently attempted to defend him. It is here, perhaps, that one might have expected the most intensive criticisms of bias. Yet (as in their other discussions) this group consistently employed the 'civic frame' and barely acknowledged the possibility of bias. Shawn argued that the programme-makers were simply 'showing the different views of Farrakhan', while Noah concluded that 'they were trying to get it across, like, that [the marchers] were just trying to make a difference'. Significantly, this group's high level of investment in the issues almost led them to *talk past* the programme itself. It was not so much, perhaps, that they read the programme as in some way 'transparent' rather than as 'mediated' (cf. Richardson and Corner, 1986), but that they were simply not interested in the question of mediation.

As these examples indicate, the relationships between viewers' *existing* knowledge or attitudes and their perceptions of media bias are not straightforward. 'Political literacy' does not necessarily translate across into 'media literacy', or vice versa: both need to be seen as forms of *discourse* which are crucially dependent upon the social purposes for which they are used.

Nick News: Militias

Summary

[*Linda Ellerbee (in studio) delivers an introduction to camera. She begins by asking whether patriotism is a matter of love of one's country or loyalty to the government. She explains that the Bill of Rights, which is a part of the Constitution, allows citizens to own guns and form civilian armies or militias. The bombing of the federal building in Oklahoma City in 1995 was attributed to such private militia groups. This led to calls for militias to be outlawed. Members of such groups argue that they are protected under the Constitution, and that they will fight to protect that right. Militia groups, and others such as 'survivalists', do not trust the government, but still maintain that they are patriots. Is it possible, she asks, to love one's country but hate its government?*]

[*Music, shots of Washington, soldiers, militia members being arrested, statutes of law.*]
Voice-over: Government's getting too big and out of control ... They're getting too nosy, getting into affairs they don't need to get into.
Bo Gritz [*on screen*]: The reason we have militias today is because the government has run amok.
Bill Clinton [*speaking at university ceremony*]: I say this to the militias and all others who believe that the greatest threat to freedom comes from the government instead of from those who would take our freedom away. [*Shots of soldiers in fatigues, guns shooting, militia conventions, patriot literature.*] If you say violence is an acceptable way to make change, you are wrong. If you say the government is in a conspiracy to take your freedom away, you are just plain wrong.

[*In interview, Chip Burlay, a political analyst, distinguishes between the patriot movement, 'which is concerned about the government using too much power to assert itself', and the armed militias, 'who fear that the government is going to use troops to put people down'.*]

[*Militias swearing oath of allegiance.*]

Voice-over: There's at least one armed militia unit in nearly every state. They say the Constitution gives them the right to be in a militia. [*Shot of Constitution.*] Not everybody agrees.

[*Burlay says that constitutional experts dispute the idea that the Constitution gives people the right 'to get together over a beer in a local tavern and announce that they're a militia'. Over shots of the Bible, focusing on the book of Revelation, he describes the 'apocalyptic viewpoint' of people in the militia movement.*]

Voice-over: While some are dressing in camouflage uniforms and calling themselves militias [*shots of militia members in fatigues*], thousands of others, sometimes called survivalists, are retreating to the hills to live apart from the rest of us. [*Shots of Bo Gritz's training camp.*]

Gritz: My name is Bo Gritz. I'm supposed to be the most decorated Green Beret commander of the Vietnam War. [*Shots of medals and Gritz's book* Called to Serve.]

[*Voice-over describes Gritz's community 'Almost Heaven' in Idaho.*]

Gritz: People are saying 'we want to move up here because we will stand in the protection of every other neighbour's constitutional rights'.

[*Teenage members of a family living in the community deny that they are part of a militia. One says that the Constitution says the government should help and protect, but 'the government has been so corrupt lately, they're doing more harm than help right now'. Shots of the Constitution and of government ATF officers.*

Another boy, who lives nearby in Idaho, expresses concerns about Gritz's group 'taking the land'. He expresses fears for his safety, citing the siege at Waco. Over shots of David Koresh preaching, followed by the Branch Davidian compound in flames, and a copy of a Time *magazine cover, the voice-over explains the events at Waco.*]

Voice-over: . . . When the government learned that Koresh was storing high-powered weapons they raided the compound. In the chaos, the building ended up in flames, killing men, women and children. Some people believe the Branch Davidians set their own compound ablaze. Others blame the government.

Chuck Schumer [*New York congressman, in studio*]: David Koresh did a lot of very bad things long before the government ever came on his property. [*Shots of Koresh preaching.*] He kept and hoarded a lot of machine-guns. This man is not a hero. He broke many laws and did many, many bad things.

[*Voice-over explains the events at Ruby Ridge, over shots of Randy Weaver being arrested and going to court, and a* Newsweek *cover. The boy in Idaho expresses further fears for his safety.*]

Schumer [*in studio*]: Don't worry, because your house is safe, your lives are safe, and the government is trying to make your life safer from people who would violate the law.

Gritz [*in studio*]: I've trained elite armies all over the world. Now I'm training American families the same way we train those elite armies.
[*Dramatic music, shots of training, mountaineering, SPIKE graphic. Voice-over and Gritz explain his SPIKE training: SPIKE is Specially Prepared Individuals for Key Events.*]
Gritz [*over shots of 'key events'*]: It means an earthquake in LA. It means a hurricane in Florida. It means a flood in the Midwest. Anything that might imperil your family or your well-being is a key event. Now SPIKE teaches you self-reliance.

[*Over a montage of the training, including several shots of guns and target practice, members explain what they have learnt in SPIKE: self-defence, gardening, emergency birthing, using a gun, defence against an armed weapon.*]
Burlay [*in studio*]: I was a Boy Scout and I did training for emergencies. He's not talking about training a bunch of people to be concerned about an earthquake. The whole training is aimed at focusing people to use arms to resist the federal government. [*Shots of shooting, ATF agents, police.*]
Gritz: I've told people, 'Don't ever look to me to ever attack anything – I don't believe in it.' But we have a righteous right to defend what is ours. I just want to see America continue. [*Urgent music.*]
Clinton: There is nothing patriotic about pretending that you can love your country but despise your government. [*Shots of Washington, American flag.*]
Schumer: I would think that George Washington and Thomas Jefferson would want citizens to work hard to protect the Constitution. But the way to do that is the old American way – debates, voting, town meetings – not marching around with a lot of guns. [*Shots of people protesting against nuclear weapons, debating, etc. Then shots of people in fatigues with guns: freeze-frame.*]

Duration: 7 minutes, 10 seconds.

Readings

[Note: This item was used only with Grade 5, Grade 8 and Pilot groups.]

To a greater extent than in the case of other items, there were some marked age differences in these discussions. As I shall indicate, similar processes were occurring in both age groups; and several of the judgements made by the younger children were equally as astute and sophisticated as those of the older ones. In general, however, the differences between them were more striking than the similarities.

These differences could partly be understood in cognitive developmental terms. Broadly speaking, the older students found it easier to 'decentre' –

for example, to take account of opposing views, or to balance two sides of an argument. They were also more assiduous in employing forms of logic – for example, in seeking out causal motivations for a particular viewpoint, or in identifying inconsistencies.

However, these differences also have to be explained in terms of the students' prior access to information. I began these discussions by asking the students about the Oklahoma City bombing: the bombing had taken place several months previously, but the story was being covered widely as the principal bomber, Timothy McVeigh, was about to be brought to trial. All of them had heard about this event, and in many cases were able to describe what had happened in considerable detail. However, the Grade 5 students were much less capable of explaining the *motivations* of the bombers. By and large, they could only say that they were 'crazy' or 'sick' – or, more grandly, 'psychopaths' or 'pyromaniacs'. Mark suggested that such people 'just like the fun of blowing things away'; while Birgit compared them to 'bullies – they just bully people to feel big'. Only two students suggested that they might have had a more political motivation: Shawn suggested they were 'trying to get back at the government' because they had lost their jobs; while Justin proposed that the bombers might have been people 'from a foreign country' seeking revenge against the US for interfering in 'their matters', 'trying to take back what the Americans were doing in their own country'. (In fact, this was a theory which had initially been proposed in the days following the bombing, although it was quickly rejected.)

By contrast, the Grade 8 students knew that the bomb had been planted by a domestic terrorist who 'disagreed with the government'. In many cases, they went on to identify the bombers as members of a militia, and to discuss the political motivations of such groups – although there was some disagreement about whether they were 'anarchists', 'right supremacists', or motivated by religious beliefs. There was also some discussion here of other incidents involving militias, and of the constitutional issues. Insofar as the Grade 5 students knew about militias, their understanding was solely derived from their social studies classes, in which they had recently been learning about the role of the militias in the Revolutionary War: with the exception of Justin, none of them seemed to know about the existence of contemporary militias.

These different levels of prior knowledge clearly affected the students' ability to understand the item, and the strategies they used in debating it. The Grade 5 students appeared confused on several points, and explicitly admitted as much. Birgit, for example, said that she was not clear about whether Bo Gritz was 'running a militia or against the militia'; Noah was confused about the difference between militias and survivalists; while Monica was unsure whether Chip Burlay (the political analyst) was for or against them. In some cases, such confusions seemed to lead to outright misinterpretations: for example, in reference to the short sequence about the apocalyptic viewpoint of the militias, Justin argued that 'they showed the

Bible, how it is evil to do something like that'. Significantly, however, the relationship between the students' engagement with the content and their perceptions of bias were not so straightforward – and in some respects, went against what might have been expected.

Debating the Issues: Fifth Graders

The item explicitly set out to present viewers with a conundrum – which is stated in the closing sentences of Linda Ellerbee's introduction. In a sense, however, the dilemma is even broader than this suggests. The issue of militias evokes fundamental tensions between the rights of the citizen and the rights of government – tensions which focus particularly on questions about freedom of speech and about gun control. These tensions are central to US political life.

For most of the Grade 5 students, the item generated a considerable degree of confusion on these points. They understood that militias were opposed to the government, but they were unclear about what had motivated this view. Even where they were able to hypothesize about this, they were still uncertain about why they had chosen to express their opposition through resorting to arms. As a result, they tended to focus more on the rights and wrongs of weapons in themselves – in a sense, on the symptoms rather than the causes.

On one level, this emphasis reflects that of the item itself. There is very little explanation of the reasons why militias are arising, other than general statements by their members that the government is 'getting out of control'. The only instances of the government (arguably) 'getting out of control' which are actually shown are those of Waco and Ruby Ridge – where the government's intervention could be seen to be justified in any case, as a response to the stockpiling of weapons. The item focuses centrally on the issue of guns, both in its repeated footage of armed militia members and firing ranges, and in the commentary – not least in the closing statement and the freeze-frame.

For most students, the question of guns was the deciding factor in the debate. Yet for some of the younger ones, it was the beginning and end of it. For Birgit, Christine and Monica, the central issue here was one of allocating blame. They accepted that the militias felt the government was not 'handling the soldiers or the way to protect people right', and that 'the government can make bad decisions at some times'. But they placed the responsibility for violence fairly and squarely with the militias themselves, even in the case of the events at Ruby Ridge:

> *Birgit*: It's just because of [the militias] that people are getting killed ... If there were no militias, no one would ever have done that.

This group spent some time pondering the origins of the militia movement. They speculated about whether it had arisen following the government shut-down, or whether it was a result of the 'bad government' of Richard Nixon. As Christine said, 'They probably started for a reason, and . . . it would be interesting if we knew what the reason was.' Ultimately, in the absence of such information, they could only explain the motivations of the militias as a preoccupation with violence *per se*:

> *Monica*: It's an excuse for people to go out and get guns and kill people and then say 'we're not doing anything, we're just protecting ourselves'.

Likewise, Bediah, Shawn and Noah expressed considerable confusion about the motivations of the militias. Unlike the other group, they were more sympathetic to the possibility that the militias had valid points to make, and that their frustration at being unable to do so had led them to violence:

> *Noah*: They missed their chance . . . Like all those things [demonstrations?] they show on TV about peace and stuff, they should – like, instead of like beating people up or something. So it's like they missed their chance to speak, they go and kill people.

As self-declared 'activists', Shawn and Bediah could conceive of a situation in which they were critical of the government; but they felt that the way to deal with this was, in Shawn's words, to 'write to the government or something, speak your mind about what you think'. Ultimately, they perceived a logical contradiction between the aims and methods of the militias:

> *Bediah*: If you want your country to be so good, then why are you creating war? You know, because that just doesn't make any sense.

The remaining Grade 5 group, Justin, Brian and Mark, were more able to articulate the point of view of the militias, although they were no more inclined to support them. Throughout the discussion, they self-consciously presented both sides of the argument, balancing opposing viewpoints and weighing the good against the bad. Like the previous group, they felt that the emphasis on self-reliance and self-defence in Gritz's training was positive, but that it was wrong to teach people 'to hate the government and to fight against it any chance they get'. Again, guns were a deciding factor:

> *Brian*: I think that [Gritz] was half and half. He was teaching them how to use self-reliance and about teaching them to know what to do in hurricanes and the rest of the stuff. But he shouldn't have taught the kids to use the armed weapons and all that other stuff ... If I was a parent, I would have dropped that quick.

Brian's statement is typical of this group in its even-handed structure. What is also striking is his emphasis on the position of *children* – and indeed, how he assumes the role of a parent. This theme recurred throughout this group's discussion. There was anxiety about the abuse of children at Waco, and the fact that they were killed in the raid; concern about the possibility that the militias would 'influence' children to commit murder; and a feeling that Gritz was encouraging children to fight or shoot people they disagreed with, rather than to 'talk it over'. Such statements imply that children are highly vulnerable and impressionable, but also that they are in some sense *other* people. While this may partly be seen as a claim for one's own superiority (they themselves, presumably, would not be influenced in this way), it also reflects a kind of decentreing; and it is worth noting that such arguments were more widely voiced among the older students.

This group tried hard to explain Gritz's motivations, albeit by pathologizing him:

> *Justin*: I think he's going to break. I think he's going to have to start shooting people. Because he's been in Vietnam, he's probably had trauma, you know, seeing everyone killed ... A lot of people are crazy when they come out of the war.

As we shall see, this kind of argument was also more characteristic – and more subtly argued – among the older students. It too could be seen as form of decentreing, or at least to reflect an ability to hypothesize about causal motivations on the basis of the (limited) evidence available. Nevertheless, Gritz's protestations of innocence were not recalled. By contrast, several echoed the words of Chuck Schumer, the congressman, arguing that the government 'is trying to help you'. It was only among the older students that the role of government – and particularly of politicians – was overtly criticized.

In general, then, the Grade 5 students were confused about the political motivations of the militias. If anything, what they saw tended to confirm their initial suspicions that they were simply 'crazy'. Nevertheless, they worked hard with the information provided, attempting to resolve the dilemmas the item raised: they hypothesized about causes and motivations; they sought consistency, and exposed logical contradictions; they balanced positives and negatives; and they attempted to account for positions that were different from their own. Their failure to make much headway was, perhaps, not so much a failure of cognition as of information.

Debating the Issues: Eighth Graders

These forms of political reasoning were more apparent among the eighth graders. In general, these students made more nuanced judgements, which were expressed as matters of degree rather than as absolutes. Many of the central dilemmas raised by the item were, they argued, incapable of easy resolutions. These students were more inclined to hypothesize about the motivations of the militias (particularly Bo Gritz) and were more openly critical of the government representatives (particularly the congressman, Chuck Schumer). They were also more concerned to expose what they saw as logical contradictions in the positions of both parties.

Freedom of speech was much more of a central issue in these discussions, although again it was the issue of weapons that was the deciding factor:

> *Nicole*: They don't have to blow up things to make their point, or whatever. Like, they [can] do what they want to do in a little space. They don't have to be loud about it, and marching around saying 'this is our place and we don't want to listen to the government'.

For Nicole, it would seem, freedom of speech is acceptable within bounds – 'a little space' – and so long as it is not 'loud'. It becomes unacceptable when it is associated with weapons. Ultimately, Molly argued, it was an 'illusion' for such groups to think that the government would take their land – unless, of course, 'they do something illegal, like have that many guns'.

Likewise, Brandon, Ed and Jumatatu began by affirming the right to freedom of speech, and to self-protection:

> *Ed*: They can think what they want. There's nothing wrong with it. It's just, like, if the government tries to take over that place, they will retaliate.

A little later, however, they agreed that the government had been right to invade Waco, on the grounds that 'they were storing a lot of weapons', and that this was unlikely to have been merely in self-defence. For them, the Branch Davidians' use of weapons was inconsistent with their religion: 'you're teaching them peace and everything while you have all the weapons'. Nevertheless, these students agreed that the power of the government could be 'misused', and that it should be restrained – although there was some debate about how this should be decided. As Jumatatu pointed out, there is room for disagreement about what constitutes people's 'best interest', and whether the government is best placed to identify it.

Both these groups were inclined to favour the government's intervention in Waco, although they agreed that it represented a difficult dilemma. The girls argued that Clinton was in a 'tough position', and had to make some 'hard decisions', particularly in the face of public criticism. Nevertheless, there was some criticism of Clinton on the grounds that he was merely talking about the problem, but not really 'doing anything'. These girls were even more critical of the congressman, Chuck Schumer:

Nicole: He sounded like a politician, like 'everything's all right' and everything.

Molly: I don't trust him. Everything is not all right. The government is not perfect ... I don't trust the government that much. He was too confident.

DB: Yeah, so he sounded like a politician? Say more about what you mean.

Nicole: Like, he wasn't really telling us about what was going on.

Molly: Like a salesman.

The boys expressed similar views, arguing that they did not know whether to trust Schumer. Like the girls, they suspected that he was not entirely honest, and that this might have been because 'he wanted to keep his job' and 'get re-elected'.

Jared, Michael and Seth were more explicit in their criticism of the government. Although they broadly supported Clinton's position in the item, they criticized the decision to invade the Waco compound, arguing that it had been based on slender evidence. Like the other students, they argued strongly for freedom of speech and belief, at least so long as it was not harmful to others: it was fine, they argued, for the Branch Davidians to believe that Koresh was Jesus Christ, as long as they were not committing crimes. Michael argued that the best way to express one's disagreement with the government was by 'speaking out', and that this was 'more effective than blowing up buildings and shooting at people'. However, Jared argued that governments themselves were sometimes violent – as when they waged war on other countries – and that 'speaking out' could get you into trouble:

Jared: Now they will even come up and arrest you even if you are speaking. And they will like start things in a crowd. Like with the protests and stuff. They were like college students who got shot. And the college students weren't really doing anything, they were just in the crowd and they were like innocent bystanders. They got shot by federal agents.

The specific incident Jared is referring to here is not clear, but his argument exposes the limitations on 'free speech'. In responding, Michael argued that it was through such acts of martyrdom that 'the civil rights were passed' – 'your life stands as a symbol of what's wrong with the government, and should give more fuel to your cause'. However, as Jared replied, 'that's why people start militias sometimes, they see someone get shot that's important'.

As this implies, this group was also more inclined to sympathize with Bo Gritz's motivations, if not his methods. Where the girls hypothesized that Gritz had psychological motivations – 'something must have happened to him, that turned him against the government ... like a family member got killed and the guy who did it got off' – this group suggested that his motivations were more political. However, they also challenged Gritz's individualistic strategy. Jared argued that Gritz had 'a good cause', but that his approach would undermine social cohesion and nationhood: 'if everybody thought like him, then America would be gone, 'cause everybody would be different, everybody could believe in different stuff'. Finally, this group also engaged in an extended debate about gun control. Here again, their position was complex. They argued that the Constitutional 'right to bear arms' had been formulated several centuries before, at a time when weapons themselves were fairly unsophisticated. While they were in favour of increased gun control, they also pointed out that this would lead to an increase in the illegal gun trade. As with several other issues, they concluded that the central dilemma here was one of interpretation: the Constitution might give people the right to oppose an unjust or ineffective government, but (as Michael put it) 'people interpret what the government does in different ways'.

In general, then, these students displayed a high level of political reasoning. They were able to identify and debate underlying philosophical principles; to weigh evidence, to identify logical inconsistencies, and to perceive the nuances of an argument; to understand the motivations of others' decisions; and to think through the consequences of their own and others' positions. While several of these qualities were apparent in the younger students, they were more evident here. These students were much more independent – and critical – of sources of authority; and yet they were also more aware of the unresolved – and perhaps unresolvable – nature of the dilemmas faced by governments. These differences were, as I have indicated, partly a matter of their access to information: the older students (and some of the boys in particular) simply knew much more about recent political events, about history and about the structure of government and the law. This enabled them to pick up on, and develop, some of the rather vague and generalized material presented in the item itself.

Reading Bias

In several respects, my analysis of these discussions appears to confirm a cognitive developmental model of 'political literacy'. From this perspective, the development of children's understanding of politics might be seen as one aspect of their broader intellectual growth. In fact, as I have indicated, this is only part of the story. The younger children's confusion was also partly a result of their lack of prior knowledge, and the failure of the item to provide an adequate explanation of the *motivations* of the militias.

This developmental model is further complicated by the different ways in which students discussed the issue of bias. Broadly speaking, it was the younger children who were more likely to perceive bias – in this case, against the militias – and to offer evidence in support of this claim; while the older ones were more likely to conclude that the item was 'balanced'.

Thus, among the fifth graders, a majority argued that the item was opposed to the militias, on the grounds that more time was given to their critics, and particularly to Bill Clinton, who again appeared to be invested with considerable authority:

> *Birgit*: They had President Clinton's speech, parts of it, everywhere. And they showed parts of it where he said 'you are wrong, wrong, wrong'. And they also showed a lot of stuff, like people attacking the militia . . .

> *Christine*: They were saying like all this stuff, fires, people being blown up, killed . . . They didn't really show anything that showed it was helping.

Even those who disagreed with this view, and pointed to the positive comments on the militias, eventually agreed that (in Monica's words), 'if you put it on a scale, the bad would outweigh the good'. Even Shawn and Bediah, who consistently maintained the 'civic frame' in other discussions, reached the same conclusion. As Shawn implied, this was also about the sequence of elements within the item: 'When they were going to say the good stuff about them, they kind of said a thing or two and dismissed the whole idea and went back to the bad stuff.'

From this perspective, bias was defined primarily in terms of 'balance' – an approach which is encouraged by the programme's characteristic attempt to show two 'sides' of a debate. In common with the younger students' discussions, the emphasis here was primarily on the amount of time given to different viewpoints, and the selection of speakers. There was very little discussion of issues such as editing or the combination of sound and image.

By contrast, the Grade 8 students were less certain on this point. Among the girls, Amy and Nicole felt the item was in favour of Clinton's view, although they also complained that there was not *enough* argument against the militias. Michael argued that Clinton's opinions were 'stereotyped', because 'they only showed the parts of his speeches where he spoke directly against those people', and that this reflected a more general media bias against Clinton. As these comments imply, much of the criticism here derived from the 'civic frame'. Several of the students argued that the item did not give enough information. Molly, for example, said she would have liked to know more about the impact of the militias on people in the surrounding area; while Brandon wanted to know more about how Chuck Schumer would have sought to curb their activities. Ed argued that programmes like this were aimed at 'kids' and hence could not 'get that deep'; but that, nevertheless, 'it was pretty informative'.

As these comments indicate, the use of the 'civic frame' serves to position the speaker as a sophisticated, rational political actor – and, in this case, as more 'adult' than the children at whom they perceive the item to be aimed. However, the older students' unwillingness to engage with the issue of bias seems somewhat at odds with their more sophisticated discussion of the issues themselves. Here again, it may have been that they were simply 'reading past' the form of the item in their efforts to engage with the content. By contrast, the younger students experienced greater difficulty in understanding the content; and this might have made them more aware of the form than they would otherwise have been. As this implies, such responses do not easily translate into a neat developmental model: the relationship between understanding or interpretation and critical judgement is not necessarily straightforward or direct.

Nick News: The Paper Mill

Summary

Linda Ellerbee [*in studio, to camera*]: Everyone knows that trees are good for the environment and cutting trees is bad, right? Ah, if life were only that simple. The place is Apple Grove, West Virginia. There are a lot of trees there. Which makes it the perfect place to build a paper mill, because paper is made from trees. A paper mill will mean jobs for people who need jobs. A paper mill will also mean pollution. Start there, and see what you think.

[*Dreamy piano music, shots of sun through trees, Julie Fletcher walking with her dog through the woods.*]
Julie Fletcher: I'm Julie Fletcher and I'm an environmental activist, because I've grown up with a love for the land in West Virginia, and I care about what happens to it. They want to build a paper mill which will cut 10,000 trees a day, seven trees a minute. The proposed Apple Grove Pulp and Paper Mill is to be built in Apple Grove, West Virginia.

[*Shots of cutting trees, close-up of Apple Grove town sign.*] *The voice-over explains that Apple Grove is a small town on the Ohio River. It is here that the paper company Parsons and Whittimore wants to build a very large pulp and paper mill. [Shots of open country, cows; then large paper mill.] Logs would be purchased from local landowners, and then ground up to make pulp, which is used to make paper products. [Shots of logging; paper products in supermarket.] The pulp is bleached with chlorine at the mill. [Shots of bleaching pulp.]*

Fletcher: If you research pulp mills, if you use the chlorine bleaching process, you will get dioxin. *['Danger' music.]* Dioxin is a chemical that would be emptied into the river and into the earth, and causes cancer and other health problems in humans. *[Outflow into river.]* There are so many polluting industries around here. The river is already extremely polluted. When you have dioxin in the river, you can't tell it's there. *[Factories, river, 'danger' music.]* You don't know you're being affected by it until you already have so much in your body that it's too late. *[Fletcher by river bank.]* My biggest fear is they'll pollute our rivers, they'll pollute our air, they'll take our trees, they'll leave us sick without money or jobs, and we won't have anything.

Ken Goddard, a Parsons and Whittimore employee, is shown doing paperwork in his office, wearing a suit. In voice-over, he denies that the mill will create pollution, or that it will produce 'measurable' amounts of dioxin. He asserts that minute quantities of this chemical can be detected. [Shots of testing for dioxin.] Julie Fletcher is then shown rejecting this claim, and the suggestion that there will be no side-effects. Goddard then argues that there is a debate among scientists about how much dioxin is safe, and that this debate has still not been resolved. [Shots of press reports, factories.]

Fletcher [walking dog]: They don't live here. They don't have to worry about this sort of thing. They aren't losing any money on the deal – obviously. And we're going to be the ones who are down and out.

Goddard [over shots of him lecturing at dinner with local residents]: Many local people do believe that they're going to benefit from this. I had dinner with 450 people in Mason County and they were totally satisfied that the company is going to do what it says it is going to do. *[Environmental activists demonstrating.]* There are many people who have other concerns, who will oppose this project, no matter what we say.

The voice-over notes that there are different views about the value of the scientific evidence. Campaigners against the mill have produced a video about pollution. [Shots of newspaper article, videotape inserted into VCR.] There is then a brief extract from the video, showing shots of logging, and a large mill. The voice-over on the video urges that the mill should be built 'dioxin free'.

Voice-over [shots of Ohio River, Amanda Horvath reading]: Other residents along the Ohio River are learning about the mill from information produced by the pulp mill owners.

Amanda Horvath [sitting on porch]: I am in favour of the mill. People say that the river is already polluted, and I'm worried about that. But the pulp mill will not really have an impact on the river ... [*Riding bike in street, voice-over:*] I have all that I need. I have a nice house, nice clothes and enough food to eat. But a lot of people don't. A lot of people in West Virginia are poor.

[*Banjo music, shots of abandoned barns, trailer homes, rusting cars, broken-down farms, cat on rusty tin roof.*]
I see a lot of people who really are in need of things they don't have. It's really important to bring jobs to West Virginia, because the unemployment rate in the state is 12 per cent, which is high. I actually think that we really need the jobs, even though it might pollute a little.

Steve White, an organizer for the construction workers' union, is then shown. He argues that the company has not promised to provide jobs for local residents. He fears that, like other companies, they will bring in construction workers from other states. [Shots of local residents, construction workers.] Goddard (again shown in his office) disputes this. He asserts that the company wants to employ local people, and that West Virginia was chosen partly because of the availability of skilled labour.

Fletcher [in forest]: And what if, one day, they decide they've eaten all the trees here, there's nothing left for them to take, so they leave. We won't have anything, we'll be left with nothing.
Horvath [on porch]: Some people think that the pulp mill should not come to Mason County, but other people do. I can see both points, but I think it would help our community more if we had the pulp mill.

[*Dreamy piano music, shots of sun through leaves.*]
Fletcher: A clean environment is a nice dream. It probably won't happen in my lifetime, but maybe within my grandchildren's. So a clean environment is something I always wish for.

[*Close-ups of leaves in sunlight, dew on spider's web.*]

Duration: 6 minutes 20 seconds.

Readings

The discussions of this item were remarkably uniform. With very few exceptions, the students were strongly opposed to the building of the paper mill; and they perceived the item itself to be biased in the same direction. There were some age differences here, both in terms of the arguments that were employed and the kinds of evidence that were offered in support of claims about bias. There were also some exceptions to this general picture, which raise interesting questions about the relationships between the reader's *existing* bias and their perceptions of bias in the text. In general, however, this item seemed to be largely preaching to the converted.

Environmental Logic

The majority of students seemed to be already highly committed to the environmentalist position. There was some passion here, most overtly expressed among the younger students and the girls, although by no means only there. The certainty and intensity of the 'environmental activist', Julie Fletcher, particularly seemed to have commanded their support. Several of the younger students directly echoed her words and intonation. She was described as 'more intense than the city girl', 'truly sincere about how she felt' and as 'giving her real opinions': Charlene and Reginald (17) even said that they had thought she was going to 'cry' or 'break down or something'.

By contrast, the advocate of the mill, Amanda Horvath, was seen as somewhat equivocal, and even rather gullible. In comparison with the certainty of Fletcher, she was described as 'whimsical' and 'naive' – or, as Layli (17) suggested, 'she was in la-la land'. Amy and Molly (14) noted that she had received her information from the company, and so 'she only saw one side of the argument' – despite the fact that, in the item, she explicitly says that she can 'see both sides'. By contrast, Julie Fletcher was described as somebody who, in the words of Mark (11), 'didn't fall for anything'.

However, these perceptions also derived from the locations in which the two girls were shown. Many of the students concluded that Amanda Horvath did not in fact live in Apple Grove, on the grounds that she was seen in her house and in a suburban street. By contrast, Julie Fletcher was seen exclusively in the forest, to the point where most students were convinced that she lived there. This argument extended to some of the other people featured in the item. Thus, it was argued that the company representative, Ken Goddard, did not live in Apple Grove either; and neither did the several hundred people whom he entertained over dinner. A particular confusion arose here because the item does not explicitly state that Apple Grove is a town in Mason County. Several students were therefore able to conclude that they were quite different places; and the fact that Amanda Horvath and the people attending the company dinner were identified as residents of Mason County further undermined their credibility. It was repeatedly argued that, since such people did not live in the area, the mill would not affect them, and so they should have no say in the matter.

To some degree, the students appeared to have been persuaded by the visuals here – or at least were inclined to use this evidence in support of their argument. Visual evidence was also explicitly cited in relation to other issues, sometimes on the basis of very short sequences. Molly (14), for example, referred to a brief shot of an outflow pipe, 'with water from the factory just rushing into the river', and used this to challenge the results of the scientific tests which suggested there was very little dioxin in the water. Likewise, Monica (11) argued that the people attending the company dinner were in fact 'representatives of corporations' or 'very rich' on the grounds that 'the women wore dresses and big earrings and pearl necklaces' and 'the men wore very good tuxedos' – which she took as further evidence of the fact that they did not live in the area. (In fact, there are no close-ups of these people, which would suggest that Monica is at least embroidering the evidence to fit her own case – as her friends went on to imply.)

There was a considerable amount of cynicism about the company representative, Ken Goddard. To some extent, this derived from a straightforward suspicion of commercial self-interest: Christine (11), for example, suggested that 'he was greedy and wants to make a lot of money'; while Amy and Nicole (14) suspected that he was 'just interested in making money' and that 'he lives in a big house'. Others argued that his role was simply to offer PR for the company, and as such he was not to be trusted: Monica (11) suggested that he was 'probably the communications person' and therefore 'all he is going to say is the good things'; while Molly (14) provided the ultimate condemnation – 'he sounds like a politician'. Ed (14) argued that the people attending the company dinner had effectively been bribed – 'the people were happy, they probably paid for their food and dinner'. This scepticism extended to the scientific evidence introduced by Goddard: Seth (14) argued that 'they pay scientists to say anything'; while Michael (14) asserted that 'there are scientists paid by Marlboro cigarettes [to say] that you can smoke your way to good health'.

As some of the Grade 11 students implied, however, there might have been a more generalized form of scepticism here:

> *Charlene*: Me personally, I don't really want to make any decisions about his character, because I think we are unfairly biased [against] the heads of companies – people in authoritative positions, because they're making decisions for us ... A lot of people's first thought would be 'oh yeah, he's lying, he's the head of the company' ... It's the corporate monster. It's the principle of the thing.

Charlene's contribution here is remarkably 'decentred', in that she is able to identify and distance herself from what she perceives to be her own 'bias'. While her instinct is to be suspicious, she self-consciously attempts to reserve judgement, arguing a little later that 'I don't know him, and you can't tell that much from a five second little clip'. As we shall see, this type of self-reflexive argument was typical of the older students' judgements of bias.

While the students were generally sceptical of the evidence produced on behalf of the company, they were not above inventing – or at least hypothesizing – some of their own in support of the environmentalist position. Several fifth graders asserted that people would die as a result of drinking the water from the river, and that the stock of trees would quickly be exhausted; while one group of Grade 8 boys expressed great concern about the fate of the (entirely hypothetical) local fishing industry. Many students asserted that the effects of the mill would be cumulative and irreversible, and that the area would simply be destroyed. Likewise, opposing views were deliberately parodied or misrepresented: Monica (11), for example, argued that Amanda Horvath was simply welcoming the mill 'because we are going to have more paper'.

Although the students were fairly unanimous in their support for the environmentalist position, there were some interesting exceptions or qualifications. Several younger students, in particular, were keen to identify alternative solutions to the problem. Some of these entailed accepting the existence of the plant, while attempting to minimize environmental damage – for example, by replanting trees, purifying the water, or avoiding the use of bleach. Others addressed the problem of unemployment, hence making the building of the mill unnecessary in the first place – for example, training people for different jobs, or encouraging rich people to help out the poor. It was also suggested that the company might be obliged to sign a contract with the town to employ local people; or that some of its profit should go into finding ways of avoiding pollution. Some older students took a wider view, making connections between this issue and broader economic and environmental problems, such as over-population. Acacia (17) argued that America was 'an impersonal land', and that most people would not be willing to use recycled paper just because it would be better for the environment several hundred miles away. Lisa (17) saw the central problem as one of industrialism, 'the factory system': 'we create the society that needs these jobs, instead of living off the land'. In all these ways, the students drew on their existing understanding of environmental issues in order to move beyond the information – and, in many cases, the terms of debate – provided by the item itself.

The most explicit doubts about the environmentalist position were voiced by those who were more aware of the issue of employment – and this in turn seemed to derive partly from a form of class politics. Charlene (17) had personal experience of the economic decline and depopulation of West Virginia, arguing that it was even worse than the item suggested. Jared (14) also asserted that it was more important to 'give some people the opportunity to have some things that they couldn't get, because they never had a job'. However, it was the Grade 5 'activists' who were most explicit in defining this as a class issue; although there was some debate about whether the plant would in fact give jobs to those who needed them most:

Noah: The paper mill would probably give jobs to the upper class. They would probably barely consider the lower and middle class. Because, I mean, those people in trailers and all, they could just get the brush off or something. [They could] say 'get out of here' . . .

Bediah: I don't really agree with that. Because maybe, OK, because they don't want to pay people that much, maybe they want to give the lower class [jobs]. Because the lower class needs to be paid more, but because they are lower class, they probably want to keep them lower class.

Despite their differences, both students clearly are bringing a class analysis to bear on the situation: they are aware of class divisions and inequalities, and of how corporations can sustain them through their policies on hiring and pay differentials. In this respect, they display a profound suspicion of corporate capital which was shared by the large majority of students here.

Reading Bias

The students' attributions of bias were much more certain and well-supported here than in the case of any other item. It was widely agreed that the item was biased against the building of the paper mill, despite its apparently even-handed approach. In general, the younger students tended to justify this view in terms of the balance of time given to each side, and the weight and author-itativeness of the evidence. Only among the older students was there much reference to the *visual* aspects of the item. However, some students dissented from this view; and, particularly among the older age group, there were several who displayed a more generalized and self-reflexive approach to the issue of bias itself.

Thus, it was generally agreed that the item gave priority to Julie Fletcher, the 'environmental activist', both in terms of the amount of time she was given, and by allowing her the last word:

Mark (11): They did a whole lot more on her than they did on the other girl. They only had a few questions on the other girl, and they had a whole lot with her. And they knew that she was right. So they get a point of view, and they want to see everybody's, but they went back to her. Everybody, a lot of people, a majority of people would think she would be right, so that's why they did it.

Interestingly, while Mark clearly perceives this bias (and shares it himself), he argues that it is effectively an attempt to please the audience: the programme-makers are almost duty bound to present 'everybody's' point of view, but they return to the one which they and their viewers prefer. It was generally agreed that the opposing position was given less time, and some even suggested that the presenter's introduction favoured the environmentalist position:

Molly (14): They showed more people for than against.

Amy: Like, when she was saying in the beginning, she was saying, like, we all know that trees are good for the environment and everything. So she said it right there.

Amy was not the only student who effectively ignored the presenter's account of the opposing view, and simply took what she wanted from it – although it is ironic that this then led her to accuse the item of bias. In fact, even these assertions about the amount of time given over to the different sides of the argument are somewhat questionable: simply on a time count, the ratio in favour of the environmentalist position is something like 8: 7 – although Mark's point about Julie Fletcher having the last word is well taken.

Nevertheless, the *selection* and *portrayal* of the participants clearly favoured the environmentalist position, and several students were well aware of this. Thus, while many were influenced by the physical locations in which the two girls were shown, they also viewed this as a deliberate choice on the part of the programme-makers:

Brandon (14): They showed how the girl lived in the trees, like walking through the woods and stuff ... And they would show just how it would affect her life. But it showed the other girl just skating, riding her bike in the street, not knowing what would happen to other people.

As Brandon implies, the use of these locations lent a very different degree of credibility to the two girls. For some, this seemed almost symbolic: according to Monica (11), for example, it was a matter of 'farms and animals and grass and trees and stuff' as opposed to 'paved sidewalks'. The belief that Amanda Horvath did not live near the proposed site of the mill led some students to argue that she was very much a biased choice: as Birgit (11) said, 'they should have picked someone who was against it that lived there, close to where she [Fletcher] lived'.

This was partly a matter of location, although it was also to do with the girls' self-presentation. As I have noted, many of the students argued that Fletcher was much more 'sincere' and 'intense' than Horvath, and many saw this as a further instance of bias. Likewise, Jumatatu (14) argued that Amanda Horvath 'sounded kind of selfish, like the way that she said 'I have a nice house and nice clothes' and all that stuff ... I think they wanted to purposely, like, find someone that sounded selfish to prove their point for the other side.' Patrick (17) summed this up, albeit somewhat cynically:

Patrick: [They were] definitely biased against the pulp millers. Number one, they used a very cute little girl, walking her dog in the woods, beautiful camera angles on the trees, the sun coming in like this, OK, and then she talks about it. And then they get this guy in an office, with a computer and talking all this technical jargon nonsense, all right, that kids don't care anyway, they're like 'what does that mean?' ... And then you get this other girl, who's not so good-looking, talking about it. [Laughter.] No, I'm serious. Kids see this.

Again, while Patrick himself is sympathetic to the environmentalist position, he also perceives the item as manipulative. It is significant that he identifies 'kids' as the ones who will be most at risk from this; and while this is partly a matter of being influenced by 'beautiful camera angles', it is also a result of their own laziness (they 'don't care' about technical matters) and superficiality (they are more likely to believe people who are 'cute' than those who are 'not so good-looking'). Later in the same discussion, Acacia went further, arguing that 'it's all about advertising', and that the programme-makers had deliberately chosen 'the cute girl' to 'push their point': 'you don't see big old ugly people selling clothes and bathing suits and stuff'.

As Patrick implies, the company representative was a less-than-effective advocate in this context: 'a guy in an office with a computer' was not fair competition against a 'cute girl walking her dog in the woods'. Again, while many of the students were clearly biased against him on principle, they also argued that he had been deliberately chosen or portrayed in such a way as to discredit the company's position. Dartagnan (17), for example, argued (with some self-conscious exaggeration) that 'they made him seem hard, ruthless, impersonal, heartless' and that the people attending the company dinner 'all seemed like business, uppity people'.

All these comments suggest a very clear awareness of how news stories are selected and constructed. Many of the students implied that the programme-makers had made a great deal of effort to find the right individuals and the right supporting material to represent particular positions – and indeed to support their own bias. In general, the older students seemed to be more aware of how *visual* evidence was used, and of the potential inconsistencies between visual and verbal elements. This was partly a matter of what was included and excluded: Kyle (17), for example, noted that they showed 'what they perceived as the impact of the factory, smokestacks and fires burning and all this' (in fact, this was in the extract from the campaigners' video), and yet they did not show 'the impact of joblessness – people on the street starving'. Patrick and Dartagnan (17) went further, identifying a kind of visual rhetoric in the images themselves:

Dartagnan: Did you see the outline of the bridge and the lake and everything, with the sun setting? And then you see the tops of waste plants, something dumping into the lake ...

Patrick: Yeah, but they showed some other plant, where it was a huge plant and nothing around it, it was just like mud and dirt and nothing and just dumping and the smoke coming out. And it wasn't a very good picture ... They used really good camera angles, I thought, in there, especially with sun and everything. I mean, everybody pictures that – you look up, these big, tall trees and then the sunshine through, and it's beautiful.

Dartagnan: That's something they teach you in photography school.

Of course, these students are self-consciously displaying their own sophistication here. And yet their powers of observation, in relation to quite fleeting images in a brief sequence they have seen only once, are fairly remarkable. For example, the shot of the factory Patrick describes, which is taken from the campaign video, is indeed more grainy than the surrounding footage; while the shots of the sunset and the sun in the trees clearly do derive from a pictorialist style that might well be taught in some photography schools (although there are probably many others that might teach one to avoid it).

Reflecting on Bias

These latter comments imply a recognition that bias is not necessarily overt, and indeed that it may sometimes be deliberately disguised. Many students seemed to begin from a position of principled scepticism here. Not surprisingly, this was most evident among the eleventh graders. In some instances, the existence of media bias was proposed as a general truth: Dartagnan, for example, argued that invariably 'the media have an agenda before they do something'. In others, the media were accused of a particular bias, as in Kyle's assertion that 'more news shows are for environment than they are for industry'. Nevertheless, it was agreed that programme-makers were likely to conceal the more obvious manifestations of bias:

Acacia: People who do this have their own point of view and their own opinion. And if you have the power to show other people your point of view and your opinion, I mean, you camouflage it so that it looks equal, you put both sides in, but if you want, put your little hint of your side you agree with.

This argument was supported by some of the eighth graders, particularly in relation to the inclusion of Amanda Horvath. Nicole suggested that she had been included because 'they wanted to have both sides of the story, so nobody would complain'; while, even more cynically, Ed suggested that she had been 'paid off' in order to appear, and that she might really live in Texas.

It was also the older children who were most likely to employ the 'civic frame' in this context, arguing that they needed more information before they could make up their minds. There was a clear sense that the item was aimed at a younger age group, and that it was therefore inclined to over-simplify. Michael and Jared (14), for example, argued that the item 'left out a lot of facts' that the main evening news would have provided and that 'you really need to know a lot more to choose a side'. Likewise, Charlene (17) argued that she would have liked to know whether the people who had attended the company dinner were those who would be most directly affected; and that she did not know enough about the bleaching process to be able to evaluate the evidence. As Layli (17) put it, 'I don't think they give you enough information to make your own opinion, but they gave you enough to know that it's a confusing situation.' Nevertheless, the older students also argued that the programme was comparatively 'mature' for its target age group, and praised it for not being 'condescending'.

This use of the civic frame became rather more problematic in another of the Grade 11 groups, which consisted of two boys (Kyle and Paul) and one girl (Lisa). Lisa was clearly very committed to the environmentalist posi-tion, but the boys persistently sought to marginalize her by pointing to the inadequacies of the item. Paul condemned the programme as offering merely 'a generic kind of argument', without sufficient 'specificity' or detailed infor-mation. Kyle went on to argue that Amanda Horvath was more effective in presenting her case because 'she had a more open mind'. This placed Lisa on the defensive: she had to acknowledge that her own response to the item – for example, her suspicion of the company representative – was based on her personal 'opinions'. She also took a more distanced stance towards the environmentalist representatives: Julie Fletcher, she argued, had 'compas-sion', but she was also 'exaggerating to get people to understand'. By contrast, the boys implicitly claimed to operate from a rationalistic (and distinctly gendered) position which was somehow beyond bias and opinion. From this perspective, commitment was seen as somehow immature: Kyle sympto-matically argued that the 'kids' in the item were 'misinformed and too emotional' – although he added, with the wisdom of advanced years, 'that's how we all were at that age'.

As this implies, judgements of bias – and 'critical' discourse about the media more broadly – can serve complex functions in the context of viewers' debates about television news. What was particularly striking here was the ability of many students to 'decentre', to identify and to distance themselves from their own self-declared biases. This was particularly apparent among the older children; and, as in the case of Lisa, it was sometimes forced upon them as a result of pressure from others.

In general, students who were already strongly biased towards the envi-ronmentalist position were more likely to perceive bias in the item than those who were not. This is perhaps paradoxical: one might logically have expected them to ignore the bias of the item because it coincided with their own.

Even more paradoxically, those who were less favourably disposed towards the environmentalist position were less likely to perceive the item as biased in favour of it. Thus, the Grade 5 group of Bediah, Shawn and Noah, who were more sympathetic than most to the argument about jobs, were also more inclined to agree that the item was balanced; while the same was true of the Grade 11 group of Reginald, Layli and Charlene, although their position was more clearly based around the civic frame. This was by no means universally the case, but it does imply that the relationship between viewers' *existing* biases or commitments and their perceptions of bias in the media may be more complex than one might initially assume. Selective perception certainly plays a role here: as I have indicated, students who strongly favoured the environmentalist position may have simply filtered out information that contradicted their views, and when asked about bias might therefore have been inclined to argue that the opposing view was less adequately represented. Alternatively, students who were more interested in the issue in the first place may just have paid much closer attention, and hence have been more likely to perceive bias.

The possibility that this item might have been preaching to converted was one which several students explicitly raised. As in the case of the Million Man March item, several students implied that bias was simply a matter of reflecting what were seen to be the majority views of the target audience – in effect, a form of reassurance or flattery. Molly (14), for example, argued that Nickelodeon as a channel was 'environmental oriented' – which she suggested was 'a good side to be on, considering it's like a kid's channel'. Kids, she argued, were more likely to favour the environment over jobs. As Kyle (17) put it more directly, 'kids can afford to care about the environment 'cause they're not looking for jobs'. For Patrick (17), this was more of a social class issue:

> *Patrick*: You have to look at the audience and where their socio-economics is. People who have cable [and hence have access to Nickelodeon] aren't usually that poor. These kids are like 'they are gonna kill trees, where am I gonna walk in the woods?' . . . It's like [if] my mom and dad are out of a job, then I don't care about the environment, I want to eat, I want to have clothes, I want that new red bike, so I don't care about the environment.

While Patrick's point is persuasive, it is notable that he exempts himself from this charge. There is a distinct anomaly here: if *these* students oppose the mill, they do so because of their superior knowledge and research; whereas if *other* members of the audience do so, it is because of their class.

These observations begin to suggest a rather different approach to the issue. Bias is clearly not something inherent in the text which simply imprints itself on viewers' minds. Viewers bring their own forms of bias *and* their strategies for identifying bias to their reading of text. Yet on the other hand, viewers are not simply autonomous 'meaning makers', whose readings are all equally valid. As I have shown, viewers can deliberately or inadvertently *mis*interpret what they watch: they can ignore or fail to understand things, and even invent or imagine them. There are also clear instances in which they have been persuaded, or even positively misled. To be sure, this is partly a matter of whether they are 'paying attention' – although attention is not simply a passive reflex that operates independently of the search for meaning. As these students suggest, what people see is partly what they want to see – although this is also a matter of what the producers have decided they *ought* to want to see. Judgements about bias are thus not simply a reflection of what is or is not 'there' in the text – even assuming that we could agree about this. Nor are they simply a matter of viewers' levels of 'critical awareness' – as though this were a quality that viewers simply possess, like a kind of intellectual muscle power, and which can be objectively assessed.

As I have implied, judgements of bias need to be understood in terms of the social contexts in which they are made, and the social functions they serve. 'Exposing' bias – or at least alleging that it exists – is a powerful discursive move. It seems to place the speaker in a position that is distanced from the text, and by implication less vulnerable to its influence than others who fail to perceive it. In certain situations, such as those analysed towards the end of this chapter, it can appear to place the speaker in a position which is somehow beyond the domain of mere personal opinion. At least, it represents a powerful *claim* to such a position – even though it cannot guarantee that this claim will be accepted by others. While we need to account for the power of the text, we also need to account for the power of the viewer – not merely in relation to the text itself, but also in relation to other viewers, both real and imagined.

Chapter Seven

Reading Interpretations: The UK Study

This chapter presents findings from the UK discussion groups, again focusing on the students' readings of four news stories. In the first interview, the students watched two items from *First Edition*. The first focused on the need to encourage young black people to vote in the forthcoming general election, while the second looked at responses to youth crime. In the second interview, the students watched two items from *Wise Up*, one on the issue of curfews for young people and the other on the National Lottery. At the beginning of the second interview, held one week after the first, the students were also asked to recall what they could from the items screened the previous week.

Here again, the items were selected in an attempt to cover different *types* of 'political' issue. As in the US study, the sequence moves broadly from 'public' politics (as conventionally defined) towards more 'personal' politics. Thus, the first item is centrally concerned with the election, and with the relationships between politicians and young people. The second and third items, on youth crime, provide contrasting treatments of an issue that has become a central focus of political debate and social policy in the UK in recent years – albeit one of which many of these students also had first-hand experience. The fourth item, on the National Lottery, is concerned with an issue that was again part of many students' personal experience, and which might well have been perceived to be quite remote from 'politics'. As with the US stories, this selection of material raises important questions about the relationships between the 'personal' and the 'political', and how connections between them might be forged.

The students' discussions of these items inevitably throw up a series of specific – albeit overlapping – issues. The young black voters item explicitly raises questions about young people's orientations towards the official domain of politics; and about the nature of contemporary discourses about race and racism, among both black and white students. Discussions of the second and third items focus on how political issues relating to young people are typically framed, both within public debate and specifically within news. Age differences within the sample are especially significant here. At the same time, the contrast between these two items also raises broader questions about news formats, bias and credibility. These latter issues come to the fore in relation to the National Lottery item, where the overtly polemical approach has significant implications in terms of its ability both to inform and to persuade the viewer. The last two items in particular also raise the question of what it means to 'think politically', and what might be gained and lost in doing so.

Many of these themes echo those discussed in the previous chapter. Here again, the contrast between the students' responses to the two programmes is particularly important. As my analysis in Chapter 4 suggested, *Wise Up* and *First Edition* define and address their target audience in very different ways. They invoke or assume different kinds of 'media literacy' – that is, different understandings of, and orientations towards, television as a medium. They also imply different forms of 'political literacy', by positioning young people as political actors or subjects in quite different ways. As I shall indicate, however, the consequences of these different approaches are not necessarily straightforward or predictable.

First Edition: Young Black Voters

1 Jon Snow (presenter)

2 Operation Black Vote meeting

3 Vox pop

4 Interviewing Bernie Grant, MP

Summary

Studio presenter: Sometime this spring there will be a General Election, and the three main political parties are all working hard on how to appeal to the voters. Probably the most difficult group to attract is the young, especially young black people, traditionally the most reluctant voters in the country. This time, over eight out of ten have said they might not vote at all. As the election campaign hots up, Oliver King has been finding out how some people are trying to change that, particularly in the 50 odd seats where black and Asian voters could decide who wins.

[*Shots of Operation Black Vote meeting being set up.*]
    Reporter: A public question time in Regent's Park, North London, organized by Operation Black Vote. It's a chance for local black voters to question prospective parliamentary candidates.
    Anthony Wade, Operation Black Vote: Well, what we have demonstrated is that up and down the country in many marginal constituencies there are large, large black and Asian communities who can determine who actually wins that seat at the next General Election.
    Reporter: The candidates were questioned on housing, the teaching of black history and crime, but still managed to get across their Party message.

[*Brief sound-bites from three main political candidates at meeting, intercut with shots of audience.*]
    Reporter: But here's the problem [*shot of young Black people in audience*]. Out of an audience of 70, there were fewer than 10 young black voters. And what did they think?

[*Vox pop outside meeting.*]
    Black Voter 1: Well, me personally, I think they're just waffling, to tell you the truth.
    Black Voter 2: To the youth and to the people they're trying to get at, they're talking like a totally different language.
    Black Voter 3: Well, like, you can vote – but at the end of the day nothing's going to change. You're still going to get stopped by the police or arrested or something, for stupidness.
    Reporter: To change those attitudes, activists for Operation Black Vote know they have an uphill task. A recent survey found that only 16 per cent of blacks aged under 25 were certain to vote, as compared with 36 per cent of under-25s in the whole population. Amongst black people of all ages, only 40 per cent told MORI they would definitely vote. The main reasons they gave were lack of time and information and no interest in politics. [*Graphic: summary of above points.*] [*Cut to reporter standing opposite Houses of Parliament.*] At the moment, there are six black MPs in the House of Commons, but that could change at the next General Election, as the

Conservatives are fielding 10 black candidates and Labour 11. However many succeed in winning seats, young black Britons in particular want to see many more black MPs if the gulf between them and Parliament is to be bridged . . .

[*Studio:*]

Presenter: Well, joining us now is the MP for Tottenham, Bernie Grant, and Poppy Perret from Camden School for Girls, who's going to question him . . .

Perret: I was just wondering, why don't many black people register to vote in the first place?

Grant [*black Afro-Caribbean Labour MP*]: I would think that quite a lot of black people are disenchanted with politics. They feel that the parties don't pay enough attention to black issues.

Perret: In general, young people aren't really interested in politics so, I mean, that's because the policies don't really relate to them very much. So shouldn't governments or parties be reviewing their policies to help young people?

Grant: Absolutely right, and certainly they should have specific policies for young people. Young people are concerned about issues like the environment, they're concerned about homelessness and they're concerned about drugs and all these issues MPs tend to avoid if possible. But I think that certainly there is a case, particularly nowadays, for Members of Parliament and politicians generally to begin to concentrate on issues that affect young people.

Presenter: Bernie, don't you find Parliament a very white place? I mean, how do you make it relevant to the ethnic communities in this country?

Grant: Well, Parliament is very white, but quite a lot of institutions in this country are also that way. I think that two things have got to happen. I think that the MPs themselves have got to pay more attention to the issues to do with race, and secondly, I think that the political leaders need to give a high profile to the question of race, because then the media picks it up and then everybody feels that they are included in it.

Perret: So what's the point in young black people actually voting if, like, 'cause, I mean, promises have been made before but I don't know if much things have changed. Why should they vote?

Grant: Well, they should vote because most of them have never seen a Labour Government and people have thought 'we've had a Conservative government for 18 years' and most people think that that's the way all politicians are.

Perret: Why are there so few black and Asian MPs?

Grant: Well, because of racism, I mean, this is a racist society. And black people are discriminated against. Not only in politics but in schools and the police force – all over the place. So that there's a constant struggle that we have to engage in.

Presenter: Poppy, do you feel it's a racist society? I mean, growing up in a multi-ethnic school in Camden?

Perret: I think – I don't think everyone's racist, but I think people can be racist. But not everyone is. I mean, like, younger people, teenagers and stuff, they're much more aware of not being prejudiced and not being racist. I think older people are more racist than younger people.

Presenter: Do you think that's true, Bernie?

Grant: Oh, yes. Absolutely true. And I think – when I talk about racism I don't – I'm not speaking about persons as individuals, I'm talking about the institutions within the society . . . And I agree totally with Poppy. Young people, they're a real breath of fresh air. And certainly in my area, in Haringey, in Tottenham, you know, the people get together tremendously well. They get on really well, particularly young people. It's not a problem.

Presenter: . . . We'll end on that optimistic note.

Duration: 6 minutes.

Readings

This item was chosen as a counterpart to the US Government Shutdown item discussed in Chapter 6. While both share an explicit concern with politics – in the sense of the party political system – this item also focuses directly on the relationship between young people (and specifically young black people) and politics. It thus also invokes the issue of 'race', albeit in a less overtly controversial way than the Million Man March item.

Like the Shutdown item, this item generated the least interest and enthusiasm of any of those discussed with these students. While some praised the emphasis on young people's perspectives, the item was judged by many to be 'boring'. Comparatively little was recalled when I asked the students about it the following week. Nevertheless, the students' responses raise some interesting questions about their perceptions of the domain of 'politics', and further illustrate some of the tensions that often characterise discussions of 'race'.

Talking Election Politics

Before screening and discussing the item, I asked the students to offer some observations on the forthcoming general election, which was then only a few weeks away. Some of their more general observations were discussed in Chapter 5. Responses to the election specifically were predictably alienated and sceptical. While some (perhaps politely) said that it was 'interesting', the overriding response to the topic was that it was 'boring'. Many expressed their dislike of the *amount* of election coverage in the media, complaining about '12-page spreads' in the newspapers, and dismissing it as (in the words of Daniella, 14) a lot of 'palaver'. Predictably, some of the older students were more interested and well-informed, although in several cases this appeared to amount to little more than an expression of citizen-like duty: as Nandi (17) put it, the election was boring, 'but I suppose they have to do it for democracy and everything'. Jack (12), one of the more middle-class 'civic-minded' students here, said that he was interested 'to know what's going to happen to my country, and what they're thinking to do', but even he was very forthcoming with his criticisms of politicians and of election coverage.

This sense of boredom and alienation derived from several sources. On the one hand, there was the generalized distrust of politicians that was manifested throughout these discussions. Politicians were routinely accused of dishonesty, incompetence and self-interest, and of making promises they couldn't or didn't keep. Even if you were able to vote, said Daniel (14), it was hard to know who to vote for 'because they've all really made a mess'. According to Colin (17), politics was simply a game:

> *Colin*: When you watch politicians, it just seems ridiculous to me. When they're having arguments, they're just playing games with each other. And in real terms, I think their arguments, when it comes down to actual results, physical things, I don't think it stands for anything, what they say. Most of what they say is lies.

At the same time, the students were directly critical of tendencies within the campaign itself – tendencies that were widely attacked by political commentators at the time. Thus, students in all age groups condemned the emphasis on negative campaigning. As Keirra (12) put it:

> *Keirra*: How can you be interested in politics when you see them saying 'I'm pretty crap myself, but he's crappier than me.' And that's about all they say. And you don't know what they're going to do.

Others criticized the emphasis on the personalities of the party leaders: as Siobhan (17) put it, 'It's not really Labour or Tory, it's John and Tony.' The emphasis on 'sleaze', which was a key feature of the campaign, was also commented upon by several students, although some were far from clear what it meant. There was considerable confusion about 'cash for questions', although more obvious forms of scandal-mongering were also condemned:

> *Jake (14)*: They usually talk about stupid things like some politician's gone off with some other woman or something like that. We don't really want to know that. We just want to know who's running the government ...

Several mentioned one particular publicity stunt in which the Tories has paraded a person dressed up as a chicken in response to Tony Blair's refusal to participate in a televised debate with John Major. Interestingly, this was condemned by some of the younger students as 'childish': as Anna (12) said, 'they don't have to be serious and be adults', but this was going too far.

While some of this criticism was directed at the media, much of it focused on the actions of politicians themselves. In general, it was argued that the style of campaigning was distracting attention from the policies – which, like Keirra and Jake, many students claimed they wanted to know more about. This desire to know more was often expressed as a need for some straight talking. Daniel (14) complained about politicians making 'long, boring speeches' – 'they should just cut it down, just say what they mean'; while Chris (17) said he would like the newspapers to print concise one-page summaries of the main parties' policies. Imran and Matt (12) argued that the politicians were simply 'talking to the parents', and that the parties should 'get things to children in schools' to explain how their policies would affect them. Despite such complaints, few students actually seemed to have made the effort to find out more themselves: Olivia (17) was one of the very few who claimed to have done this, and it may be significant that she had used the Internet rather than traditional media.

Very few of the students here professed any political preference, and those who did often put this down to the influence of their parents. One of the older students, Ben (17), commented ironically that he would vote if he could 'but more because my parents have drilled in Labour to me over the years, rather than my own decision.' Among those who did express a preference, there was a notable presence of Liberal Democrats. While some recognized that this might be a 'wasted vote', others argued that the party was somehow rising above the trivial conflicts and publicity stunts being pursued by the two main parties.

On the other hand, much of the students' sense of alienation from the election debate derived from a sense of their own position as 'kids' or 'young people'. Broadly speaking, they argued that the outcome of the election would make no difference to them, and that they would not be able to make any difference to it: as Isaac (14) succinctly put it, 'I'll only care if I can vote.' As several students pointed out, much of the campaign had focused on the issue of taxation, which did not directly affect them – although, as Darren (12) suggested, it might do so if their pocket money was reduced as a result of rising taxes. Few were able to identify policies that would make much impact upon them, although some noted with trepidation the Labour Party's emphasis on homework, and their proposal to introduce curfews. Others argued that Labour might devote more money to education, and that they were committed to maintaining comprehensive schools, though Jack (12) criticized the fact that some Labour politicians had sent their children to grammar or selective schools. Ultimately, when it came to defining the differences between the policies of the main political parties, several of the students maintained that they were 'just the same', while Keirra (12) cynically pointed out that Blair and Major do have 'different colour hair'.

Several students expressed the belief that they would become more interested in politics when they got older, if only because they would have to pay taxes. For the moment, however, their position was effectively that of a disinterested spectator:

> *Jack (12)*: I'm not totally concerned with it, because of the fact that I have no say in what's going to happen ... [If I could vote], then I would be thinking about what I want, rather than what's going to happen to the whole country. Because if I vote in it, it's like 'what should I say, what should I say, do I want this, do I want this?' But now I'm just thinking, 'what's going to happen?'

While this lack of interest was seen by most as simply a function of their inability to vote, others argued that it was a more general characteristic of their age group:

> *Nandi (17)*: You have other things on your mind. You don't really want to engage in politics or anything ... Why at seventeen would that be the most important thing on your mind? [*laughs*]

As we saw in Chapter 5, Nandi and her friends also suggested that factors such as social class might contribute to this. Having grown up under Conservative governments, they clearly found it hard to imagine what it would be like to have anything different; as Suzanna put it, 'We've had a Conservative party for so long, nothing's gonna change.'

In many of these statements, therefore, there was a mixture of alienation and confusion. On the one hand, the students claimed that they were not interested in politics, and that they were sick of hearing about it; yet on the other, they claimed that they were not being sufficiently well informed about the policies of the parties, and that they would like to know more. In these respects, the students' responses echo the findings of research into adults' perceptions of election coverage conducted during the 1997 campaign. Jane Sancho-Aldridge (1997) found that viewers in general – and particularly first-time voters – wanted less coverage, less negative campaigning and less emphasis on the main leaders, but that they also called for better explanations of the policies, more coverage of minor parties and more straight answers to questions. In these respects, the responses recorded here may be rather less specific to their age group than some of the students themselves suggested.

Reading Intentions

Most of the statements discussed so far were made before the students had seen the item, although in several respects, the item merely tended to confirm their position. The issue of 'race', which was the main focus here, will be considered below, but the argument that young people in general lacked interest in politics was accepted without question. Very few of the students argued that the item had a particular 'point of view'; it was described by many as 'showing both sides', 'playing it safe' and even as showing 'blatant truths'. One or two tentatively suggested that it might have been pro-Labour, because of the inclusion of a Labour MP; but this may have been because they felt required to produce an answer to my question.

There was some uncertainty about the motivation behind the item, however. Many argued that it was trying to encourage young black people to vote, or at least to make them more 'interested' or 'aware of what is going on'. However, some doubt was expressed about whether this was an effective strategy: Nandi (17) perceived the programme as a whole to be 'aimed to 12 years old', and argued that it was therefore 'pointless' to include such an item that 'had nothing to do with 12-year-old people'. Colin (17) argued that the item did not give any details of policies that would be relevant to young black voters, and hence 'there was nothing actually there to encourage them to vote'. Indeed, several students perceived this encouragement to vote as simply another manifestation of politicians' self-interest:

> *Parastoo (14)*: I think they're kind of forcing them to vote. I think they're just saying it 'cause they want our vote. I don't think that it's true, because they just get a lot of young people and just sit them there and just keep on talking about the Labour and the Conservative. They just want their votes.

In effect, Parastoo is accusing politicians of using 'race' as another electoral ploy – they are simply interested in black people as, in the words of Sarah (17), 'just a different group of people you need to get to vote'. Some students also reacted negatively to the politicians featured (albeit briefly) in the news report. Keirra, Imran and Matt (12) – whose generally subversive stance was discussed in Chapter 5 – displayed considerable lack of interest during the screening, but went on to mimic and mock the speakers in great detail, interpreting one of the candidates' brief glance towards another as clear evidence that 'she fancied him'.

This somewhat literal – and indeed, rather contradictory – interpretation of the motivations of the item was fairly widely shared across all age groups. Even Olivia (17), one of the most sophisticated and well-informed students here, condemned it in these terms:

> *Olivia*: They wanted to make people more aware of the issues without going into too much depth. It's kind of fashionable at the moment, isn't it, to have stories like that ... It gets people, it's a race relations thing, got to watch it, kind of thing. They're

playing on our kind of people's insecurities as well. 'Cause it came across as trying to target the black audience, to get them interested into watching it. But it didn't actually give you any answers.

Like the other students in her age group, Olivia clearly perceives the item to be aimed at children younger than herself, and uses the 'civic frame' to accuse it of superficiality: elsewhere in the discussion, she argued that it merely 'skimmed on a few topics' and failed to 'go in depth'. Yet she also seems to see it as directed at her (she is British/Asian) and as somehow making unreasonable accusations; it was perhaps this perception that led her and her friends to develop a more sustained critique of the item, as we shall see below.

'Race' Talk

It was the issue of racism, rather than electoral politics, which generated the most substantive debate here. As in the case of the Million Man March item, discussions of 'race' were fraught with tensions and contradictions. On one level, hardly any of the students directly disputed the explicit assertions made within the item. Both black and white students supported the points made by Bernie Grant, that young black people would be more likely to vote if politicians made a greater effort to address their concerns, and if there were more black and Asian MPs. Yet the topic of 'race' was not an easy one to talk about in this context. These groups were more mixed than the Philadelphia groups, and more ethnically diverse, with several students of Asian and Afro-Caribbean origin, as well as several of mixed race. As with the Million Man March item, this led to a complex mixture of disavowal and acknowledgement of racism and of racial difference. 'Race', it appeared, was something that both did and did not matter.

This was particularly – but by no means exclusively – the case for the white students. Especially in ethnically mixed groups, the white students clearly found the experience of talking about 'race' an uncomfortable one. In one instance, Liam (14) struggled to talk about the 'vox pop' of black youths, and began to turn red in the face. He seemed unsure about whether to talk about young black voters as 'they' or 'we', and eventually opted for the latter – as if aware that talking in terms of a 'they' who could not understand politicians could be construed as insulting. Several white students echoed Bernie Grant's argument that 'we live in a racist society', while others were keen to repeat his claim that young people were less racist – as though this somehow exonerated them from blame. Others extended this argument, pointing to racism in the police or the incidence of racist attacks; although here again, the racists were always *other* people. On the other hand, some sought to challenge the emphasis on race, arguing (for example) that people should not be put forward as candidates simply because they were black, but because they were 'clever enough' or 'good at what they do'. Chris (17, white) was particularly disturbed by the presenter's use of the word 'fielding' in this context: people should vote on the basis of policies, he argued, not because of the colour of the candidate's skin.

Both implicitly and explicitly, the students debated whether or not dis-affection from politics was a 'race issue' or a 'youth issue'. In some cases, they simply slipped from one to the other, talking about 'black people' at one moment and 'young people' at another. In others, they directly chal-lenged the emphasis on 'race': Nandi (17), who is black, argued that class and education were more significant in determining people's interest in poli-tics; while Sarah (17), who is white, pointed out the absence of women in the 'vox pop', arguing that gender was also a factor here. Parastoo (14), who is British/Asian, even refuted the programme's assertion that young black people were less likely to vote than whites: 'I think they're paying more attention because they're black, it's racist.' Such statements are diffi-cult to interpret, however. On the evidence of these interviews, for example, it is not clear whether Parastoo defined herself as 'black': for example, in discussing the 'vox pop' she talked about 'them' rather than 'us', although (as discussed above) she also criticized the politicians because 'they just want *our* vote'. Symptomatically perhaps, her challenge to the programme's statistics was prefaced with the classic statement 'I'm not racist or anything, I'm just saying, as a manner of speaking . . .'

At the same time, several students implied (in my view correctly) that the item itself fudged the issue by selecting a white girl to interview a black MP. The girl herself was perhaps the most memorable aspect of the whole item for most of the students, not least because she attended a local school – and one that several clearly regarded as 'posh'. Several students expressed approval of the use of a young interviewer, even if some of the older ones were sceptical about whether she was putting forward her own questions; while Keirra (12) was especially impressed by her 'cool T-shirt'. Nevertheless, many students – both black and white – questioned the use of a *white* inter-viewer in this context, and felt that she should have been black. It was argued that she did not have any right or authority to make judgements about racism, because she did not have any experience of it. The choice of a white inter-viewer was seen as a kind of denial of the issues:

> *Keirra (12, white)*: I don't know why she was white. But [they were] talking about people being racist, and there was this white girl sitting there saying 'well I don't think I'm racist.' Some people *can* be racist . . . She ended up talking about young people's issues rather than black issues.

> *Imran (12, British/Asian)*: She could only talk for herself. She can't talk for black people.

On the other hand, some students adopted a more generalized 'multi-culturalist' position, arguing that the programme should have included people 'from all different backgrounds'. The most sustained example of this argument came from two students, Jake (14), who is white, and David (14), who is black (Afro-Caribbean). They argued that this section of the programme should have included a broader range of perspectives:

> *David*: Not just white and black, there should've been Asian, perhaps Chinese, Bangladesh also and a white MP. Not to have a battle, but to discuss problems and different issues.

These boys also argued that one of the points made in the 'vox pop' should have been extended by interviewing the police, on the grounds that this would have been fairer; while David facetiously suggested that they had chosen a white interviewer 'because she might speak proper English' – a point that was greeted with laughter. Whether or not David and Jake might be interested to watch a programme that contained a more extended debate of this kind is a moot point; but it is clear that the emphasis on diversity and 'fairness' – and the humour – provides them with a way out of a potentially awkward encounter.

Aside from Poppy and her cool T-shirt, the one element of this item that did appear to speak directly to these students was the brief 'vox pop' with the young people attending the Operation Black Vote meeting. This item was recalled and quoted by several of the students the following week. It was clear that many of the students shared the stance articulated here, particularly the point about politicians 'waffling' and 'talking a different language'. Chris (17, white) saw these interviewees as possessing a greater degree of authority than any 'expert':

> *Chris*: They could have got an expert in to say, 'We think it's this. We've done studies to show that de-da-de-da-de-da.' But they'd actually gone to the roots. If you've got a problem, the root is that they don't understand it, and don't want to understand it. And why should we vote? . . . They got them to say that. They actually got it on camera. That is so much more than some guy sitting there saying, 'I think this is what should be.'

Chris is aware that this material has been selected and constructed (he later speculated, jokingly, about whether the interviewees had been paid); and he went on to argue that 'black youth' were 'an extremity' in terms of their alienation from politics. Nevertheless, these interviews seem to possess a kind of 'ethnic' authenticity for him, which is implied by his use of the term 'roots'.

By contrast, Olivia, Colin and Sarah (17) argued that black voices were marginalized in the item as a whole (Olivia is British/Asian, the others are white). They were much more critical of this sequence, and were particularly scathing about features that might have led Chris to perceive these interviewees as somehow 'authentic':

Colin: They've obviously picked out those sentences to represent the people in some way, they most probably had a big interview or a small interview with each of them and picked out those few sentences.

DB: So why do you think they've picked out those particular sentences?

Sarah: [To show?] they didn't know what they were talking about, they were ignorant or something like that . . .

Olivia: But it comes across as really like a stereotype, these are like the things that people –

Sarah: And they chose, they all wear baseball caps as if they're gonna rob something [laughter] . . . They chose them all with baseball caps and hiding themselves, and one of them saying, 'We are still gonna get stopped by the police.'

This argument implies, not merely conscious manipulation on the part of the programme-makers, but also the existence of an audience that will not recognize this – that will, in this case, simply have its stereotypes confirmed. Here again, this 'media literate' discourse creates a powerful position for its users – even if it possesses its own stereotypical script ('the media always portray black youths as trouble' and so on).

While this group's discussion obeys the general rules of this script, it also displays some of its contradictions. Thus, Chris accused the report of saying that 'it was . . . the black youths' fault that they weren't voting', while Sarah criticized it for not including 'the black youths who *were* interested in politics'. They also argued that the interviewer should have been black, on the grounds that the presenter 'could have asked them what do you want, what changes do you want?' Black people, they argued, were effectively excluded, even though (according to these students) they were the primary target audience: as Sarah put it, 'They're talking *for* them, but we don't get to hear them talk for themselves.' On the other hand, the focus on black people was seen (as it was by Parastoo, p. 161) as itself evidence of racism; this group argued that the item should have focused on young people in general, 'from all different backgrounds', rather than identifying blacks as the problem. There was too much 'black, black, black', said Olivia.

There is a fundamental paradox here, which I would argue is characteristic of much popular debate about 'race' and the media. In effect, the students are calling simultaneously for *more* representation and for *less* – for 'race' to be emphasized and for it to be effaced. As in the case of the

Million Man March item, these contradictions reflect both the broader social and political tensions that surround the issue, and the specific interpersonal tensions of the interview context. Here again, perceptions of media bias – and hence their relationship to the development of political understanding – need to be interpreted in relation to the social and discursive contexts in which they are articulated.

First Edition: Youth Crime

Summary

Presenter: Did you know that one quarter of all the crimes in this country are committed by people under 18? And more and more by children under 13? So how should we deal with these young people and how should they be punished? Should their parents be punished too? Politicians have started suggesting big changes in the law to try to deal with people's fears of youth crime.

Reporter: [*Shots of children rioting, setting fires, dancing on tops of cars*] Out of control, children like these are a menace for local residents. Youth crime costs its victims three billion pounds a year and the police and courts one billion. Politicians want a crack down to force parents to take more control. Some recent cases of crime shocked the whole country. The London head teacher Philip Lawrence was stabbed by a gang member outside his school gates. His killer Learcho Chindano was only 16. But when 2-year-old Jamie Bulger was murdered by two 11-year-olds, the police had to prove the killers knew they had done wrong. [*Shots of Lawrence, Chindano, Bulger: surveillance camera stills and crime scene.*] That was because a 600-year-old law says that a child under 13 doesn't always know the difference between right and wrong. [*Jack Straw on walkabout.*] The Labour Party plans to change that age limit to 10, and the Government also has plans for young criminals.

Michael Howard [*Home Secretary, in studio*]: I am hoping to tackle the problem of child crime at its roots. I want to give help at as early a stage as possible to children who are in danger of going off the rails, and to their parents.

Reporter: So what do they want to do? The Conservative plan includes getting police, social workers and others to work in Child Crime Teams to identify unruly children. They can suggest that the court imposes a Parental Control Order to force parents to keep control of their children. But if the parents fail to obey, the court can impose fines, curfews and electronic tags on them. [*Graphic of Conservative policies: Child Crime Teams, Parental Control Orders, fines, curfews and electronic tags.*] Labour also want curfews and their plan involves family training sessions to try and stop the child offending. If this fails, the child could receive a formal final warning instead

5 Youth rioting

6 Electronic tagging

7 The Youth Centre

8 Interview with Jack Straw

of multiple cautions at present. If both these measures don't work, the Juvenile Courts will receive extra powers to put offenders in secure accommodation. [*Graphic of Labour policies: family training sessions, formal final warnings, extra powers for courts.*] The Government thinks tagging parents would force them to stay at home and control their children because the police would know where they were. [*Shots of electronic tag being attached.*] They should also pay for their children's crimes.

The main aim of the politicians is to prevent young children ever getting involved in crime and growing up into full time adult criminals. But what's the best way to do that? [*Reporter in playground. Shots of playground, children playing snooker, arriving in playground.*] Here at Camden's Fairfield Centre in North London, kids from local inner city estates can play with their friends in safety. It takes them off the streets and keeps them busy in the afternoons. The Centre is a refuge from Camden's problems of drugs, graffiti and gangs. It believes children won't commit crime if they have good alternatives and are kept active.

Pip O'Byrne [*Camden Community and Leisure Services, in playground*]: The solution cannot be in punishing parents – it has to be around parents understanding what their children's needs are and how they can get involved in their children's lives to prevent their children getting involved in crime.

Reporter: The children here say that kids should be punished if they do wrong. But what do their parents think about punishing parents?

Mother: [*in youth centre*] I think they should leave it to the police. It's not the parents' fault.

2nd Mother: My kids can be naughty the same as anybody else's, but it doesn't say, like, that my kids are bad.

3rd Mother: I do think that the parents should be responsible and should be made responsible for young children.

Reporter: Good centres like Fairfield, they say, are a better way of preventing their kids committing crime than any ideas of a crack down from the politicians.

Studio:

Presenter: Jack Straw is the Shadow Home Secretary – that means that he's the man who speaks for Labour on law and order. Lizzie Greenaway comes from Bishopton Comprehensive School in Swansea. Lizzie, what would you like to ask Jack Straw?

Greenaway: What do you think should happen to children who commit crime?

Straw: Well, when they first commit crimes – a trivial offence – they ought to be given a warning by the police and the parents ought to be spoken to. But if they go on and commit more crimes, or more serious crimes, then the Court should listen to the case and if the Court decides that they are guilty of the crime then the Court should decide on both the punishment and the means of trying to stop them doing it again.

Greenaway: Why do you think that young children commit crimes?

Straw: It's a variety of reasons. It's often got to do with the fact that their parents don't give them a proper framework, an idea of what's right and what's wrong. And if you look at the background of a lot of what we call persistent offenders, young children who commit a lot of crimes, you often find that their parents one moment are very harsh towards them and another moment are indulgent, being soft on them. So that's part of the reason why we think that there ought to be much better parenting education. Another reason why children commit crime is because they get into bad company of elder children, and that's also why we think it's very important to give these firm final warnings early on so that children just don't drift into crime.

Greenaway: Do you think it's fair that parents should be punished for their children's actions?

Straw: In very extreme cases, yes. But I think what's much more important is that parents should be held responsible for what their children do. Particularly if the children are younger. I've got teenage children and I know that it's quite difficult bringing up children, particularly looking after teenage children. But parents are responsible for their children, they ought to be held responsible for their children. And if they're failing, then what we're suggesting is that the parents might be subject to what we call a Parental Responsibility Order where the parents would get some counselling, some help and advice about how to be better parents.

Greenaway: Do you think that all children know the difference between right and wrong?

Straw: Most do. And I think most aged 10 and upwards do. Some don't, but they ought to. I accept, of course, that a child aged 10 or 11 has a different idea of what is right and wrong from an adult aged 20 or 21. But I think that most children know that if they go into a supermarket and take goods that they haven't paid for, that's wrong. If they break into a car or house and take things that don't belong to them, that that is wrong.

Presenter: Lizzie, Jack Straw, thank you both very much indeed.

Duration: 6 minutes 15 seconds.

Readings

This item and the next provide contrasting approaches to the question of youth crime – an issue that has become a major focus of political debate in the UK in recent years (Pilcher and Wagg, 1996; Scraton, 1997). The differences between the two items and the students' responses to them raise interesting questions about the formal strategies that are used in presenting such issues, and about how young people in particular are represented and addressed. In addition, the issue of bias is again a central concern here. Broadly speaking, both items were perceived to be biased towards a point of view which the students themselves were inclined to share; they were effectively preaching to the converted, albeit in quite different ways – and with different consequences.

Defining the Problem

Prior to viewing the item, the students were invited to discuss briefly three main questions: Is youth crime increasing? What are its causes? What can be done to prevent it? Most students agreed that youth crime was indeed increasing, although their evidence for this was essentially anecdotal. In some cases, particularly among the older students, they were able to draw on personal experience: Chris (17), for example, described how he had been a victim of bullying by local gangs in his previous school; Nandi (17) recounted how she had witnessed a fight on a late night bus journey. Among the younger children, the evidence was more likely to be based on rumour, or possibly media coverage: Dean (12), for example, recounted the story of a fight between local graffiti gangs, which had led to a stabbing. As these examples suggest, 'youth crime' was defined in some rather diverse ways here. Perhaps predictably, the criminals concerned were always *other* people, although several students claimed that they knew people who had been involved in crime of various kinds. In general, the students seemed to take the perspective of potential *victims* of youth crime – which makes an interesting contrast with the majority of media coverage, which tends to represent youth as perpetrators and adults as the primary victims.

However, only a few students directly challenged the idea that youth crime was increasing. Jack (12) argued that it had simply been taken up by politicians as a means of gaining votes in the run-up to the election:

> *Jack*: They always seem to say that it's more of a problem. But I think it's not so much more of a problem, it's more of an *issue* now.
>
> *DB*: What do you mean?
>
> *Jack*: Now they're taking note of it. Before, they weren't so much ... It's got great in just the last year or something. It's become completely massive. And everyone, every kid's a criminal ... [It's] another way of getting votes. Saying 'we're going to stop this happening'. Because if one big thing happens, where there's a youth crime, then it's like a major issue all across the country and so the government raises it. 'We'll pick up on this, it's another thing we can use' ... Anything they can use, they'll use to win votes.

Jack's comments display the kind of scepticism about politicians that informed several of these discussions, though he also shows a much rarer ability to question the ways in which 'issues' are defined within the political domain – particularly striking given his age. However, there were other students in each age group here who questioned the construction of 'youth crime' as an issue, both in general and within the item itself. Ben, Chris and Leo (17), for example, echoed Jack's points about the self-interest of politicians, and extended this to a critique of the role of the media in amplifying such problems (cf. Cohen and Young, 1972):

> *Leo*: Maybe that's just the media, though ... If something triggers off – there'll be a little row happen somewhere and the media will pick that up. Then once the media picks it up, it's a concern, everyone's talking about it. The government will then go, 'Oh! we must do something about youth crime!'
>
> *Ben*: If there was a big racial attack today, the media would blow it out of proportion tomorrow and then it would be a political issue the next day.

In fact, this group did not simply dismiss the idea that youth crime was a problem; all of them claimed to have some personal experience of having been victimized, or having 'hung around with some bad crowd', as Leo put it. But they were cautious about generalizing from this experience:

> *Leo*: I can't say. I mean, I've been a victim, but I'm sure quite a lot of people have. I can't say that just because, like, I was mugged a year ago and I wasn't mugged five years ago, that [crime] is growing.

Clearly, many young people will have some direct experience of 'youth crime'. As we shall see, the students tried to make sense of the political debate in terms of the general lessons they felt they had learned from personal experience – and particularly from their relationships with their parents, with the police and with other sources of authority. What distinguishes the comments recorded here, however, is an ability to 'decentre', to perceive the limitations of personal experience. These students are obviously employing a more or less routinized form of critical discourse – a form of 'in-principle' scepticism – about both politics and the media. Yet their ability to look beyond immediate experience allows them to adopt a more generally critical stance towards the ways in which social problems are defined. These kinds of observations were comparatively rare in our initial discussions, although (as we shall see) they emerged more strongly in response to the item itself.

Causes and Solutions

All the students here took a broadly liberal stance on the question of crime and its prevention. Significantly, their responses were also very much 'child-centred', that is, they sought to explain the causes of youth crime and to evaluate potential solutions from the perspective of young people themselves. It was this perspective that also informed their responses to the item, and (in some cases) their critique of its approach.

Thus, the causes of youth crime were predominantly defined in terms of 'peer group pressure'. It was a matter of 'getting into bad company', 'acting cool for your mates' or trying to 'get in the gang and be one of the hard people'. A number of the younger children particularly explained this in terms of attempting to emulate a leader, often an older person: Darren (12), for example, argued that 'a lot of kids idolize older people' and hence might be led to copy their criminal behaviour. Very few sought to explain the causes of crime in terms of broader structural problems, such as poverty; and even here, poverty was generally defined as a matter of individuals not having enough money. Only Jack (12) attributed this directly to broader political processes – 'the way the country's being run, people are getting poorer, that's creating more thieves'. In general, youth crime was seen to result from *individual* weaknesses, and from interpersonal, rather than more broadly social, influences.

However, it was generally agreed that disciplinary responses to the phenomenon were unlikely to succeed. Thus, several students argued that encouraging parents to become more strict would simply cause children to react against them. Curfews were seen as ineffective for the same reason:

> *Liam (14)*: That's gonna anger them and make it worse. Because people are gonna go out more before 7 o'clock because there's a curfew.

> *Jake*: Yeah. It's like when people say in school 'don't smoke cigarettes'. It's like telling them to smoke cigarettes.

Caroline (12) offered a further instance of this kind of deviance amplification theory, arguing that curfews would lead to more young people being arrested, which would lead in turn to a perceived increase in youth crime. 'It would be on all the surveys and people would just say that crime is rising – but it's not.' In general, it was argued that people who were going to commit crimes would do so in any case – and indeed at any time of the day – and were unlikely to be deterred by their parents or by the police.

In general, the favoured responses to youth crime were those which addressed causes rather than symptoms. Before they had seen the item, several students argued that increasing leisure provision and education, rather than punishment, was the answer. David and Liam (14) proposed that there should be 'more places to go' and 'more youth centres'; while Rosie (14) argued, 'They should educate and encourage more: if [young people] could be more interested in getting a good job and everything, they wouldn't turn to crime.' As with the students' accounts of the causes of crime, therefore, their preferred solutions focused primarily on providing positive support for young people, rather than on ways of strengthening social control.

These existing biases were largely confirmed by the students' readings of the item itself. One aspect of their broadly 'child-centred' approach was that the students largely attributed responsibility for crime to young people themselves. Thus, several of them explicitly supported Jack Straw's argument for lowering the age at which children were seen to understand the difference between right and wrong. In this context, Parastoo (14) argued that children today were more 'mature' than their counterparts in earlier times, and that they should have to face the consequences of their actions.

Likewise, solutions to youth crime that focused primarily on parents rather than children were generally rejected as ineffective or irrelevant. Some suggested that it was not the parents' fault if their children turned to crime; others argued, more pragmatically, that some children simply could not be controlled. Here again, it was suggested that disciplinary measures might prove counter-productive: Parastoo (14) argued that children of parents who were electronically tagged would be more likely to resist their authority, because they would be confined to the house; Abigail (12) even suggested that such children might turn to crime 'just to get their parents into trouble'. Some argued that it would be much more logical to tag the children, since they were the ones committing the crimes, though tagging was explicitly rejected by the large majority. Even the softer option of 'counselling' was challenged by some:

> *Liam (14)*: I think parents know how to raise their children. They've known their children better than anyone else. They know how to look after the child and tell them what's right and wrong and whatever. I don't think anyone can tell them how to look after their child.

In general, however, it was the more liberal solutions, aimed at addressing causes rather than punishing symptoms, that were more widely supported. All of the younger groups favoured the idea of providing more youth clubs, on the grounds that it would 'get kids off the streets' where they might get 'bored' and be more likely to 'get in trouble'. Some also appeared to have been influenced by the positive representation of the youth club in the item; Liam and Jake (14) commented several times on the brief shot of the snooker game, arguing that youth clubs would 'encourage kids to go and do something good like playing snooker instead of going out and breaking into cars'. Only some of the older students questioned this approach, on the grounds that it would only be effective with younger children; as Chris (17) pointed out, anyone over 13 would be unlikely to respond very positively to being told to attend a youth club. In general, the older students seemed to be more aware of the intractability of the problem and less convinced about the possibility of finding an easy solution.

Reading Bias

As I have indicated, the students' existing views on these issues were largely confirmed by their readings of the item. This can be explained in two ways. We might argue that the students exercised a form of selective perception, paying closer attention to material that could be taken to support their existing views, and ignoring that which could not. Alternatively, we might conclude that the students read the item 'transparently'; since they shared its bias, there would have been no reason for them to come to any explicit awareness of how it had been selected and constructed. The latter explanation necessarily presumes that the item is biased in a particular direction, whereas the former one does not. Nevertheless, both positions would lead to the conclusion that, if their viewing of the item had any effects, these were principally a matter of reinforcement rather than persuasion.

In fact, the data here pose obstacles to both these interpretations. To be sure, there were some students who argued (albeit rather uncertainly) that the item was not biased. Others (particularly the older students) tended to use the 'civic frame', arguing that the problem was not so much one of bias as of inadequate information; it was argued, for example, that the item did not focus sufficiently on the causes of youth crime, or (more simply) that it tried to cover too much in too short a time. However, few students expressed much doubt that the item *was* biased: when asked, the large majority agreed that it was in favour of more liberal responses to youth crime, *and* in favour of Labour Party policies. The evidence for this was, they argued, fairly straightforward. Several students pointed out that the item spent more time on the youth centre than on other methods, and discussed it in a more positive way. This was partly a matter of 'tone and expression', as Abigail (12) put it; although it was also because, as Jack (12) pointed out, 'they had the parents saying it was a good idea'. Many students also argued that the item was biased towards Labour policies; for example, they pointed out that, as in the Youth Crime item, the interviewee was a Labour MP.

These are all, in my view, justified arguments, although they also reflect a degree of confusion which the item itself may have introduced. Significantly, many of the students identified the youth centre as an example of Labour Party policy, although the item provides no justification for this. Indeed, I would argue that the item rather obscures the considerable *similarities* between Labour and Conservative policies on youth crime. It notes that both parties favour curfews, for example, though the word is included on the graphic of Conservative policies and not on that of Labour policies. The item also fails to explain the difference (if there is any) between Labour's Parental Responsibility Order and the Conservatives' Parental Control Order. In this context, it is easy to see how most students were led to believe that Labour favoured the more liberal solutions that they themselves preferred, *and* that the programme-makers did so too.

One group of Year 12 students reflected in some detail on this issue. Ben began by arguing that the item was clearly pro-Labour:

> *Ben*: I thought that they did have kind of political views. They presented Labour's whole solution to the problem as a lot more gentle than the Conservatives.

These students were particularly struck by the images of the electronic tag being fitted, even rubbing their ankles as they discussed it. They argued that tagging was 'barbaric' and an 'invasion of privacy'. On the other hand, they acknowledged that the programme itself did not explicitly condemn tagging: 'They didn't actually say "this tag, which by the way is bad" – they just said "this tag".' Nevertheless, as Leo pointed out, 'the tag almost speaks for itself' – or at least it seemed to have done for these students. It was,

they argued, 'a harsh image'. Yet, as they ultimately recognized, their interpretation of the item depended partly on their existing views:

> *Leo*: If you think tags are bad, then you could say it's got a pro-
> Labour view, because it didn't [associate] Labour with the tags
> bit. If you think tags are good, this is just an example of tags,
> then you could say it's a good view of the Conservatives ... In
> that sense, they don't really have a view ...

> *Ben*: That's why maybe I took their point of view [to be] Labour
> strongly, because I thought it looked like Labour's policies were
> better in the way of dealing with that.

These students display the kind of 'decentering' which I have argued is
characteristic of the older age group here; they are able to identify their own
biases, and to reflect upon the consequences of this in terms of their interpretation of the item – and, in Ben's comment here, in terms of their
perceptions of bias within the item itself.

However, this relativistic view of bias as merely a matter of selective
perception is only partly supported by the data here. In some cases, the
students did effectively seem to have 'filtered out' elements that did not
conform to their existing viewpoints. For example, none of them referred to
the interview with the Home Secretary, Michael Howard, or to the discussion of the Conservatives' plans for Parental Control Orders – although these
were, admittedly, quite brief. On the other hand, while some of them referred
to the interview with Jack Straw, he too was perceived quite negatively:
Abigail (12) was one of several who complained about how 'he just kept
going on and on and repeating himself'. Some of the older students were
more sympathetic, particularly because of Straw's reference to his own children: Rosie (14), for example, said that this made him seem 'friendly', and
that it 'related to other children'; although Nisha (14) questioned whether
he was representative of parents in general. Significantly, Parastoo (14)
suggested that the interviewer 'should've asked more personal questions
about his opinion [rather] than what the Labour wants' – illustrating (yet
again) the need to connect the personal and the political, and the fact that
the generic 'politician' tended to be perceived very negatively. Nevertheless,
none of the students were able to recall anything of what Straw had said
the following week, aside from the point about lowering the age of responsibility; the highly authoritarian nature of some of his other proposals seemed
to be ignored in favour of a view of Labour as, in Ben's words, 'a lot more
gentle'.

As this implies, interpretation is rather more complex than simply a
matter of 'selective perception'. One significant issue here (as with several
of the other items, notably the Paper Mill, see Chapter 6) was the relative
importance of the *visual* aspects as compared with the verbal ones. Three

sequences in particular were recalled and discussed by several groups: the brief scene of children rioting and dancing on cars; the shot of the electronic tag being fitted; and the sequence inside the youth club, particularly the children playing snooker. These sequences were all very brief – much briefer, for example, than the discussion of Conservative Party policies – but they were inherently more visually striking, particularly when compared with the preponderance of talking heads that surrounded them. In some respects, these sequences seemed to have been highly influential – at least in reinforcing, or providing further evidence in support of, the student's existing beliefs. Thus, as we have seen, the image of the electronic tag fed into criticisms of punitive responses to youth crime; while the image of the snooker game encouraged the view that youth clubs were all about 'kids enjoying themselves'.

On the other hand, the meaning and impact of the scenes of children rioting – with which the item began – were rather less predictable. This sequence was the one most frequently recalled the following week, and was described by several students as 'shocking'. Yet responses to this sequence also fed into a more critical response to the item itself, which focused on its allegedly negative representation of young people. This response was most fully articulated by one group of Year 11 students. Right at the start of their discussion, they referred to the sequence as follows:

Olivia: To highlight the point that we're a menace to society, really bad people, they show footage of people –

Chris: Riots on the street or something –

Olivia: That could be about something different, like some situation different to that –

Chris: Could be completely out of context and we don't even know.

Sarah: That clip they showed of all the children, like as if there was a riot going on, they portrayed it like it always happens.

According to this group, the item systematically excluded and misrepresented young people. Thus, they complained that it did not include any interviews with young people themselves: as Sarah put it, 'they didn't talk to the children, they were accusing them but they didn't give them a chance to answer for themselves'. The item's 'point of view', they argued, was to 'blame the parents': 'all they did was ask the parents how they should prevent it ... the children weren't involved at all'.

These points were echoed by other students in all three age groups. As with the previous item, they generally welcomed the use of a young interviewer, although here again there was some suspicion that she was simply reading lines that had been written for her. In addition, it was felt that adults should be interviewing children rather than the other way round: Parastoo

(14) suggested that 'they should've chosen someone who was in crime already, someone who does that sort of thing'. While some students were keen to draw a distinction between 'good kids' like themselves and the 'bad kids' shown in the item, others argued that it was portraying children in general in a bad light. David (14) argued that this might have a negative influence on adults:

> *David*: I disliked [the item] 'cause it kind of stereotyped young chil-
> dren. If a group of children were walking down the street and
> there's a policeman, he'll assume you're causing trouble. But
> he'd never think 'Oh, you're nice kids, you're going to the
> library' or anything. They'd assume you're causing trouble.

Likewise, Darren (12) argued that the item – and particularly the rioting sequence – 'made it look as if the kids did worse than the adults', while his friend Jack criticized the way the programme had selected two 'massive' incidents (presumably the murders of James Bulger and Philip Lawrence) from among 'lots of minor incidents'. These boys too were implicitly concerned about how this kind of representation might influence adults; they spoke at considerable length about how shopkeepers viewed them with suspicion and would not allow them to linger in their shops.

On one level, these are somewhat ritualistic complaints, although this in itself does not necessarily render them inaccurate or invalid. Perhaps particularly for the older children, they derive from a generalized suspicion, in which the media are routinely condemned for misrepresenting young people. They also depend upon assumptions about a vulnerable audience that will somehow substitute media stereotypes for their own everyday perceptions – although ironically in this case, that audience is made up of adults rather than children.

In some respects, however, these critical responses also derive from the same 'child-centred' position which, I have suggested, characterized the students' discussions of the issues themselves. They indicate a significant gap between the ways in which political issues relating to young people are framed within news and the ways in which they are perceived by young people themselves. The fact that this is a news programme which is directly targeted at young people indicates the scale of the problem; even here, it would seem, politics appears to be framed in adult terms. My analysis suggests that if young people are to perceive news – and indeed politics itself – as 'relevant' to them, a more radical approach is required. Relevance is not simply a matter of *content* – that is, of which stories are chosen – but also of *form*. The attempt to connect with young people's perspectives requires more than simply using them to read questions in an interview. On the contrary, the students here demanded that young people should be heard and represented on their own terms. The following sections of this chapter discuss some of the possibilities and limitations of one attempt to do just that.

Wise Up: Curfews

Summary

9 Phillip and Gary (presenters)

$\left\{ \vphantom{\begin{array}{c}10\\11\end{array}} \right.$ 10

11 Interviewing the police officer

12 Interviewing the parent

[*Title: Time Out. City street, night: presenters to camera.*]
 Phillip: Hi, my name's Phillip.
 Gary: My name's Gary.
 Phillip: We're in Orlando, Florida. We're reporting on the curfew put on children in downtown Orlando. If you are 17 or under and it's past 12 a.m., whether it be 12.01 or 12.02, you're taken to the downtown police department where your parents are called. If your parents refuse to pick you up, you're taken to a shelter. This really puts a restraint on kids in Orlando.
 Gary: I think the curfew really does suck.
 Phillip: It's a violation on our rights as kids and our rights as citizens.
 Holloway: [*Interviewed in office.*] Hello, I'm Sergeant Mike Holloway with the Orlando Police Department.
 Phillip: What exactly is a curfew?
 Holloway: The curfew is actually designed to cure a particular criminal problem in the downtown area. We don't want people to be in an area where

we know there has been criminal activity. Of course, there are many kids that probably would not be causing the crimes – they're not criminals and have no criminal intent. But the flip side of the coin is that everybody under the age of 17 who's down there is a potential victim.

Phillip: If I was to walk out right now it would be 12.05. How would you apprehend me?

Holloway: The officers that walk the streets would come over and ask you what you're doing and also what age you were. And if you were under 17 years of age they would ask you to come with them. They'd escort you down to the office we're sitting in now and they'd hold you here until they contacted your parents.

Gary: What if your parents can't come and get you?

Holloway: Then they would ask for any other reasonable adult. Now if there is nobody, then they would take you Great Oaks Village, which is a shelter on Michigan Street where we house kids that are runaways or kids that are having some kind of family problem.

Gary: OK. My friend went to a White Zombie concert, downtown. The concert got over at, like, 12.05. He was heading home and he told the cop that but still he got arrested.

Holloway: The law says that you have to be out of the area at midnight. Not 12.05, not 12.10.

Gary: The concert wasn't over then.

Holloway: It was his responsibility to be out of the area ahead of time.

Gary: It's still – if I paid for a three dollar ticket, I'm going to stay for the whole concert.

Holloway: Well, that would be fine, but you'd still be violating the curfew. If you're caught then you would be held until your parents could come to get you.

Phillip: Many times you never know when it's going to end.

Holloway [*smiling*]: But you do know when midnight is. And if you know how to tell the time, you know when you've got to get out of the club. So that's the bottom line.

Gary: It seems like you're acting like parental figures.

Holloway: Yup. That's what government is about.

[*City street, night: presenters interviewing.*]

Kursky: Hello, my name's Chris Kursky and I'm a parent of two children here in Orlando.

Phillip: As a parent do you think the curfew's a good idea?

Kursky: I think the curfew's a good idea and I want my child home at midnight from downtown. I just don't think it's a good place for them to hang out. That way, anything they want to do downtown they can do before midnight.

Gary: What do you think about raising the curfew to maybe one o'clock, two o'clock?

Kursky: I think midnight works. It worked for Cinderella – it'll work for kids in Orlando.

Gary: I know you have a daughter. Say she goes to a White Zombie concert and the concert – most of them end like one a.m. Are you going to want to let her go? Or are you going to be willing to go with her to the concert?

Kursky: Now that's a great idea. Invite your parents along. Have some family fun. But I don't think they're going to arrest you if you're walking from a concert door to the parking garage.

Gary and Phillip: They do.

Gary: They'll arrest you in a second.

Kursky: Well then, she won't be attending any White Zombie concerts after midnight. The law is the law, you know. The curfew's the curfew. So while it's in place you have to obey it. And if you don't like it, when you're 21 you can vote out the people who voted in the curfew.

[*City street, night: presenters to camera, shot from below.*]

Phillip: After talking to a policeman and a parent, they still have not convinced me that the curfew should not be abolished.

Gary: I agree. The policemen haven't said anything that proved that they are right. Or even slightly convinced me that, hey, the curfew should be in.

Phillip: OK. We've got to go now, 'cause if we hang around here too long we'll get arrested.

[*Presenters walk away from camera; sound of siren over.*]

Duration: 3 minutes, 34 seconds.

Readings

This item was chosen primarily in order to provide a direct contrast with the previous one. As I indicated in Chapter 4, *First Edition* employs a fairly conventional news format, carefully avoiding overt signs of bias. Its address to young people is most obviously manifested in its selection of topics and in its use of young interviewers, but young people do not themselves play a particularly prominent role. By contrast, *Wise Up* uses the conventions of access programming, rather than news; it presents a series of young people's personal views, without the appearance of adult mediation. There is no studio presenter; young people address the camera directly, read the voice-overs and conduct the interviews. The programme uses hand-held cameras, jump-cut editing and hand-written captions.

The content of this item overlaps to some extent with that of the previous one; while curfews were only briefly mentioned in the *First Edition* report, many students were familiar with the idea. However, the treatment of the issue of youth crime and its prevention is distinctly different in the two items. Where the students accused the *First Edition* story of effectively neglecting young people's perspectives, here young people are the key players. While a range of views is again presented, the bias of the item is overt and unambiguous. In general, the students significantly preferred this item to the one from *First Edition*, although, as I shall indicate, they were far from uncritical of its style and approach. Here again, their readings of the item raised some complex questions about bias and persuasion.

Taking a Stand

Unsurprisingly, the large majority of the students shared the perspective of the two boys featured in the item. Several were prepared to accept that there was a problem with youth crime – a view they also rehearsed in response to the *First Edition* report. Some were even prepared to grant that there might be good intentions behind the curfew. Nevertheless, it was generally agreed that it would prove ineffective:

> *Anna (12)*: They're only trying to do it to protect the children, you know, to keep them out of trouble there. And so it is, in a way, a good idea ... It's got good meanings behind it, but the way they've done it doesn't work.

As several students implied, the central problem here was that the curfew applied to *all* children simply on the grounds of their age, and as such, it did not directly address those who were committing the crimes. As Colin (17) put it, it was a measure that did not address 'the real issue' of crime, which, the students argued, was caused by a small minority – and not only by the young. As such, therefore, curfews were seen as a form of age discrimination. This dimension was most explicit among the older students, which is perhaps ironic in light of the fact that (as some of them acknowledged) they were least likely to be affected by such measures. Siobhan (17), who had experienced curfews when she had lived in the US, condemned them as 'a disgusting violation of liberty'; while Olivia (17) dismissed the idea as an attack on children's rights:

> *Olivia*: It's just because you're young, you have no rights, you can't think for yourself, *we* must protect you. It's a load of rubbish.

In general, therefore, it was felt that the argument for a curfew unfairly stereotyped and scapegoated young people. As Olivia pointed out:

> *Olivia*: They wouldn't dream of doing it to adults. You can imagine them in bed by 10.30 with their slippers and their hot chocolate. D'you know what I mean?

Even before they had seen the item, students in all age groups were ready to produce some powerful arguments against curfews. The Year 7 students, for example, argued that they would unfairly penalize those who had perfectly valid reasons to be out late at night; that they would simply lead to crime being committed at other times of the day; and that it would be impossible for them to be imposed right across the country. As in the discussion of the *First Edition* item, many argued that imposing stricter discipline would prove counter-productive: curfews would encourage some people to come out after dark, and create more opportunities for committing crimes in unpatrolled areas. Ultimately, most agreed that curfews would not work; while there might be a short-term impact, young people would easily find ways of violating them. As Siobhan (17) concluded, 'kids do what they do'.

Many of the students supported these assertions with evidence from their own experience: they described how, on certain occasions, they returned home late from an evening class or sports club, arguing that this would be impossible if there had been a curfew. Keirra (12) went further, arguing that this would give the police too much power:

> *Keirra*: In other countries ... a lot of people are against giving the police so much power. Because, like, there are some countries where the police completely took over. Like in [East] Germany, you couldn't listen to the radio stations. If the police didn't like it, they could arrest you.

Matt (12) supported Keirra's point by describing his own experience of being searched by the police, on suspicion that he had been painting graffiti. Even where they had not had such experiences themselves, many students were willing to hypothesize about them; and in this respect, the idea of the curfew seemed to evoke a more general sense of resentment at adults' unfair and arbitrary abuse of authority.

Thus, while there was some acknowledgement of the 'problem' of youth crime, hardly any students were prepared to accept any kind of rationale for a curfew, and those who did so invariably displaced these arguments onto those younger than themselves. Chris (17), for example, said he would support curfews as a 'short-term solution' for children younger than about twelve – although he accepted that it would be impractical for older children, who in fact represented the most significant threat. Meanwhile, some of the 12-year-olds believed that it should be applied to those aged eight or nine, on the grounds that they did not have 'much awareness'. Yet the logic of this move was quite transparent:

> *Caroline*: ... they should have it for the younger children.
>
> *DB*: So what do you mean by younger? What age should it be?
>
> *Caroline, Abigail*: Stop at eight, eight or nine or something.

DB: So why do you say that age?

Anna: So that we can go out! [*Laughter*]

Several of the older children accepted that they could afford to take a more distanced view, since they were unlikely to be affected by a curfew. As Colin (17) pointed out, similar arguments applied to adults – and indeed to politicians:

> *Colin*: Just 'cause we're older now than people who are say 13 or 14, we can easily say 'keep them in the house'. But if we were 14, we wouldn't be saying that. The people who run the country, they're obviously older than us, so it's easy for them to say 'let's keep people under eighteen in their houses'. But when you are actually those people, it's a lot different.

Given this comprehensive rejection of curfews, the item could be seen to be preaching to the converted – and in a much more direct manner than the *First Edition* report. In fact, the item does give a considerable amount of time to the opposing view, albeit in the confrontational style which is characteristic of the programme. Broadly speaking, however, the students read the item in line with their existing views, seeking out further ammunition in support of their arguments and ignoring or dismissing those with whom they did not agree. Thus, after watching the item, several of them commented on how 'harsh' and 'rigid' the curfew appeared to be, and argued that the police should allow more flexibility. Many echoed the points made in the item about the unfairness of detaining people shortly after midnight, particularly if they were on their way home. Several argued that the police should 'make allowances' or have a 'buffer zone' in which they might issue warnings rather than arresting people – an argument that was also accepted by the small minority who broadly agreed with the need for a curfew. Meanwhile, the (limited) details of the operation of the curfew provided by the item seemed to provoke further questions. A couple of students wondered what might happen if your parents did not have a car, and were unable to collect you from the police station; others questioned the wisdom of imposing a curfew only in a 'downtown' area, when crime might be more likely to occur in less well-lit and less busy areas away from the centre of town. Interestingly, many of the students implicitly adopted the position of the potential *victim* of crime here: it was a question of where you yourself would feel 'safer'.

Unsurprisingly, little sympathy was expressed for the item's two main interviewees. The parent, Chris Kursky, was condemned by some as 'too strict', though others argued that, as Anna (12) said, 'He has every right to care about his child.' Mike Holloway, the police officer, was more wholeheartedly condemned. The older children in particular condemned him as 'patronizing', commenting with some irritation on the way he smiled. Here again, this was seen as an issue of age discrimination: as Dean (12) put it, 'he didn't think much of the children's rights'. While a couple of students did take up his point that young people were also potential *victims* of crime, Colin (17) argued that people should be free to take such risks:

> *Colin*: If you're a potential victim, then it's your choice, You know there's a risk there ... You shouldn't be stopped going there in case you get attacked. That's your choice to make.

While most were prepared to take the speakers' observations at face value, others disagreed about their credibility. Some of the Year 9 students saw the selection of these speakers as an illustration of the more 'natural' or 'realistic' style of the item as a whole. While they did not agree with them, they were seen as more honest and direct than the politicians featured in *First Edition*:

> *David*: With parents, you can understand them, more than politicians really.
>
> *Liam*: They're saying what they feel, and politicians are saying, um, what they want, or stuff that's not going to – 'cause they always pass the question, they won't answer your question directly. But when they're asking the parents and that, they will [answer], 'cause nothing's going to happen to them if they say their mind. Whereas the politicians, they might get kicked out of the party or whatever.

On the other hand, Chris (17) – who was more inclined to favour the idea of curfews – was somewhat less convinced about this: he suggested that 'they' (the interviewers or the programme-makers) might have 'bullied' or 'prodded' the speakers into saying what they wanted them to say. Somewhat facetiously, this group suggested that the parent was just 'some guy they'd grabbed off the street' and speculated about whether he was drunk. In this case, the apparently spontaneous style of the item did not appear to guarantee its credibility.

Styles of Credibility

This leads on to an issue that was a major focus of discussion right across the three age groups. When asked for their immediate responses, several students commented not on the content of the item, but on its style – for example, the use of graphics and music, the camerawork and the editing. Keirra (12), who was one of the most consistently cynical students here (see Chapter 5), saw this as evidence of the programme's low budget: 'they didn't have enough film to retake ... it looks like they had a £3 budget and they had to keep to it'. Despite these comments, none of the students was seriously under the illusion that this style was anything other than a deliberate choice on the part of the programme-makers; and their overall response to it was generally very positive – particularly in comparison with *First Edition*, which was widely condemned as 'boring news'.

There were some variations with age, however, in the students' accounts of the reasons why this style had been chosen. For the Year 7 students, the use of hand-held cameras and jerky editing was primarily an attempt to 'keep you interested' and to 'catch your eye':

> *Ryan (12)*: The cameraman must have been really cool camera ...
> He didn't just, like, focus it right at the person, he kept it from different angles and stuff like that. That programme was more exciting than normal programmes that they do on TV.

Some of these students also argued that the rapid-fire editing enabled the programme to 'get to the point quickly' without 'wasting time' – and hence that it was less likely to 'bore children'. Only the 'media cynics', Keirra, Matt and Silas were less enthusiastic:

> *Keirra*: They're trying to do it so that it looks kind of rough. But it doesn't – it just looks ripped up.

> *Matt*: It's OK if you're doing skateboarding films or something, 'cause that's the kind of thing it is. But this is more like – I dunno, news or something, it's not the style you should film it.

> *Silas*: It's a bit of a protest ... It's like they want to change things.

Interestingly, these students speculate about the motivations for adopting this style *as a style* – in other words, as something distinct from 'content'. Matt explicitly separates style and content, although Silas's comment may imply that there is more of a fit between style and content (or purpose) here.

By contrast, the Year 9 students appeared to read the style of the programme more naïvely, as a kind of guarantee of realism or authenticity. It was argued that it showed more 'direct information' and 'real life':

> *Daniella*: They had no set, they just moved around ... [It made it seem] more true, in a way. Because you know they haven't put anything in.

> *Nisha*: It's not been made up, you can see it's not been falsely made.

While these students were aware of the *potential* for manipulation or deception – they speculated, for example, about whether the interviewees were actors – the stylistic claim to realism seems to have exercised more of an influence upon them, compared with the younger students. At the same time, they did comment on how the interviews had been shot, describing how 'they changed their view, they went closer or they took the camera out'; although, as with the younger students, this was seen primarily as a means of 'catching your attention'. Perhaps ironically, the very things which provided evidence of the constructed nature of the programme – such as the hand-held camerawork and the jump cuts – were also seen here as guarantees of its authenticity.

Among the Year 12 students, however, there was much more explicit discussion of this approach as an aesthetic *style* – and while some praised this as 'up-to-date and funky', others implied that perhaps the programme-makers were trying too hard to be 'hip'. As this suggests, it was acknowledged that this approach was more likely to appeal to young people; Sarah suggested that it was similar to the style of young people's magazines, 'just like little segments, so you don't get bored with one section'. Several students also commented on the similarities to fictional programmes such as *Homicide* and *NYPD Blue*; while Nandi argued that this approach worked less well in British programmes such as *This Life*, where there was less 'action', and perhaps also in non-fictional programmes (and in this respect, her comments echo those of Matt, p. 183).

In addition, the older students seemed to be more aware of the potential for manipulation through editing. While some of the younger students understood this in principle – suggesting that the programme-makers could 'keep the best parts that they like' or that they could take out 'mistakes' – the older students were more alert to the issue of bias here:

> *Sarah (17)*: They probably cut out what the policeman really had to say, which might have been good. They wanted to show it negatively ... They've probably cut out certain parts to go in their favour.

These students also speculated about the possibility that the presenters had not actually edited the piece themselves, but that 'TV people' might have done so in order to convey a 'set angle' – and indeed that this was why the two presenters had been chosen 'out of hundreds of people' in the first place.

There were similar age differences in the students' responses to the use of young presenters. In general, the younger students accepted the idea that, as Anna (12) put it, 'the kids *make* the story'. This approach was explicitly seen as a matter of 'children's rights'; the programme was praised for enabling children to 'say their views', particularly on issues that concern them. This led some students to assert their own identity very strongly as *children*; as Matt (12) put it, 'it's got the child's point of view – it's got *our* point of view' rather than 'stupid newsreaders talking'. Several students also suggested that the presenters were more 'natural' and 'comfortable' than the young interviewers on *First Edition*.

Interestingly, those elements of visual style that were seen as evidence of spontaneity and authenticity were also seen as evidence of the fact that children were responsible for producing it. Liam and Jake (14), for example, noted that the 'jerky camera' made it 'feel quite real' and 'like it's made by kids'; while Nandi (17) made a similar argument, albeit with a little more scepticism:

> *Nandi*: It looks like a home video, like a child's really made it. I don't know if it had children editing it, but it looks like it is.

At the same time, some students were more sceptical about this claim, and about who was actually responsible for producing the programme. This was particularly the case among the older students, but not only there. Interestingly, the visual style was also a major issue here:

> *Abigail (12)*: I think it's adults, but they're moving [*the camera*] around to look as if it's kids ... I think they're fooling us by saying that it's – maybe the kids don't even write the script, you know ... Because the camera – you know how they were moving it around, as if the kid was holding it, and couldn't hold it steady? [*laughter*] Well, if the kid was holding it, it wouldn't move around like that, it would just be moving around a tiny bit.

Likewise, Caroline (12) argued that 'they've just gone a bit over the top trying to make it look as if kids have done it'. Nevertheless, both girls enjoyed the item, and seemed reluctant to accuse the programme makers of deliberate deception; indeed, they went on to argue that the programme-makers 'know you're not going to be fooled by it', and that it was simply 'the style of the programme'.

Likewise, Chris and Ben (17) argued that the jump cut editing effects would have required several cameras in order to be able to edit between different angles during the same stretch of dialogue, and that the item could therefore not have been made by an 'amateur'. Here again, they argued that it was 'made to look' as though it had been made by children, and that this supported its broader claim to be presenting the child's perspective. Interestingly, however, these students argued that younger people, less 'clued up' than themselves, might be deceived by this – although, as Abigail's comment indicates, this was not necessarily the case at all.

Responding to Bias

Unlike the other items considered thus far, the bias of this item was clear and overt; the central question was not so much whether the students would perceive it, as how they might respond to it. As I have indicated, almost all the students were sympathetic to the opinions of the two presenters. They were generally positive about the style of the item and its claim to be representing young people's point of view. As such, it was perhaps not surprising that they expressed support for the overtly polemical approach.

Reflecting generally on this issue, several argued that having such strongly argued viewpoints was more 'interesting' than the more sober, 'balanced' approach of mainstream news – and, indeed, of *First Edition*. Siobhan (17), for example, argued that this 'opinionated' approach was much better than the 'bland' or 'subdued' approach of mainstream news, because it invited the viewer to respond:

> *Siobhan*: I just think when they do it and they don't show opinions
> – like if they talk about youth crime and they don't have any
> definite opinion – I dunno, it just doesn't jump out at me. I don't
> think, 'Oh, that's true' or 'I don't agree with that.' Whereas
> if those kids [the *Wise Up* presenters] were doing that, kids
> watching are gonna think, 'Oh my god, that's so true, I'd hate
> that [curfews]'.

As Siobhan implies, it is not necessary (at least in principle) that one agrees with the views presented; the mere fact that they are so strongly expressed invites a more intense response than the 'boredom' that most students here saw as characteristic of mainstream news. Indeed, Chris (17) did not agree with the boys' position, but he argued that they were right to be 'selfish' in presenting their own views, and in talking about their own experiences.

Criticisms of the item tended to focus more on its brevity and superficiality. Several students expressed the desire to see more documentary evidence of the police apprehending people. Matt (12) even suggested that they should 'get arrested on purpose and go to the shelter and show the conditions', possibly using a hidden camera. As Keirra (12) graphically put it:

> *Keirra*: I'd like to see what *happens*! Again, it's the same with the
> news, innit, like when they have the white sheet over the bodies
> and you don't actually get to see what has happened.

However, the overt bias of the item led some students to suspect that important information had been omitted. Rosie (14) was not alone in pointing out that 'you didn't hear how bad the crime was', and hence that it was hard to judge whether a curfew really was necessary. She argued that the item did not really 'let you make up your own mind, because you don't hear everything'. Like most of the students, she agreed with the two presenters – but she also suspected that, if she were to hear more, she might change her mind. As Nandi (17) argued, this failure to present (and refute) opposing evidence meant that the item was unlikely to persuade those who were not predisposed to agree with it – particularly adults:

> *Nandi*: They've said their opinion, fine. But they're not persuasive. If you didn't agree with them, you'd think, 'Who are they? They're just kids, what do they know?' Especially adults watching them … They didn't back anything up with facts.

As this implies, the confrontational approach of the programme may have been somewhat counter-productive. Particularly among the older students, it seemed that the discussion of the item itself drew attention to some of the limitations of the presenters' case, hence led them to be more sympathetic to the opposing view. The more the students talked about it, the more suspicious they appeared to become. Even those who were most strongly opposed to the idea of curfews were led to suspect that a curfew might be justified under certain circumstances.

Abigail, Caroline and Anna (12) engaged in a complex debate about whether this overtly polemical approach made the item more or less likely to influence the viewer. On the one hand, Abigail argued that the programme challenged you to 'make up *your* mind about what *you* thought'; she also pointed out that the presenters were 'trying to see if they can change their opinions' by interviewing people who did not agree with them. On the other hand, Caroline argued that this was simply designed to prove them right:

> *Caroline*: I think they're doing that just to show that they're right. They interview people [*laughs*] that they kind of know what they're going to say, basically. And then, so they know that they're always going to be right [*laughs*].

Caroline and Anna argued that if the presenters were genuinely interested in allowing viewers to form their own opinions, they would have interviewed more *young* people who disagreed with them – although of course, as Anna pointed out, this 'would undermine their argument'. Caroline argued that it was much easier to use adults to represent the opposing view, since most viewers would be inclined to reject them – 'they know that's what their viewers are going to think'. Significantly, Caroline also vociferously complained that the programme was 'fixed', in that it tried to deceive the viewer into thinking that it had been made by young people themselves. While she did not ultimately disagree with the position taken by the two presenters, she did accuse the item of preaching (somewhat dishonestly) to the converted, and of exploiting viewers' assumed identification with other young people in the process.

For all sorts of reasons, then, overt bias of this kind may have contradictory consequences. The failure to *appear* balanced or even-handed – and particularly to deal in 'facts' – may weaken one's argument, even among those who are predisposed to agree with it. On the other hand, this directly polemical approach may encourage a kind of distancing or 'decentring', which was apparent even among the youngest age group here. Thus, the overt bias of the item may have forced the students to recognize their *own* bias, even where this was effectively the same; it may also have encouraged them to reflect in more detail on how the item was constructed – for example, on its mode of address, its use of evidence and its distinctive visual rhetoric. As we shall see, this issue became even more acute in relation to the final item, on The National Lottery.

Wise Up: The National Lottery

Summary

13 Kylie (presenter)

14 Interviewing the lottery manager

{ 15

16 Interviewing William Waldegrave, MP

[*Title: Everyone's a Winner? Presenter to camera, in charity shop.*]

Kylie: Hi, I'm Kylie. I hate the lottery and I'm here to tell you why. Charities have missed out big time since the lottery began. People don't realize when they're buying their tickets how much charities are missing out. A recent survey showed that people actually thought that 22p in every pound was going to charity. The fact that it's only 6p and the fact that the government gets 12p makes me feel very, very angry.

[*Interview with Mark Phillips, Chief Executive of cancer charity Ten of Us, in charity shop:*]

Phillips: ... We've lost one-and-a-half million pounds in the last 12 months. There's only so much spare cash in people's pockets. And a lot of that spare cash is going towards the national lottery.

Kylie: Do you think you should be compensated for the amount of money you've lost?

Phillips: The government has said that we must learn to live with the new situation.

Kylie: Do you think that the national lottery has been unfair to medical charities from the start? You know, with excluding them from even applying for grants?

Phillips: Clearly that was very unfair.

[*Interview with Gillian Greenwood, National Director of Alexandra Rose Day, umbrella organization for charities, conducted in street:*]

Kylie: ... Do you think people realize when they are buying a ticket what an extreme detrimental effect that the lottery is having on charities?

Greenwood: No, I don't think they do. I do think a lot of people have given to the Lottery honestly believing that the good causes were getting the money. They didn't realize how few do. We've got 800 charities under our umbrella and after the first allocation of grants only 17 were given a grant. Now that's 2 per cent and it's not enough ...

[*Interview with Brian Dickens, South West Regional Manager for Camelot, licensed operators for the National Lottery, conducted by lottery sales point:*]

Kylie: Do charities really benefit on the whole from the national lottery?

Higgins: Well, if you've got to give money to charity, don't play the lottery, give it direct – it's the most effective way of doing it. We get blamed for all sorts of things. We've been accused of affecting the gaming industry as far as pools, bingo, betting shops, etc ... The charities have lost money. And overall if you take the amount of money that's supposed to have been lost in the UK since the lottery started, it comes to over 8 billion. Now we haven't sold 8 billion pounds' worth of tickets.

[*Interview with William Waldegrave MP, Chief Secretary to the Treasury, conducted in his office:*]

Kylie: Do you think the government could allow charities to receive more if they reduced the amount of tax that they took?

Waldegrave: The amount of tax we take is supposed to make up for the tax that we predict that we would lose from there being less gambling of other kinds. If you look at lotteries abroad – say the famous one in Spain –

Kylie: Yes, but Spain don't tax –

Waldegrave: Don't they?

Kylie: No, Spain's government do not tax and so charities do receive a lot of money.

Waldegrave: Well, they're getting quite a lot of money here too.

Kylie: A recent survey showed that people actually thought it was 22 per cent that charities receive, not less than 6.

Waldegrave: Mm, mm.

Kylie: Don't you think that people could know more about the Lottery? You know, you could advertise better? Make things clearer?

Waldegrave: I think that's sensible, yes. I think we probably could do more.

Kylie: So why don't you?

Waldegrave: Well, [*smiling*] perhaps programmes like this will help . . .

Kylie: You agree that some charities have lost out?

Waldegrave: Well, some charities certainly seem to have a convincing case for saying that.

Kylie: Do you think they're entitled to compensation? Do you not think it's a moral obligation?

Waldegrave: I think that it would be quite difficult to say that – to prove that a charity which is getting less money this year than last was doing so solely because of the lottery. That would be the difficulty. I believe that there isn't evidence that the big cancer charities have so far lost money.

Kylie: That's strange, because I read in the *Independent* that they thought it was a monstrous rip-off.

Waldegrave: Well, let's have a look and let's see what the research shows.

Kylie: What about all the others that claim to have lost out? The British Heart Foundation haven't received anything. They weren't even allowed to apply for a grant until now. Why?

Waldegrave: Well, because, um, it was thought that those huge charities with –

Kylie: That they didn't need it?

Waldegrave: With their enormous flows of money were of less importance than some of the small ones. Now, they –

Kylie: Don't you think –

Waldegrave: Well, they are now getting – the medical charities *are* now getting money, aren't they?

Kylie: Less people are giving money to charity than *ever* before.

Waldegrave: Well, that's not yet proven. No. And you have to judge –

Kylie: Well, figures have gone from 81 per cent to 67 per cent. I think it proves it. Don't you?

Waldegrave: 81 per cent of what?

Kylie: Of the population giving money to charity.

Waldegrave: Well, that is not yet shown. That, I think, comes from the NCVO . . . initial work [*Caption: National Council of Voluntary Organizations*].

Kylie: So are they not telling the truth then?

Waldegrave: No, no, they just haven't completed their work yet. You don't need to be so confrontational about it. [*Cut to end of interview.*]

Thank you, nice to see you [*laughs, they shake hands*] ...

Kylie: [*To camera, on street:*] After talking to William Waldegrave, I'm still not convinced. Charities are really missing out. And I really thought that Mr Waldegrave really wasn't as aware as I thought he would be of the effects it's had. THE LOTTERY IS JUST NOT FAIR!

Duration: 5 minutes, 20 seconds.

Readings

Like the *Nick News* story on the Paper Mill, this item attempted to draw out the broader social and political dimensions of an issue that might initially have been perceived primarily in terms of its effects on individuals. In this respect, it offers a case study of how connections between the 'personal' and the 'political' might or might not be forged. As with the previous item, there were many positive comments on the *style* of presentation, and on the central role of young people; although in this case, the 'personal view' approach seemed to prove rather more strongly counter-productive. Here again, there are significant questions to be raised about the effectiveness of this approach, both in terms of *informing* the audience and in terms of *persuading* it.

Debating the Lottery: The Personal and the Political

Responses to my initial question about the students' views on the lottery were somewhat mixed. Several argued that the lottery was a 'waste of money', given that the chances of winning were so small: as Abigail (12) put it, 'it's like chucking stuff down the drain'. Others condemned it, somewhat moralistically, as a form of gambling, arguing that some people might become 'addicted', and even (in one case) that gambling was 'a sin'. Several students also expressed dislike of the TV show in which the winning numbers were announced. On the other hand, several were more positive. Some of the older students in particular argued that it was simply 'fun' – although only a few admitted that their parents bought tickets, and only one student claimed to do so himself. (The legal minimum age for purchase of lottery tickets is in fact 16.) Of course, many students commented on the possibility of winning prizes – even though, as David and Jake (14) argued, such new-found wealth might have its disadvantages; it would be hard to avoid being pestered by long-lost friends, particularly if you were to 'suddenly come to school in a big limo'. Finally, several students praised the lottery for making money available to charity, and some groups were able to think of several examples of such donations.

In general, these responses derived from what might be termed a 'consumer' perspective – that is, from the point of view of potential purchasers of lottery tickets, or users of lottery-funded services. In some other cases, how-ever, the criticism was rather broader and more 'political' in nature. Particularly among the older students, there was some debate about whether the lottery money had gone to the *wrong* charitable causes – an issue that had been the focus of some media coverage. Thus, for example, two groups criti-cized the use of lottery money to purchase the Churchill papers; while others argued that it was wrong to fund the Royal Opera House rather than the homeless, for example. Colin (17) suggested that such choices probably reflected the interests of 'the people who make those decisions'. Several stu-dents criticized the substantial profits being made by the lottery operator, Camelot, and the limited proportion which was given to charity; although only one group of Year 7 students contrasted this with the alternative, non-profit proposal to run the lottery which had been made by 'that Virgin dude' Richard Branson. (This proposal had been rejected by the Conservative Government.)

Meanwhile, Nandi and Siobhan (17) offered a much more explicitly polit-ical – and indeed, almost classically Marxist – analysis:

Nandi: I'd love to win. I'm always saying, 'when I win the lottery, blah, blah, blah.' But at the same time, I don't think it's right, 'cause I think the government should just pay for – like, I believe in charity [beginning] at home, but ... there shouldn't have to be charities for worthy causes ...

Siobhan: ... all working-class England's gonna buy, because they wanna win the lottery, where the upper class rich guy won't really care because he's loaded anyway ... I guess it is bad because it's wasting people's money, but I think people have that in mind ... Obviously you're going to get weak-minded people and all that, but I don't really care [*laughs*].

DB: So do you not think it's good that the lottery gives money to charity?

Nandi: Well ... most of the money will go to the chairperson [of Camelot] ... I mean, I don't think people should stop doing charities or anything. I just think charities and the lottery are just excuses so the government doesn't have to pay anything.

While these girls' resentment against the excessive profits of the lottery oper-ator was shared by several of the students here, their explicit analysis of the class dynamics of the lottery – and particularly of its *functions* for a govern-ment committed to reducing public spending – were effectively unique. Nevertheless, there is a certain ambivalence here. Nandi 'confesses' to par-ticipating in the collective fantasy of winning, even though she condemns it as an attempt at political deception. Likewise, Siobhan suggests that 'weak-minded' people might be led to waste their money, although she also argues that people are aware of what they are doing – and hence by implication that they are not simply being duped. As we shall see, this question of whether ticket buyers are or are not aware of this broader picture was to become significant in the students' responses to the item itself; while many were predisposed to favour its critical stance, they also argued that it should have taken more account of what I have termed the 'consumer' perspective.

Information and Persuasion

While many of the students were aware in broad terms of how the profits from the lottery were spent, the item forced them to address this in more detail. As we shall see, almost all of them were extremely critical of Kylie, the presenter, though several said they had been informed and even persuaded by her argument nonetheless. Her use of statistics carried considerable weight here; several students quoted (and in some cases misquoted) the statistics she provided, and argued about what proportion should be given to the various parties concerned. Several said they had not realized that such a low proportion of lottery profits was going to charity, and some also explicitly mentioned the fact that the government taxed lottery income, which had not been mentioned prior to viewing. As we shall see, however, the students were not necessarily inclined to believe all the 'facts' that were quoted, and some of them remained confused about how the money was divided up, arguing that the item should have presented this more clearly.

One further source of confusion here surrounded the figure of William Waldegrave, interviewed at the end of the item. While this interview was very much the longest, and several students commented upon it in some detail, very few seemed to have a clear idea of who Waldegrave was. (As is conventional in *Wise Up*, as in *Nick News*, interviewees introduce themselves; and there are no captions to identify them.) Some thought he might be the person responsible for allocating lottery grants, while one even suggested he was a Labour MP. Nisha (14) and her friends were rather embarrassed to be told that Waldegrave was in fact a government representative, and complained that there should have been a fuller explanation of his role. As in the case of the statistical information, it was suggested by some that a more conventional style of presentation – such as captions and charts – would have been more useful. In general, as with the Curfews report, the style of the item was praised for contributing a sense of spontaneity and 'attention-grabbing'; and yet it was this very approach that appeared to undermine its effectiveness in providing basic information.

However, the most vociferous criticisms here were directed at the unfortunate Kylie, who was condemned in no uncertain terms by the large majority of both boys and girls. Among the words used to describe her were: rude, uppity, bossy, uncivilized, annoying, stingy and mean. In general, the students argued that she presented her case in much too aggressive and exaggerated a manner. They accused her of shouting, and suggested that she would have made her points more effectively, both to the viewers and to Waldegrave, if she had 'calmed down a bit'. Several argued that she had been wrong to interrupt Waldegrave, and that this would only encourage him to 'look down at her'. There was a general sense that she was 'going over the top' or 'showing off', and that this undermined her credibility; as Caroline (12) suggested, 'she was taking it so seriously that she was taking the mick'. Others condemned her for, as Olivia (17) put it, 'wanting to come across as the young intellectual', while Matt (12) was particularly scathing about her claim to have read *The Independent*. In some cases, this criticism extended to more personal abuse of her accent (which is actually vaguely Scottish), her hairstyle and her clothes. The fact that one of the interviews was conducted in a charity shop, amid racks of second-hand clothes, led some to accuse her of buying her clothes there – which, in these students' world of designer sportswear, was sufficient justification for accusing her of the cardinal sins of being both 'posh' and 'uncool'.

Interestingly, some of the older students also dismissed her as 'childish' or 'immature', and even of 'throwing tantrums'. Nandi (17), for example, who was highly critical of the lottery, dismissed Kylie as 'an irritating little brat' – 'I just hate little children like that . . . I felt she embarrassed herself, I felt a bit sorry for her.' Others argued that she was making 'a big deal' of an issue that actually did not concern her (or indeed her audience) directly – both on the grounds that children were not allowed to buy lottery tickets and on the grounds that she did not actually work for a charity. (In this respect, the boys in the curfew item were seen as more sincere, on the grounds that they were addressing issues that affected them directly.) According to Colin (17), raising the issue in this context was 'promoting it to the wrong people – like advertising a razor on children's TV'.

There is an interesting contrast here with the responses of adults to whom I have shown this item and others like it from *Wise Up*. Some adult viewers seem to particularly enjoy watching young people talk back to adults in this way, whereas young people themselves may find it rather embarrassing. As I have noted, many of the students here explicitly praised *Wise Up* for allowing young people's voices to be heard – which is, of course, one of the producers' central claims (see Chapter 4). Yet the mere fact that the presenters were young did not necessarily make them any more inclined to believe or support them than if they had been adults. It may be that this notion of young people rejecting adult authority is one which reflects and appeals to *adult* fantasies about the young.

On the other hand, there were some students who expressed admiration for Kylie. She was praised by many for 'knowing her facts', 'studying her position' and 'organizing her questions'. Others clearly appreciated her interviewing style: Ben (17) described her as 'the next Jeremy Paxman', while Colin (17) was one of several students who expressed pleasure at how she had made Waldegrave 'squirm'. Dean and Ryan (12) felt that she did not 'respect' Waldegrave, and that she was 'rude' to him, but that this was partly justified: as Ryan said, 'She didn't need to be so aggressive . . . but she was really trying hard to achieve something, and to get something for the charities.' As Leo (17) put it, Kylie was clearly 'on a mission', and this in itself deserved admiration, even if she was widely perceived to be 'going about it in the wrong way'.

The predominant rejection of Kylie herself as irredeemably 'uncool', 'childish' and 'uncivilized' did not seem to prevent the students from taking on board at least some of what she had to say. Nevertheless, there was a general sense that the forcefulness of her approach rather undermined her case: as Colin (17) put it, 'it just blatantly has the opposite effect'. There was certainly evidence of this in the students' responses. In several cases, the students' rejection of the presenter's style led them to suspect that she was being deliberately misleading – even where they were inclined to support her. While some were persuaded by her use of statistics, others refused to grant them complete credibility:

> *Colin (17)*: She was a tiny bit immature . . . the way she just used the statistics and nothing else really. It was just that. And the thing about statistics is that they can be fiddled. You can get them to say anything to prove your point, whatever it is. So it seems as though she just heard a few statistics about the charities dropping and 6p in the pound as opposed to 12p to the government, and from that small information she's got up on her high horse and decided to make the whole programme.

While Colin's scepticism derives partly from a generalized suspicion of the use of statistics, it is also clearly cued by his response to the presenter's style.

In some instances, this rejection of the presenter led the students to develop more substantial counter-arguments. Even those who were disposed to agree with Kylie began to provide good reasons why she might be wrong. For example, Nandi (17), whose quasi-Marxist critique of the lottery was quoted above, ended up arguing in favour of the government taking more than charities:

> *Nandi*: I think the government should keep 12 per cent and give less to charity, because that's just right, you know. 'Cause in the end, the government's gonna help us anyway – well, they're meant to. So by taking the 12 per cent, they're doing the same thing as a charity would . . . When it comes down to it, we have some sort of control over the government. We don't know what those charities are gonna do.

Likewise, Siobhan, who was more equivocal about the lottery, argued that there might be other reasons why donations to charity had fallen, 'like changing income, jobs, anything ... there could be a million reasons why people aren't donating to charities'. Indeed, some students went so far as to invent hypothetical evidence that would undermine her argument: Daniel (14), for example, who was broadly in favour of the lottery, suggested that children were now no longer 'wasting their money on sweets' and putting it on the lottery instead; while Isaac (14) argued that lottery winners were donating some of their prize money to charity.

As this implies, the forceful stance of the presenter may well have 'back-fired', as Sarah (17) put it. Several students criticized the item for failing to include opposing views, arguing that a more even-handed approach would have been more persuasive. This was partly a ritualistic complaint, which was made in relation to many of the items considered here, whether or not they were perceived as overtly biased. This criticism derives from the 'civic frame' (Corner *et al.*, 1990); it draws on a generalized belief that public communication should allow space for a range of perspectives, and that media such as news should not be overtly partisan. Thus, several students argued that the presenter should have given more space to Waldegrave, or at least 'let him finish'; and others were directly critical of the way in which he was 'cut off' by the editing. Here again, this led some to suspect that he might have had some persuasive things to say, which had been removed because they would undermine the presenter's case:

> *Chris (17)*: They cut him off before he could finish his answer ... He went to say something and before he could continue and maybe make a valid point, he was cut off, and she threw something back in his face again. That made him look really poor ... I'd like to have seen the uncut version, because I reckon he probably came out with something ... but they wouldn't let it say it, probably because he was [right] and she was gonna get blown out.

As an advocate of the lottery, Chris was obviously more likely to favour Waldegrave – while most students were more inclined to reject him as a 'typical politician'. However, several students who broadly supported the presenter's position also argued that she should have spoken to more people who were in favour of the lottery, and particularly to people who bought the tickets. While this was to some extent a ritualistic call for the inclusion of more points of view, it also reflected the absence of a particular view-point, which I have earlier called the 'consumer' perspective.

This absence was partly reflected in the widely expressed view that the presenter was 'mean', and that she was attacking the right of ordinary people to enjoy the 'fun' of participating in the lottery. However, there was a more substantial criticism here, which focused on the presenter's claim that people who buy lottery tickets believe they are giving more of their money to charity than they actually are. Such people, it was argued, were implicitly condemned as ill-informed, if not positively deluded. A few students agreed with this view, although most directly contested it; as Caroline (12) put it, 'The majority of people do the lottery to win, not to give to charity.' Many also repeated and expressed agreement with the lottery manager, Brian Dickens, who argued that people who wanted to give to charity should (and would) do so directly. Chris (17), himself a lottery punter, made the same argument. He acknowledged that 'it makes you feel better when you know some of the money is going to charity'; but he also argued that Kylie had not managed to persuade him because of what he saw as this flaw in her argument:

> *Chris*: The points she was making were true, but they weren't enough to persuade me. Because I don't think I'm giving money to charity when I'm paying that pound.

While Chris's comment leaves open the possibility that *other* people might not realize where the money goes, this assumption was directly questioned by Olivia (17):

> *Olivia*: If they had actually asked people who had paid for the lottery, they could have said, 'What do you think? where do you think your money goes?' But they were just like 'only 6p goes to charities and people don't know that'. Well, ask the people if they know that or not, or when they buy their ticket if they know that ... They had the statistics, but the thing is, they could have just asked people.

As Olivia and her friend Sarah suggested, the programme could be seen to imply that ordinary people were 'a bit ignorant for not knowing where their money was going', or even that they were 'uncaring' – a view that several students were concerned to challenge.

Bias and Persuasion

As with the curfews item, none of the students was under any illusion that this item presented a balanced view. Yet while some of them praised the forcefulness of the presenter's approach, and the way she had researched her argument, several argued that the overt bias of the item was ineffective in terms of persuading them, and even that it was counter-productive. This debate was particularly explicit among the older students, though the relationship between students' responses to the polemical style of the item and their prior commitments was far from straightforward, as the following selection of extracts from the 17-year-olds shows.

On the one hand, several argued that it was good for young people to 'have their say', even if they did not like this particular presenter. This applied to those who were strongly opposed to the lottery, but also to those who were not. Colin and Sarah, for example, opposed the lottery and disliked the presenter, but praised the overall approach:

Colin: You don't often get a chance to see young people's point of view. So if you look at it like that, it could be seen as a good thing that they're only showing one point of view.

Sarah: It shows that we are here, that we should be heard, not just seen. If we have things to say, we can contribute things. If it affects us, why shouldn't we have our say?

Interestingly, these students were among those who condemned the presenter as 'immature'; yet here they express a solidarity with 'young people' – most obviously in Sarah's 'we'. On the other hand, although Chris claimed that he was not ultimately persuaded to agree with her, he too supported the partisan approach:

Chris: I was thinking to myself, 'this is gonna be bad for me, because I'm gonna be totally biased from the beginning' because I like the national lottery . . . But she was really good, she was brilliant.

Meanwhile, Siobhan, who was fairly indifferent about the lottery, argued that this approach was more engaging: 'It gives you room to agree with them or disagree with them, and therefore you think about it more.'

On the other hand, this polemical approach was seen by some to imply an intolerance or disrespect for others' points of view – and again, this was not directly dependent upon the students' views of the lottery or of the presenter. Olivia was broadly opposed to the lottery, but she resented the overt bias of the item:

Olivia: It's trying to force-feed and shape your views, and sometimes you can't do that. Because you hear somebody's opinion, but other people are always going to have different opinions to yours, and you should try to hear those arguments, and not shout out above all the others. I think it's so terrible.

Likewise, Ben, who was somewhat equivocal in his view of the lottery, argued that a less partisan approach might have been more effective in persuading him:

Ben: She didn't give me any other options, really, but to believe her. If maybe she had presented a more objective view, I would have possibly taken her side.

Finally, Nandi, who was strongly opposed to the lottery, complained that the bias of the item rendered it superficial:

Nandi: It was a bit one-sided. Just with the format of it, you can't get a reasonable opinion, it's just people complaining about things ... I mean, you are informing a little bit [about] her opinion, but you're not actually making, the person watching it can't make an informed choice about the subject, because there's not enough information.

As these examples suggest, the relationship between students' responses to the item and their existing views on the lottery was far from predictable; and in this respect the analysis here has parallels with that of the Million Man March and the paper mill items. One might have expected those who were opposed to the lottery to be more inclined to favour the presenter, or at least to excuse her perceived shortcomings, while those who favoured the lottery (or were indifferent to it) might have been expected to reject her. Yet if anything, the opposite was the case. Those who opposed the lottery were also more likely to reject the presenter – and, as we have seen, several of them began to develop counter-arguments – while those who were in favour of the lottery were more positive about the presenter, even if they were not obviously persuaded to change their views. This was the case right across the three age groups.

In this respect, the comparison with *First Edition* was again somewhat double-edged. On the one hand, there was a widespread view across all the age groups that this approach made a refreshing change from mainstream news. Keirra and Matt (12), for example, who were both strongly opposed to the lottery, comprehensively demolished Kylie, arguing that she should have been more 'open-minded', and yet they went on to state their preference for this approach, as compared with 'presenters who stand there with a straight face' or 'sit behind a desk'. By contrast, Nisha, Parastoo and Daniella (14), who were also opposed to the lottery, disliked the partisan approach and argued that the more 'formal and informative' style of *First Edition* would have been more appropriate, at least in the case of this topic – even though they had clearly been quite bored by their viewing of *First Edition* the previous week.

The complexity and diversity of these responses therefore resist any easy classification. Indeed, even here, I have largely ignored the contradictions and ambiguities, both in terms of what took place within the groups, and in terms of the contributions of particular individuals. As I have indicated in Chapter 5, individual positions were frequently renegotiated as the discussions proceeded: the students did not necessarily take up single, consistent 'pro' or 'anti' positions. This makes it hard to trace 'cause-and-effect' relationships – between, for example, people's existing beliefs, their perceptions of bias in messages and their susceptibility to persuasion by those messages. Manipulating such variables in a laboratory and assessing them by means of scales and questionnaires might eliminate some of these difficulties, but it would also eliminate the complex ways in which media texts are interpreted and used in real life.

What the approach adopted here does make possible, however, is an understanding of the social and discursive processes through which such readings are generated. As I have shown throughout these two chapters, there is a complex series of factors in play here. In the case of this item, for example, it is vital to distinguish between the students' responses to the presenter, to the item as a whole, and to the broader genre (the access programme, or the 'personal view') from which it derives. In each case, judgements are being made at different levels of complexity and sophistication – from complaints about the presenter's accent or her hairstyle, right through to the highly reflexive, 'decentred' comments about bias and persuasiveness discussed towards the end of this section. Likewise, it is essential to distinguish between responses to the issue itself, based on existing knowledge; responses to the new information the item presents; and responses to the item's perceived position (or positions) on the issue. Here again, these judgements are more or less complex or superficial, and they clearly derive from different discursive positions – be they overtly political or moral, or (as I have argued is significant in this case) from the position of the 'consumer'. In each case, these judgements clearly result from an interaction between the text itself and the reader's prior knowledge and experience.

This discussion begins to anticipate some of the concerns of my concluding chapter. At this stage, it is worth emphasizing that any such analysis of audience readings of television needs to be grounded in the concepts and categories employed by viewers themselves. Thus, for example, distinctions between 'form' and 'content' of the kind implicitly made in the previous paragraph might well be questioned on epistemological or methodological grounds; yet, as I have indicated, such distinctions are a commonplace – and indeed fundamental – move in viewers' interpretations of television. Likewise, a term like 'bias' has been subjected to some rigorous theoretical questioning, to the point where it is implicitly seen by the majority of academic commentators as hopelessly naïve. Yet, here again, the concept of bias (and indeed, the term itself) is an everyday aspect of viewers' judgements about what they watch. As I argued in Chapter 3, some academic analysis of viewers' relationships with television news and of their conceptions of 'politics' has tended to float free of these seemingly mundane concerns. Yet if we are concerned to explore and develop the *educational* potential of young people's relationships with television, we cannot afford to lose sight of the knowledge and understanding they bring to it.

Chapter Eight

Conclusion: News, Education and Citizenship

Qualitative research of the kind reported in this book does not always lead to neat conclusions. In some respects, this is not its aim. In attempting to represent and analyse the complexity of audience engagements with the media, such research often seeks precisely to challenge the easy generalizations that are sometimes seen to constitute research 'findings'. Yet while this can lead to a necessary rethinking of received wisdom, it can also lead to a degree of complacency. There is a kind of safety in the knowledge that everything is so much more complicated than other people imagine it to be – and that one must be so much more intelligent by virtue of the fact that one can recognize this.

Nevertheless, readers are bound to draw their own conclusions from the material presented here, and it therefore seems appropriate to outline some of my own. In this final chapter, then, I offer some general conclusions in three main areas. I look first at young people's engagements with politics; secondly, at their responses to the form and approach of the news programmes used in the study; and thirdly, at questions of 'media literacy' or 'critical viewing'. In the final section of the chapter, I consider some of the broader implications of the research for debates about the future of citizenship education.

(De-)constructing 'Politics'

As I noted in Chapter 1, popular debates about young people's relationship with politics have often reached pessimistic conclusions. Young people are frequently represented here as ignorant, cynical and apathetic. Such assertions are often part of a broader lament for the apparent decline of democracy, of 'civic virtue' and of 'social capital' – developments which are routinely blamed on the media, or on the rise of commercialism. These arguments are most familiar on the political Right, although they also form a significant theme in the 'communitarian' rhetoric that currently appears to inspire left-liberal policy-makers both in Britain and in the United States (see Etzioni, 1993).

On the other hand, some have attempted to turn this argument around, suggesting that young people are actively *excluded* from the domain of politics, and from dominant forms of political discourse. From this perspective, young people's apparent lack of interest in politics is a rational response to their own powerlessness. Why should they bother to learn about something when they have no power to influence it, and when it makes no effort to address itself to them? Young people are seen here, not as apathetic or irresponsible, but as positively *disenfranchised* (Bhavnani, 1991).

This latter argument is broadly supported by the research presented here, though, as I shall indicate, it is not without its problems. Certainly, these students' discussions of politics as conventionally defined – that is, of the actions of *politicians* – were frequently suffused with cynicism. While this was sometimes irreverent or dismissive, at other times it was distinctly bitter and forcefully expressed. Politicians were condemned, not merely as boring, but also as corrupt, uncaring, insincere and self-interested, and politics was dismissed as a kind of dishonest game, which had little relevance to the students' everyday lives and concerns. The students explained the reasons for these views in terms of their own inability to intervene or participate; since they could not make any difference to what happened, there seemed to be little point in making the effort to find out about it. When pushed, they acknowledged that political changes (for example, at the election) might have implications for themselves or their families, and yet the fact that they could not vote meant that they could only observe this process with passive detachment. Somehow, a lack of interest in politics appeared to be perceived as part of the condition of being a child.

In fact, this cynical stance became more prevalent with age, a phenomenon that can be explained in various ways. To some extent, of course, it can be seen a consequence of cognitive development; as they become more able to 'decentre', children begin to hypothesize about (and to analyse critically) the motivations of others. To some degree, this change is also a matter of access to information: in general, the older children here simply knew and understood much more about politics – and hence about issues such as corruption and media manipulation – and were therefore able to provide more concrete evidence in support of their views. However, I would argue that this increasing cynicism can also be seen as a result of young people's growing awareness of their own powerlessness. Older teenagers are frequently caught between adult injunctions to behave 'responsibly' and adult prohibitions and controls: they are ceaselessly urged to be 'mature' and constantly reminded that they are not. It is not surprising that they are often so keen to challenge what they perceive as inconsistency, complacency or hypocrisy on the part of adults – and not only politicians.

Several qualifications should be noted here, however. The first concerns the status and reliability of the data. As I have argued, discourse should not be seen as straightforward evidence of what individuals think or know, but as a form of social action. In studying how young people go about presenting a 'political self', I have emphasized how talk is used to achieve particular social purposes, for example in negotiating relations with others, or in claiming socially-valued subject positions. To this extent, such expressions of cynicism need to be seen as a *discursive strategy*.

The notion of 'cynical chic', which I have imported from similar research with adults (Eliasoph, 1990; Gamson, 1992), captures something of what is taking place here. According to this argument, such expressions of cynicism serve as a valuable – and indeed pleasurable – way of rationalizing one's own sense of powerlessness, and even of claiming a degree of superiority and control. Certainly, there is a sense in which the students' expressions of apathy or disinterest (as distinct perhaps from cynicism) should be seen as superficial. Many students expressed the view that politics as a whole was simply 'boring', and that it was of no interest to them; but, as the data here amply demonstrate, they were able to engage in some extremely complex and sophisticated debates about key political issues.

Yet in some respects, the notion of 'cynical chic' is too dismissive; it seems to imply that cynicism is necessarily skin deep – that it is merely a self-conscious, and indeed compensatory, tactic of self-presentation. By contrast, I would argue that the cynicism expressed here also needs to be respected on its own terms, as a genuine and sincere assessment of the actions of politicians and of the political system. As Bhavnani (1991) argues, cynicism implies some form of political analysis, and hence some level of engagement, even if it results in inaction (for example, not voting). In this respect, political cynicism should be distinguished from mere apathy, even if their behavioural outcomes may be the same. Indeed, as she suggests, cynicism towards established authority may be a prerequisite for becoming involved in protest movements, or a stage that one needs to pass through before doing so; and to this extent, cynicism may not be incompatible with political agency or collective action (cf. Gamson, 1992). One necessary distinction here, however, is between *cynicism* and *criticism* – and this is an issue to which I shall return below.

Either way, I would concur with Gamson (1992), that in their engagement with politics, people (in this case, young people) are by no means as stupid or as passive as they are frequently made out to be. Of course, this finding is to some degree an artefact of the research method. Very few of these students were initially enthusiastic about discussing news or politics, though it is clear from what they said that at least some of them did discuss such issues with their friends or family, in some cases fairly regularly. What the data suggest is merely that, under certain circumstances, young people may be *capable* of engaging with broadly political issues at a relatively sophisticated level – not that they necessarily do so in other circumstances, or in their everyday interactions.

At several points here, the students can be seen struggling to connect the 'political' dimensions of their everyday experiences with the official discourse of politics encountered through the media. The discussions of youth crime, for example, or of the paper mill item from *Nick News*, demonstrate both a cynicism about those in authority and a genuine attempt to think through the advantages and disadvantages of particular policies, both in the light of the evidence presented and in the light of personal experience. Several students possessed strong commitments on these issues, and few were prepared to support the introduction of curfews or the despoliation of the natural environment, yet their discussions displayed a careful concern for the validity of the evidence, a willingness to consider the consequences of particular policies, and an attempt to imagine alternative solutions.

In many instances, however, the preoccupations of national politics were dismissed in favour of the more immediate concerns of the local (for example, the local environment, crime in the neighbourhood, family histories, schooling or consumer behaviour). In the process, the potential *connections* between the two were often lost. This was most apparent in the discussions of welfare spending, and to some extent of racial politics (both in the US and the British groups). The students were effectively discussing the same issues as the politicians, although they positively refused to recognize this. This was partly symptomatic of the principled rejection of politics identified above; though, as I shall indicate below, the extent to which news might be capable of making politics *relevant* to lived experience also depended on the formal strategies of the programmes themselves.

In order to appreciate what might be taking place here, we have to adopt a broader definition of politics, which is not confined to the actions of politicians or of political institutions. As Cullingford (1992) points out, children develop broadly 'political' concepts at an early stage, through their everyday experiences of institutions such as the school and the family: notions of authority, fairness and justice, rules and laws, power and control, are all formed long before children are required to express their views in the form of voting. The choice available at school lunches, the attempt to introduce compulsory uniforms, or even the organization of the school playground are, in this respect, just as 'political' as what goes on in parliament. One might well make a similar case about sports or entertainment: the success of Tiger Woods or the Spice Girls can clearly be interpreted as 'political' phenomena, as they implicitly were by some of the students here. Nevertheless, as I have argued, one should avoid any premature collapse of the distinction between the 'personal' and the 'political'. The personal can *become* political, but this requires a fundamental shift in how issues are framed or defined; and this may in turn require certain kinds of information to be made available.

The item about the national lottery from *Wise Up* – which might outwardly appear to be the least 'political' issue here – provides a clear instance of this. On one level, the lottery can be seen as simply a matter of everyday consumption and pleasure – a question of individual choice. Yet for many students, the item provided them with new information which forced them to take a wider view; and indeed, some students already knew additional information (for example, about the Conservative government's rejection of a non-profit proposal to run the lottery) which reinforced and extended this. Significantly, however, several students criticized this move, not just because of what was seen as the strident tone of the presenter, but also because of the implicit rejection of the 'consumer' perspective. The item did connect the 'personal' and the 'political', but at the risk of rejecting the former – and hence of a form of moral self-righteousness.

Nevertheless, this kind of shift could be seen as characteristic of a distinctly 'political' mode of thinking, or at least as a prerequisite for it. Again, there are significant age differences within the sample in this respect, which can partly be explained in developmental terms. Particularly among some of the middle age group studied here (age 13–14), one can identify the emergence of a broadly consistent and even 'logical' political world-view, which relates partly to other developmental shifts – such as the ability to relate parts to wholes (for example, in seeing individuals as representative of broader social categories), or the ability to view the world from perspectives other than one's own (for example, in hypothesizing about why the experiences of members of other generations or cultures might have led them to adopt particular beliefs).

This kind of developmental explanation provides only part of the story, however; at the very least, it seriously neglects the social and discursive contexts in which such thinking is formed. As I have implied, 'political thinking' is a socio-cultural phenomenon. It implies a view of the self in social terms; and hence prepares the ground for forms of collective action (although equally, it can be developed *through* collective action). Seeing one's own experiences as representative of those of a larger social group – for example, in terms of social class or 'race' or gender or age – is thus effectively a prerequisite of political consciousness.

The media often appear to hinder this process. As Gamson (1992) argues, the media generally favour a view of people as an aggregate rather than a collective, 'a pool of individuals rather than a potential collective actor'. The media provide a discourse on 'the person as an individual', which transcends the differences of social class, gender and ethnicity (and so on) that provide the grounds for political action. However, as he indicates, the media may also keep such images of collective action alive, if only to condemn them; developing and applying 'collective action' frames may mean 'reading against the grain', but it is not impossible.

However, the position of young people may be particularly problematic here. To risk another generalization, one might argue that young people are much more rarely presented as a social collective in the media than other social groups, and that where they are, they are most frequently framed as a problem, whether implicitly or explicitly. Images of young protesters merge readily with those of young hooligans, ravers and fans. In this respect, the 'youth politics' of a series like *Wise Up* – and, to a lesser extent, *Nick News* – represents a significant exception to the rule, however much such programmes may also play up to adult fantasies of young people as automatically rebellious.

This leads on to my final qualification here. In offering such generalizations about 'young people', it is obviously important not to conceive of them as an homogeneous group. As I indicated in Chapter 5, there are distinct limitations on the representativeness of this sample, given both its size and how it was recruited – though it is no more limited in these respects than the kinds of samples on which many such generalizations are routinely made. However, within the scope of the sample, there were some clear social differences in terms of the students' orientations both towards politics and towards news. While I have not attempted to isolate such variables statistically, I have been able to cross-check and compare in a fairly systematic manner, and clear distinctions have emerged along the axes of social class and gender.

Broadly speaking, the middle-class children were more likely to express a positive interest in and/or knowledge about political issues (as conventionally defined), and there was some evidence that this reflected their own perceptions of their potential futures, as powerful figures or at least as 'stakeholders' in society. By contrast, the working-class students, particularly in the US school, appeared to be less well-informed and more comprehensively alienated. Likewise, the domain of politics (as conventionally defined) frequently seemed to be perceived by students of both genders, both implicitly and explicitly, as masculine. Girls were more likely to dwell on the 'human interest' aspects of political issues, and to express generalized alienation from or apathy towards institutionalized political activity. There was some variation here according to issues, however: ecology was implicitly seen – and, as we have seen, explicitly claimed – as more of a 'girls' issue', while the machinations of elections and party politics were more enthusiastically addressed by boys.

Again, there is a need for caution here. These broad social differences are best seen as matters of emphasis; they are in no sense absolute distinctions. There were several notable exceptions to these general trends: some of the older girls were the most articulate and sophisticated in their discussions of politics, for example, while some of the more working-class children, particularly in the middle age group, were extremely astute and perceptive. Indeed, insofar as one can make such judgements, the students who appeared to have the strongest sense of themselves as members of collectives – and hence, according to Gamson (1992), the makings of political activism – were probably more likely to come from these groups. Furthermore, it was among these groups that the discussion most often turned to what I have termed 'local' or 'everyday' politics. Their alienation was from politics *as conventionally defined* – that is, from the actions of politicians, who (not coincidentally) happen to be largely white, middle-class men.

As I indicated in Chapter 5, this definition of a 'political self' is a highly self-conscious activity, in which social identities are claimed and negotiated in the course of discussion. This can be a problematic and contested process, particularly for those who are members of less powerful social groups. In the case of gender, there were several instances here in which girls actively resisted 'masculine' values, and chose to assert the authority of what they perceived as 'feminine' values, most overtly in the case of environmentalism. By contrast, 'race' was a much more problematic dimension of identity, especially in the context of ethnically mixed groups; the explicit politics of the Million Man March item in particular created further obstacles in the way of claiming a positive 'black' identity. As these examples suggest, claiming membership of a collective is not always a straightforward achievement.

While these observations should call into question any undue generalizations about 'young people', they nevertheless reinforce the broader arguments I have been making. In summary, this study confirms the view that young people's alienation from, and cynicism about, politics should be interpreted as a result of exclusion and disenfranchisement, rather than ignorance or immaturity. In analysing the development of political understanding, we need to adopt a broader definition of politics, which recognizes the *potentially* political dimensions of 'personal' life and of everyday experience. In the process, it is important to recognize that 'political thinking' is not merely an intellectual or developmental achievement, but an interpersonal process that is part of the construction of a collective, social identity.

Programme Form: Pedagogy and Address

My analysis of the programmes in Chapter 4 pointed to some significant differences between them, both in terms of content and in terms of form. Broadly speaking, *Channel One News* and *First Edition* are significantly more conventional than *Nick News* and *Wise Up*; in several respects, they are much closer to the style and presentational format of mainstream news. Their aim is essentially to *make news accessible* to a younger audience. This does entail some departures from the conventions of mainstream news, for example in terms of the balance between 'foreground' and 'background', the kind of language used and the style of presentation. To some extent (particularly in the case of *Channel One News*), this could be seen as a kind of superficial 'window dressing', but *First Edition* also uses young people as interviewers (albeit in a rather limited way), and has begun to experiment with a viewers' access slot. Nevertheless, neither programme significantly challenges what is seen to *count* as 'news', and both appear to invite a fundamentally deferential stance on the part of the viewer.

By contrast, *Nick News* and *Wise Up* depart more radically from the conventions of the genre. On one level, neither programme should strictly be seen as 'news', in the sense that neither of them is immediately topical. Nevertheless, this is implicitly to accept a conventional definition of what counts as news in the first place, and indeed to imply that news should be weighted towards 'foreground' rather than 'background'. In fact, both programmes do cover issues which feature in mainstream news, and which are matters of debate within the political domain (that is, which are of concern for politicians). In terms of their pedagogy and their address to the viewer, however, they offer a distinctly different conception of what might count as news, and what form it might take. While this has a particular relevance to the younger audience, the more widespread turn away from news media in recent years suggests that it might also have implications for the audience at large.

Among the students interviewed here, there was very little doubt or disagreement about the approach they preferred. For the US students, *Nick News* was almost universally judged to be more interesting and effective than *Channel One News*. The programmes' address to the younger audience was a particular focus of concern here. The Grade 8 and Grade 11 students perceived both programmes to be aimed at younger children, although *Channel One News* was particularly singled out for criticism on the grounds that it was patronizing. The programme was repeatedly accused of trying (and failing) to be 'cool' or 'hip'. It was, several argued, 'fake' and 'forced'; it was like 'an adult trying to be a kid', and it was 'trying to do too much to get us interested'. This was partly a matter of the presenters' tone of voice and their attempts at humour, although there was a more general sense in which the programme was perceived to be 'manufactured' and 'slick'. Interestingly, it was judged on several occasions to be 'not really news'.

By contrast, *Nick News* was praised for not 'talking down' to its audience – despite the fact that it was seen to be aimed at younger viewers. Several students judged the programme to be more 'serious' and 'mature' than *Channel One News*; it was seen to contain a wider range of opinions, and to provide more background detail and information. There was also praise for the fact that it presented new information 'about things that you probably don't already know about', rather than simply presenting a simplified version of the mainstream news, as was seen to be the case with *Channel One News*. However, several of the younger students argued that *Nick News* was easier to understand, not least because it was 'more orderly' and had 'more of a plan' (a reference, perhaps, to the strategy of presenting two contrasting viewpoints).

On the other hand, *Nick News* was also judged to be more 'kid centred', in that it included more young people, rather than simply 'the person sitting at the desk'. It was praised for its inclusion of 'ordinary' people, rather than the 'stuck-up' people who are normally 'all over the news'. According to Winnie (13), '*Channel One News* tells you about the President and his home and his wife and the election and stuff, but this [*Nick News*] tells you about real life, the one you have to worry about.' Inevitably, there was some diversity here, although it was only boys who said they preferred *Channel One News*; interestingly, one group of younger boys accused *Nick News* of 'going way too deep ... into the personal things'. In general, though, one could conclude that these students wanted to be better informed, and that they wanted the news to be more relevant to them, but at the same time, they did not want to be patronized. This was a balance that *Nick News* appeared to strike much more successfully than *Channel One*.

Responses to the British programmes were even more unanimous. *Wise Up* was universally preferred to *First Edition*, both on the grounds of its style and its address to young people. There was considerable praise for its graphics, camerawork and editing, which were variously described as 'rough', 'cool', 'catchy', 'effective' and 'attention-grabbing'. By contrast, *First Edition* was described as 'just like boring news', and condemned for its 'stupid newsreaders ... sitting at a desk'. Its approach was seen as much more 'formal', and the young people included on the programme were perceived to be 'stiff' and 'uncomfortable'. As I have noted, the 'hand-made' style of *Wise Up* and its use of location footage were generally seen as a guarantee of authenticity – as somehow automatically more 'real' and 'true' than the seamless, more studio-bound approach of *First Edition*.

Here again, the programmes' address to the younger audience was a particular focus of concern. While there was some scepticism about *Wise Up*'s implicit claim to be providing unmediated access for children's voices, there was considerable praise for its attempt to present 'kids' point of view', and (more broadly) for its focus on 'ordinary people'. Parastoo (14) and her friends praised the fact that it included 'everyday people', as opposed to 'MPs': such people, they argued, talked much more directly and honestly, and in comprehensible language. Likewise, Liam (14) approved of the presenters' emphasis on 'emotions', arguing that such people would be more likely to 'speak their minds'. By contrast, *First Edition* was seen by many to be 'too adult' and 'not really anything to do with children'. It was pointed out that the dominant voices in the items were those of adults, and that the young interviewers were not allowed to put across their own points of view; by contrast with the 'natural' approach of *Wise Up*, the young people here were frequently accused of simply reading from a prepared script. Like *Channel One News*, *First Edition* was condemned for its emphasis on 'politics', rather than on 'things that matter to kids'; whereas *Wise Up* was praised for its emphasis on issues that were 'closer to home'.

As I have indicated, one of the most significant contrasts here was between the polemical, 'point-of-view' approach of *Wise Up* and the outwardly more neutral style of *First Edition*. Using the civic frame, several students argued that *Wise Up* should have included a wider range of views, and that it lacked detail and 'facts' – although others contested this latter point. All the students were aware that the programme was 'fixed' – for example, that the interviews were manipulated through editing in order to 'prove' the validity of the presenters' viewpoints – and in some instances (notably in responses to the lottery item), this appeared to prove counter-productive. Nevertheless, all the students claimed to prefer this approach:

it was generally seen as less 'bland' and less confusing than that of *First Edition*. While they suggested that it might be more likely to persuade *other* people, they argued that it allowed *them* to make up their own minds about the issues: as Siobhan (17) put it, 'it gives you room to agree with them or disagree with them, and therefore you think about it more'.

On one level, these comments appear to confirm commonsense wisdom among television producers who work for this age group. Being patronizing and being boring are obviously to be avoided; although this is easier said than done. Young people are very sensitive to age differences, and are particularly scathing about programmes that appear to underestimate or 'talk down' to them. They also want programmes that are relevant to their own everyday concerns, which are largely marginalized in mainstream news. Yet while they condemned the more conventional approach of *Channel One News* and *First Edition*, these students did not simply want to be entertained. On the contrary, they *also* wanted to be informed and made to think, and the more adventurous approaches of *Nick News* and *Wise Up* were praised insofar as they achieved this.

This study thus confirms the need for formal innovation if news is to reawaken the interest of younger audiences – and indeed of the large majority of viewers. Despite the general decline in news audiences, the rate of formal innovation in news has been extraordinarily slow in comparison with other genres. In the UK, for example, Channel 5's attempt to attract a younger audience by having its newsreaders step out from behind the desk has been seen as an almost dangerously radical move – a response that merely illustrates the remarkable degree of conservatism that continues to characterize the genre.

As I have implied, there is a need for much more fundamental rethinking, both of the formal strategies of news, and of what is seen to *count* as news in the first place. The deferential stance that is invited and encouraged by mainstream news formats needs to be abandoned in favour of an approach that invites scepticism and active engagement. Much greater efforts need to be made, not merely to explain the causes and the context of news events, but also to enable viewers to perceive their relevance to their everyday lives. News can no longer afford to confine itself to the words and actions of the powerful or to the narrow and exclusive discourses that currently dominate the public sphere of social and political debate.

This is certainly a call for a kind of democratization, but it is not an argument for condescension or trivialization. Young people do not deserve to be patronized any more than adults do. The young people whose views are reported in this book wanted to be entertained, but they also wanted to be better informed about the world around them; and if they were cynical about politics, or bored by it, this cannot be put down simply to their own laziness or ignorance.

The avoidance of 'entertainment' in favour of a narrow insistence on seriousness and formality that characterizes dominant forms of news production systematically alienates and excludes substantial sectors of the audience; yet, as I have argued, the answer is not simply to add sugar to the pill. None of these observations should be seen to endorse the hyperactive MTV style that has become characteristic of 'youth television'. Nevertheless, news clearly does have a great deal to learn from the genres that are most successful in engaging the younger audience. Obviously, such approaches can be a recipe for superficiality, but they can also offer new ways for news to fulfil its traditional mission to educate and to inform – a mission which, I have argued, it is performing far from adequately at the present time.

The Limits of 'Critical Viewing'

Discussions of young people's relationships with the media frequently conclude with assertions about the need to develop 'critical viewing skills'. In practice, however, it is often far from clear what is meant by the term 'critical viewing', or what difference it might make. Many such discussions appear to be based on a simplistic cause–effect model. From this perspective, critical viewing is seen as a kind of cognitive character armour, that protects the viewer against the dangerous emotional influence of the media; it is an essentially *rationalistic* strategy. Recent research in this field has significantly questioned such assumptions, however (see Buckingham, 1993a; Liebes and Katz, 1990; Livingstone and Lunt, 1994). Researchers have drawn attention to a kind of 'spontaneous' critical stance that is implicitly invited by many popular genres – responses to soap operas, for example, are characterized by a complex interplay between emotional identification and critical distance. Yet such research also raises difficult questions about the *consequences* of critical viewing, not least in terms of the potential influence of the media. How do we identify what *counts* as truly critical viewing? Is identification or intense involvement inherently incompatible with being critical? And are critical viewers any less likely to be influenced by what they watch?

On one level, there is substantial evidence of critical viewing in the data presented here. Generally speaking, these students knew a great deal about how news programmes were put together; they were alert to the potential for misleading information, inadequate evidence and bias, and they were often very prepared to argue with what they had seen, both in terms of its own consistency and logic, and by drawing on contrary evidence of their own. Their debates about these issues focused not only on the selection of information, but also on its presentation; they repeatedly drew attention to aspects of editing, camerawork and visual design which they felt were designed to persuade them to accept a particular reading of the issues.

Again, I am inclined to echo Gamson's (1992) conclusion that people are by no means as easily duped by the media as they are often assumed to be. Of course, this is not to say that the media are simply powerless; there are systematic omissions and dominant frames in media discourse that inevitably exert constraints on how particular issues can be interpreted. This was apparent at several points here, for example in the US students' discussions of the entitlement to welfare, or in the British students' understanding of the 'problem' of youth crime. Nevertheless, as Gamson argues, readers and viewers negotiate meaning in complicated ways that vary from issue to issue, and they draw on other resources, including their general knowledge of television as a medium, in doing so.

At the same time, there are some important qualifications to be made here. As in the students' discussions of politics, there was a clear developmental dimension, which is partly about access to information, and partly a function of broader cognitive achievements. Unsurprisingly, the older students here knew much more about television as a medium, both in terms of the 'language' and characteristic techniques of television texts and in terms of the operations of the industry. They were also more inclined to 'decentre' (for example, to perceive that a particular message might have persuasive intentions) and to apply criteria to do with logical consistency (for example, to point out the contradictions between verbal commentary and visual evidence).

However, there are significant methodological difficulties in identifying and evaluating evidence of critical viewing. As I have indicated, both here and in previous work (see Buckingham, 1993a), critical discourses about the media may emerge as a function of the interview context – as a response to what subjects believe the interviewer wants to hear. The phenomenon of 'cynical chic' could be seen as one example of this. As Gamson (1992) indicates, such responses arise partly from speakers' recognition that they are 'playing to the gallery'; they provide a way of saving face in a situation in which they feel they might be negatively judged by their social superiors. From this perspective, critical discourse about the media may be little more than a socially desirable response – a way of distancing oneself from the 'uncritical viewer' who is implicitly invoked and condemned in so much academic and public debate about the media. Indeed, the term 'critical' itself is often used as a means of distinguishing between 'us' and 'them', and hence of claiming social (or academic) status; people who are truly critical, it would seem, are simply those who happen to agree with us.

Critical judgement about television therefore needs to be regarded as a *discursive strategy* – that is, as a form of social action which is intended to accomplish particular social purposes. Like 'cynical chic', this kind of critical discourse is a situated response to the social context of the interview; it should not necessarily be taken as evidence of what takes place outside this context. In explicitly inviting the students to speculate about whether the programme-makers had a particular 'point of view', for example, I was directly cueing these kinds of discourses – although in many cases, they were volunteered quite spontaneously. Nevertheless, the fact that such critical discourses are *available* to viewers – that they form part of what we might call their 'discursive repertoires' – is itself significant, not least in educational terms. It implies that critical competencies can be called upon – and hence systematically elaborated – if the appropriate teaching strategies are used (see Buckingham and Sefton-Green, 1994: Chapter 7).

Nevertheless, the fact that viewers are capable of being 'critical' – or, more accurately, of mobilizing critical discourses – does not necessarily mean that they are therefore immune to influence. Like 'cynical chic', critical discourse about the media can sometimes be merely superficial, and indeed, it can serve as a rationalistic disavowal of more emotional responses (Buckingham, 1993c). Some students here were much more interested in going directly to the substantive content of the items than in displaying their critical acumen as television viewers; in other cases, the display of 'television literacy' appeared to serve as a way of avoiding any engagement with the issues themselves.

This study did not set out to assess media influence. At least in relation to attitudes or ideologies, it is reasonable to assume that influence is primarily a long-term, cumulative process – hence something that would be unlikely to be captured by the methods adopted here. Nevertheless, there were indications in several cases of at least *short-term* influence. In some instances (for example, the paper mill item from *Nick News*), visual evidence appeared to carry a particular persuasive force, whether or not this was the intention of the producers. In others (for example, the national lottery item from *Wise Up*), the provision of new information appeared to change some students' attitudes to the topic. Even here, however, the students were often self-reflexively aware of this process: they drew attention to the influence of visual 'evidence' even as they accepted its validity; and they did not challenge the accuracy of new information, even though they suspected that other information, which might undermine the argument, was not being provided.

On the other hand, influence can obviously be exerted as a result of the *absence* of information, or of alternative explanations; and this is inevitably more difficult to identify. For example, the *Channel One News* item on the government shutdown failed to address the reasons why welfare spending was rising in the first place, and the *First Edition* story on youth crime failed to present or question actual crime statistics. In both cases, the inclusion of such information would obviously have permitted alternative interpretations of the issues.

The perception of 'bias' is thus a complex phenomenon. It might be logical to expect that viewers who already know more about a particular issue (for example, those who have direct personal experience of it) will be more likely to detect bias than those who know less. Likewise, one would expect viewers who feel strongly about a given topic to be more likely to perceive bias in an item which presents an opposing view to their own. In fact, the situation here was more ambiguous: while there were instances that conformed to this pattern, a significant majority did not. This in turn raises questions about where bias is located: is it something inherent in the text, which can be recovered by the skilled analyst, or is it a function of the relationship between text and reader?

For instance, the Million Man March item was comparatively positive about the event itself, but it presented Farrakhan quite negatively, by including a series of influential criticisms of him before quoting his own words, and by selecting an extract from his speech which might have been seen to inflame anti-white feelings. The item generated a good deal of discussion, both among children who knew a great deal about the march and those who knew less, though the former were, if anything, rather less prone to read the item as 'biased' in the way I have indicated. Indeed, these children were generally less likely to discuss the item *as a text* (or as a mediated representation); in a sense, they 'read through' the mediation and went straight to what they were interested in, which was the content and the issues it raised. In the process, some of them appeared actively to 'misinterpret' the item, or at least to discount elements that did not immediately appear to fit with their existing framing of the issues.

By contrast, the paper mill item from *Nick News* was presented as a *debate* between two opposing positions. Again, my own analysis of the item suggested that it was biased towards one of the participants, through the structure and sequence of the arguments, and through the relation between visual and verbal evidence. For some of the children, notably groups of girls, the issues raised here were of considerable interest; they were keen to contest the view that the mill would not cause environmental damage. Nevertheless, these groups were not necessarily any more inclined to detect bias in the item, or to criticize its presentation of the issues, than those who knew much less about them. The most 'critical' viewers here were in fact those who appeared relatively indifferent to the issues, but criticized the item on the grounds that it provided insufficient information to enable them to make a balanced judgement. Among some of the oldest students, this exercise of critical judgement appeared to be an almost dispassionate process, unrelated to their awareness of, or interest in, the issues – and in this respect, it came closer to a form of 'cynical chic'.

Finally, the contrast between the two items on youth crime taken from *First Edition* and *Wise Up* indicates further complexities here. The bias of both items – at least as I perceived it – clearly coincided with the existing viewpoints of most of the students, and in this sense they could be seen to be 'preaching to the converted'. However, the bias of *First Edition* was much less overt than that of *Wise Up* – even though *Wise Up* also gave much more space to opposing views, albeit only to condemn them. On the other hand, the *Wise Up* item was much more 'personal' in its approach, both in the sense that it was presented by young people, and in its emphasis on the consequences of such policies for individuals. Interestingly, however, the students were more likely to react against the *Wise Up* item, or at least to question its reliability – and this was not primarily a response to the style of the presenters, as it was in the case of the national lottery item. Despite the 'personal' force of the item, the fact that it implicitly encouraged viewers to recognize its bias rendered it somehow less persuasive.

Research of this kind inevitably uncovers a diverse range of interpretations of a given text. It also raises significant epistemological issues. Crudely, how can we steer a course between the objectivist view that meaning is simply inherent in the text and the subjectivist view that the text can mean whatever the reader wants it to mean? How do we *evaluate* the different readings that can be made?

As I have shown, there were instances in these discussions where students had clearly *misinterpreted* what they had seen, or just failed to understand it – and in some cases, they themselves directly acknowledged this, or accepted it when it was pointed out. Some of these misinterpretations can be traced to particular properties of the text; its confusing use of metaphor, its failure to provide sufficient background information or explanation, or the contradictions between verbal and visual evidence. For example, the *Nick News* item on militias failed to provide an adequate explanation of the *motivations* of militia groups; while the *Channel One News* item on the government shutdown took far too much for granted about viewers' understanding of the economy. Yet other misinterpretations resulted from inattention, or the fact that students had mistakenly emphasized (or been distracted by) comparatively marginal elements of the text, or reached false conclusions from them. For example, most students mistakenly saw the *First Edition* item on young black voters as being directed at young black voters themselves; some failed to grasp the fact that the town of Apple Grove in the *Nick News* story on the paper mill was located within Mason County. In each case, these misinterpretations resulted in more fundamental confusion or incomprehension.

Such observations support a comparatively objectivist view of meaning, which I would argue cannot be simply abandoned. In other cases, however, there were significant mismatches between the way in which I read particular items (in my privileged capacity as the academic analyst) and the way in which the students did so, which cannot be put down simply to misinterpretation. These divergent responses can partly be explained in terms of the different knowledge and competencies readers bring to the text: in this respect, at least some of the differences result from the fact that as a white, male adult – and, in the case of the US study, as British rather than American – I was bound to apply or invoke different frames in making sense of the material from those of the students. For example, I interpreted the *Nick News* item about militias in terms of the frame 'individual versus government'; yet for many of the students, the dominant frame was to do with the issue of 'violence'. In some cases, these divergent interpretations appeared to arise from the fact that some students paid greater attention to the visual evidence than the verbal commentary – for example, in the case of the paper mill item, where the use of locations played a significant part in the students' willingness to favour one view above another.

These examples raise awkward epistemological questions about how we evaluate viewers' readings, particularly in comparison with the privileged analysis of the academic critic. Are viewers' responses to be seen as more or less 'critical' simply on the grounds that they succeed or fail in detecting biases that I perceive to be objectively present in the text? What if they claim to perceive biases that I myself have not detected – whether as a result of what I might see as their greater critical acumen, or of wilful or accidental 'misinterpretation' on their part? What *counts* as adequate evidence in establishing the validity of any such readings, and how are such claims to be adjudicated? To what extent does an overt recognition (or indeed mistaken allegation) of the bias of a text make a difference in terms of one's willingness to accept that bias?

These problems point to the limitations of objectivism; equally, they cannot simply be side-stepped by an appeal to relativism. Empirically, texts do *not* mean anything that readers want them to mean, and all readings are *not* equally valid. However unfashionable it may be, 'bias' is a key conceptual category in viewers' responses to television news, and to other texts that purport to be factual. Yet we cannot begin to *evaluate* such judgements without some notion of accuracy – that is, without some way of appealing to a set of facts about the text against which particular responses can be compared and assessed.

One response to these difficulties would be to break down these problematic notions of 'reading' and 'critical viewing'. John Corner (1991), for example, argues that it is possible to distinguish between three different levels of 'reading', which might be termed decoding, interpretation and judgement. The notion of decoding implies that at a certain (denotative) level, there are certain objective facts about the text to which appeals can be made; it is this that makes it possible to talk about 'misunderstandings' or errors in reading. Interpretation implies a more subjective sense-making process, which will depend on viewers' prior knowledge and cultural competencies; to a large extent it is likely to focus on the substantive content (in this case, on the issues or topics addressed). Judgement is more self-reflexive, implying a relatively distanced response to the text as a text; it is here that we should probably situate the practice of 'critical viewing'. The potential for diversity and disagreement among readers – or the balance between 'subjective' and 'objective' – is clearly different at each stage of this model. The problem, of course, is how we might analytically separate such processes, which in the act of reading (or in talking about what you have read) inevitably work together (see Buckingham, 1993b).

Likewise, we might attempt to identify different forms or levels of 'critical viewing'. In terms of this research, it would seem particularly important to distinguish between *cynicism* and *criticism*. Cynicism is both more generalized and more distanced than criticism; it implies a wholesale rejection of the text *as a text*, hence one which does not need to engage with what it actually represents in any detail. At its crudest, it takes the form of popular clichés – 'the news is all propaganda', 'everything they tell you is lies' – although it can also take more refined forms, for example, in some of the students' critiques of editing or photographic style. This stance can also be sustained through the use of the 'civic frame', in which news is perpetually condemned for not supplying sufficient information to satisfy the truly discerning reader. As I have argued, such responses may sanction a degree of complacent disengagement, both from the imagined responses of others and from the world of political action itself. As Eliasoph (1990) puts it, such critical readers are 'trapped in their armchairs', forever dismissing the spectacle of politics, as though it were simply another fictional show with no consequences in real life.

By contrast, 'criticism' implies a belief in the antecedent reality that the text purports to represent and a commitment to the idea that the truth about it can and should be told – or at least that the different ways in which that reality is represented make a difference to how it is perceived, and hence to what actually happens in real life. Criticism is often motivated by an emotional investment in the topics that are dealt with, which may be derived from direct experience; it entails a recognition that some form of action might be taken in order to change or intervene in the reality that is shown.

To sum up, this research suggests that young people develop a set of critical competencies – a form of 'media literacy' – which they are able to apply to their readings even of relatively unfamiliar texts or genres. In the case of news and factual programming, judgements about 'bias' are a central concern in this respect, but they are not simply a matter of 'detecting' something that is or is not immanent in the text. In practice, the emotional, personal or social identifications that viewers have *invested* in a particular political issue may be more important in determining how they interpret texts than any purely cognitive or rationalistic process of critical judgement. To this extent, there may be limitations in any model of critical viewing that is based merely on a cynical rejection of the medium – or indeed on the dispassionate pursuit of information. Truly *critical* viewing should be characterized not only by a form of principled scepticism, but also by a willingness to engage with the social reality that is represented, to relate it to one's direct experience and (if appropriate) to take action in order to change it.

Political Socialization for Contemporary Citizenship

Young people's relationship with the public sphere of politics is often taken as an index of the future health of our society. As I have indicated, the prognosis here is generally far from positive; young people's apparent apathy and cynicism are seen to bode ill for the survival of democracy. In responding to these concerns, more optimistic commentators tend to point to the apparent success of 'single issue politics' among the young. While they may be alienated from political parties, from voting and from other conventional forms of political activity, young people are nevertheless seen to be developing a broader, and no less valid, form of politics, that reflects changing social and historical circumstances.

This is certainly an important response, although the evidence would suggest that young people's active involvement in these 'new' forms of politics is still confined to a small minority. Involvement in environmental campaigns, for example, is actually higher among the 35–55 age group, and the profile of the women's movement is steadily ageing (Wilkinson and Mulgan, 1995). Among young people themselves, involvement in such social movements is also skewed towards the middle classes. More significantly perhaps, this optimistic emphasis on single-issue campaigns appears to leave the central institutions of politics untouched. There may indeed be a case for redefining politics, or for changing dominant forms of political culture, but 'politics as usual' will continue to exercise a fundamental influence on people's lived experiences, despite all the claims about its 'irrelevance'. The challenge, as Wilkinson and Mulgan (1995) put it, is not so much to develop alternatives to conventional politics as to find ways of 'reconnecting politics', by making it more accessible and meaningful to young people.

Likewise, news journalism remains the primary means of access to the public sphere of political debate and activity. Even for those who wish to become involved in 'single issue' events and campaigns – Live Aid, for example, or Greenpeace – the need for information remains. Indeed, it could be argued that public action of the kind espoused by these 'new social movements' requires *greater* access to information, precisely because such information is less likely to appear in the media (Gamson, 1992; Walker, 1996). To reject news as simply irrelevant to such forms of 'everyday politics' – as critics like Fiske (1989) have come close to doing – is to ignore the continuing need for knowledge. Indeed, it is hard to see how everyday lived experience can be conceptualized in 'political' terms without the ability to connect it to the wider world of collective action – and hence without access to *information* about that wider world.

There is certainly a need for some fresh thinking about the relationship between the 'personal' and the 'political', and about the potential of popular cultural forms. Fiske's call for news journalists to adopt less formal and conservative modes of address is certainly supported by the responses of the students reported here. Nevertheless, there is a need for some fairly traditional thinking also. Calls for formal innovation, for 'popularity' and 'relevance' in the news, need to be balanced with calls for a more informative, less superficial approach to political communication. In relation to young people, news has particular *educational* responsibilities, which could and should be fulfilled much more effectively than they are at present.

In this book, I have argued that young people's alienation from the domain of politics should not be interpreted merely as a form of apathy or ignorance. On the contrary, I would see it as a result of their positive exclusion from that domain – in effect, as a response to *disenfranchisement*.

This reflects the fact that, by and large, young people are not defined in our society as political subjects, let alone as political agents. Even in areas of social life that affect and concern them to a much greater extent than adults – most notably education – political debate is conducted almost entirely 'over their heads'.

The notion that young people are 'disenfranchised' necessarily implies that they should have some kinds of political rights (Bhavnani, 1991). There is a similar implication in the assertion that young people are (or should be) 'citizens' – not potential citizens, or citizens-in-the-making, but *actual* citizens. As I implied in Chapter 3, such arguments challenge the assumptions on which most contemporary (or indeed post-Enlightenment) conceptions of citizenship or political rights are based. Citizenship is predominantly perceived to be a function of rationality; it requires a fundamental distinction between public and private, a free flow of undistorted communication and a dutiful subjection to the public good. In these respects, enfranchisement, political rights and citizenship are typically defined in opposition to all the things that children and young people are seen to represent.

In some respects, then, this argument represents a broader call for the extension of citizenship rights to young people – a call which necessarily requires a certain 'optimism of the will'. While there clearly are problems with the romantic notions of 'children's liberation' espoused in the 1970s by authors such as John Holt (1975), it is hard to see why adult rights and responsibilities should not be extended at least to contemporary teenagers. As Lindley (1989) suggests, many of the paternalistic restrictions society currently places upon young children are unnecessary for teenagers, and actively undermine their efforts to take control of their own lives. In relation to politics, it is certainly debatable whether teenagers in general are any more ignorant than the majority of adults, and it is wrong for this to be used as a justification for their perpetual disenfranchisement as a social group.

At the same time, these arguments point to the need for a broader reconceptualization of citizenship itself. As I have indicated, the 'classical' notion of citizenship – embodied most clearly in Habermas's conception of the bourgeois public sphere – may never have been more than a utopian ideal. Whatever its value as a 'negation', there is a sense in which many of its implicit theoretical assumptions have now become redundant. There can be no return to the Enlightenment. Yet if we are not to reject the whole notion of citizenship as merely a 'technology of subjection' (Miller, 1993), we need to revise it (and revive it) in order to take account of the changing political circumstances.

In general terms, I have argued that the identification of the 'political' with the 'public' leads to a reductive conception of politics, from which the experiences of many social groups (not least children and young people) are implicitly excluded. As I have argued, young people develop political understandings through their everyday experiences of family life, the school, the neighbourhood and the peer group. Yet we need to resist the temptation here simply to flip the coin. The 'personal' is not automatically 'political': it only *becomes* political by virtue of the ways in which it is connected with the concerns and experiences of other social groups. John Fiske (1989) offers a useful reformulation of this distinction in terms of the relationship between 'micro-politics' and 'macro-politics'. Yet the key point, I would argue, is not to privilege the former over the latter, as some postmodernist critics seem to prefer – and as others have argued is increasingly prevalent in the contemporary media environment of talk shows and tabloid news. On the contrary, the central aim should be to find ways of building *connections* between the two domains.

This is a crucial challenge for broadcasters; but it also has particular implications for education. Both education and the media are public spheres, in the sense that they provide spaces in which people represent themselves to each other, and thereby negotiate shared values and priorities. If we are to move beyond normative conceptions of identity and civic virtue, and to develop a more pluralistic and heterogeneous conception of the public sphere, questions of access, of representation and of pedagogy become even *more* acute – however rationalistic and worthy they may seem.

In this respect, the emergence of more popular or relevant forms of politics and of news journalism will need to be part of broader – and in some respects much more traditional – forms of educational strategy. At Gilbert (1996) indicates, the notion of citizenship has been the focus of a considerable amount of educational rhetoric in recent years, not least in response to young people's perceived disaffection with politics. Yet the aims and methods of 'citizenship education' have often been inadequately defined. During the late 1980s and early 1990s, the Conservatives in Britain promoted a form of citizenship education which came close to a modern version of 'civics'; it was largely about encouraging young people to take on the necessary tasks that are left undone by the welfare state, such as picking up litter, fundraising for charity or visiting the elderly, rather than encouraging any more active and informed participation in politics. Indeed, 'political education' was condemned by the Conservatives as tantamount to an opportunity for indoctrination (Scruton *et al.*, 1985) – even though they were keen to use the national curriculum to promote a highly political and socially divisive notion of national identity, in subjects such as history and English (Harber, 1992; Kerr, 1997).

However, there exists an older, more liberal, tradition of political education (or 'political literacy') in Britain, which is based on developing political autonomy and a critical stance towards political information (see Crick and Porter, 1978). Advocates of this approach refute the suggestion that it is about 'politicizing' young people, or at least encouraging specific 'radical' attitudes; the overt emphasis here is on open-mindedness and tolerance for a diversity of beliefs. Nevertheless, as Harber (1992) points out, it is hard to see how such attempts to empower young people to participate in political activity will not result in them challenging those in authority. Indeed, as he suggests, one potential consequence of political education would be that young people would be more likely to challenge the institution of the school – an institution that is in many respects extremely authoritarian and undemocratic.

Orit Ichilov (1990) makes an important distinction here between a 'liberal' and a 'participatory' model of citizenship education. The liberal model is premised on a fundamental division between the political and the personal domains; the responsibilities of citizenship are located in the former, while self-realization and fulfillment are to be found in the latter. By contrast, the participatory model challenges this distinction, not least on the grounds that a great deal of what is characterized as 'public' (such as the work of government) impacts upon the 'private' (in areas such as sexuality). As she indicates, the participatory model implies a need for greater involvement and more egalitarian relationships in a whole range of social arenas – not just the formal institutions of 'politics', but also spheres such as medicine, education and the family.

In practice, however, there is little evidence about the extent or effectiveness of political (or 'citizenship') education, at least in British schools, although on the face of it, there would appear to be very little work of this kind being undertaken (Kerr, 1997). In seeking to avoid political controversy, schools implicitly assume that children are incapable of making sophisticated political judgements – that they are easy targets for 'indoctrination'. As Cedric Cullingford (1992) argues, this effectively leaves the business of political education to other sources, not the least the media. In the process, children may be left inadequately prepared:

> On the one hand, we expect children to have developed enough social literacy to make political judgements by the age of 18 [when they are allowed to vote]. On the other hand, we avoid giving them the means of acquiring such knowledge and analytical skills (1992: 16).

However, it is important to avoid a view of political education as simply a matter of making good the apparent deficits in young people's political knowledge. The more difficult challenge for teachers, as for news journalists, is to find ways of establishing the *relevance* of politics and of *connecting* the 'micro-politics' of personal experience with the 'macro-politics' of the public sphere. This will not be accomplished simply by dumping information on young people, or indeed by issuing them with implicit injunctions to do their civic duty. It will require a definition of politics that goes well beyond the formal operations of political institutions.

In this respect, media education is potentially a very significant site in defining future possibilities for citizenship. If, as Rob Gilbert (1992) implies, the struggle for citizenship is partly a struggle over the 'means and substance of cultural expression' – and particularly over those which are made available by the electronic media – it is essential that the curriculum should enable young people to become actively involved in the media culture that surrounds them. From this perspective, media education should not be confined to *analysing* the media – much less to some mechanistic notion of 'critical viewing skills'. On the contrary, it should encourage young people's *critical participation* as cultural producers in their own right.

Some would argue that such developments are emerging in any case. The new digital media are seen by some of their advocates to bring about precisely the kind of active, participatory citizenship that I have called for here. Thus, it has been argued that the Internet is encouraging a more open, accountable form of government; that it undermines the centralized control of information and political discourse; and that it offers new, democratic public spheres, in which previously silenced voices can be heard. These arguments have been particularly applied to young people. For example, Jon Katz (1996), whose criticisms of the 'monotonously reassuring voice' of mainstream news journalism were discussed in Chapter 1, perceives the Internet as a means of 'children's liberation'; it provides children with opportunities to escape from adult control, and to create their own autonomous cultures and communities. 'For the first time', he argues, 'children can reach past the suffocating boundaries of social convention, past their elders' rigid notions of what is good for them.' It is these children of the digital age, according to Katz, who will 'lead the revolution'.

This is not the place to evaluate such claims, though the evidence for them – and the technological determinism on which they are often based – is highly questionable. As with more general assertions about 'postmodern citizenship', such arguments tend to exaggerate the novelty of such developments, and to underestimate the continuing relevance of more traditional forms of communication and political activity. Certainly, the new forms of cultural expression envisaged by enthusiasts for digital media will not simply arise of their own accord, or as a guaranteed consequence of technological change; we will need to devise imaginative forms of cultural policy that will foster and support them. Here again, we have to insist on relatively traditional questions about who has the right to speak, whose voices are heard and who has control over the means of production. As Gilbert argues, the political and the cultural are not synonymous, and if rights of access to cultural expression are to be realized, more traditional forms of civil and political rights must also inevitably be at stake – not least for young people. In this respect, any revised – or indeed 'postmodern' – notion of citizenship must necessarily be based on an extension of traditional political rights, rather than seeking somehow to transcend them (see also Gilbert, 1996).

Postmodernity inevitably raises significant questions about the 'modernist project' of mass education, with its traditional emphasis on rationality, individual autonomy and the informed democracy. Yet it does not render such aims redundant. On the contrary, it suggests that the contemporary curriculum must seek to socialize students for the experience of social change, not to re-establish an illusory stability. It must attempt to create a multifaceted, complex self, which is appropriate to heterogeneous societies and which looks forward to innovation and change (DiRenzo, 1990; Kress, 1995). Rather than ignoring or seeking to invalidate their everyday social experiences, educators must enable students to build connections between the personal and the political, and hence prepare them for a participatory form of citizenship which can function across a whole range of social domains. Yet, in the context of increasing educational conservatism, the difficulty of developing and sustaining a curriculum that is relevant to the lives of citizens who will be coming of age in the next century is likely to become increasingly intense.

References

Adorno, T. and Horkheimer, M. (1979) *Dialectics of Enlightenment*, London: Verso.

Andreyenkov, V., Robinson, J. P. and Popov, N. (1989) News media use and adolescents' information about nuclear issues: a Soviet-American comparison, *Journal of Communication* **39** (2), 95–104.

Atkin, C. (1981) Communication and political socialization, in D. Nimmo and K. Sanders (eds) *Handbook of Political Communication*, Beverly Hills: Sage.

Atkin, C. K. and Gantz, W. (1978) Television news and political socialization, *Public Opinion Quarterly* **42** (2), 183–97.

Austin, E. W. and Nelson, C. L. (1993) Influence of ethnicity, family communication, and media on adolescents' socialization to US politics, *Journal of Broadcasting and Electronic Media*, **37** (4), 419–35.

Bakhtin, M. (1968) *Rabelais and his World*, Cambridge, MA: MIT Press.

Bakhtin, M. (1986) *Speech Genres and Other Late Essays*, Austin, TX: University of Texas Press.

Barbalet, J. M. (1988) *Citizenship*, Minneapolis, MN: University of Minnesota Press.

Barnhurst, K. G. and Wartella, E. (1991) Newspapers and citizenship: Young adults' subjective experience of newspapers, *Critical Studies in Mass Communication* **8** (2), 195–209.

Bhavnani, K.-K. (1991) *Talking Politics: A Psychological Framing for Views from Youth in Britain*, Cambridge: Cambridge University Press.

Bird, S. E. (1990) Storytelling on the far side: journalism and the weekly tabloid, *Critical Studies in Mass Communication*, **7** (4), 377–89.

Bird, S. E. (1992) *For Enquiring Minds: A Cultural Study of Supermarket Tabloids*, Knoxville, TN: University of Tennessee.

Blumler, J. (1992) *The Future of Children's Television in Britain: An Enquiry for the Broadcasting Standards Council*, London: Broadcasting Standards Council.

Blumler, J. and Gurevitch, M. (1995) *The Crisis of Public Communication*, London: Routledge.

Buckingham, D. (1987a) The construction of subjectivity in educational television. Part one: Towards a new agenda, *Journal of Educational Television*, **13** (2), 137–46.

Buckingham, D. (1987b) The construction of subjectivity in educational television. Part two: *You and Me* – a case study, *Journal of Educational Television*, **13** (3), 187–200.

Buckingham, D. (1993a) *Children Talking Television: The Making of Television Literacy*, London: Falmer Press.

Buckingham, D. (1993b) Boys' talk: television and the policing of masculinity, in D. Buckingham (ed.), *Reading Audiences: Young People and the Media*, Manchester: Manchester University Press.

Buckingham, D. (1993c) Going critical: the limits of media literacy, *Australian Journal of Education*, **37** (2), 142–52.

Buckingham, D. (1995a) On the impossibility of children's television: The case of Timmy Mallett, in C. Bazalgette and D. Buckingham (eds) *In Front of the Children: Screen Entertainment and Young Audiences*, London: British Film Institute.

Buckingham, D. (1995b) The commercialisation of childhood? The place of the market in children's media culture, *Changing English*, **2** (2), 17–40.

Buckingham, D. (1996) *Moving Images: Understanding Children's Emotional Responses to Television*, Manchester: Manchester University Press.

Buckingham, D. (1997) News and advertising in the classroom: Some lessons from the Channel One controversy, *International Journal of Media and Communication Studies*, 1, URL: http: //www.aber.ac.uk/~jmcwww/1997/channel1.html.

Buckingham, D. and Sefton-Green, J. (1994) *Cultural Studies Goes to School: Reading and Teaching Popular Media*, London: Taylor and Francis.

Buckingham, D., Davies, H., Jones, K. and Kelley, P. (1999) *Children's Television in Britain: History, Discourse and Policy*, London: British Film Institute.

Calhoun, C. (ed.) (1992) *Habermas and the Public Sphere*, Cambridge, MA: MIT Press.

Chaffee, S. H., Ward, L. S. and Tipton, L. P. (1970) Mass communication and political socialization, *Journalism Quarterly*, **47**, 647–59, 666.

Chaffee, S. H. and Yang, S.-M. (1990) Communication and political socialization, in O. Ichilov (ed.), *Political Socialization, Citizenship Education and Democracy*, New York: Teachers College Press.

Clifford, B. R., Gunter, B. and McAleer, J. (1995) *Television and Children: Program Evaluation, Comprehension and Impact*, Hillsdale, NJ: Erlbaum.

Cohen, S. and Young, J. (eds) (1972) *The Manufacture of News*, London: Constable.

Collins, J. (1989) *Uncommon Cultures*, New York: Routledge.

Comstock, G. and Paik, H. (1991) *Television and the American Child*, San Diego, CA: Academic Press.

Connell, I. (1991) Tales of tellyland: The popular press and television in the

UK, in P. Dahlgren and C. Sparks (eds), *Communication and Citizenship*, London: Routledge.

Connell, I. (1992) Personalities in the popular media, in P. Dahlgren and C. Sparks (eds), *Journalism and Popular Culture*, London: Sage.

Connell, R. W. (1971) *The Child's Construction of Politics*, Melbourne: University of Melbourne Press.

Conway, M. M., Wyckoff, M. L., Feldbaum, E. and Ahern, D. (1981) The news media in children's political socialization, *Public Opinion Quarterly*, **45** (2), 164–78.

Corner, J. (1991) Meaning, genre and context: the problematics of 'public knowledge' in the new audience studies, in J. Curran and M. Gurevitch (eds), *Mass Media and Society*, London: Edward Arnold.

Corner, J. (1995) *Television Form and Public Address*, London: Edward Arnold.

Corner, J., Richardson, K. and Fenton, N. (1990) *Nuclear Reactions: Form and Response in 'Public Issue' Television*, London: John Libbey.

Crick, B. and Porter, A. (1978) *Political Education and Political Literacy*, London: Longman.

Cullingford, C. (1992) *Children and Society: Children's Attitudes to Politics and Power*, London: Cassell.

Dahlgren, P. (1986) Beyond information: TV news as cultural discourse, *Communications*, **12** (2), 125–36.

Dahlgren, P. (1991) Introduction, in Dahlgren, P. and Sparks, C. (eds) *Communication and Citizenship* London, Routledge.

Dahlgren, P. (1992) Introduction, in Dahlgren, P. and Sparks, C. (eds) *Journalism and Popular Culture*, London: Sage.

Dahlgren, P. (1995) *Television and the Public Sphere*, London: Sage.

Davies, M. M., Berry, C. and Clifford, B. R. (1985) Unkindest cuts? Some effects of picture editing on recall of television news information, *Journal of Educational Television*, **11** (2), 85–98.

Davies, M. M. and Corbett, B. (1997) *The Provision of Children's Television in Britain 1992–1996*, London: Broadcasting Standards Council.

Dennis, J. (1986) Preadult learning of political independence: Media and family communication effects, *Communication Research*, **13**, 401–33.

DiRenzo, G. (1990) Socialization for citizenship in modern democratic society, in O. Ichilov (ed.), *Political Socialization, Citizenship Education and Democracy*, New York: Teachers College Press.

Dominick, J. R. (1972) Television and political socialization, *Educational Broadcasting Review*, **6** (1), 48–56.

Drew, D. G. and Reese, S. D. (1984) Children's learning from a television newscast, *Journalism Quarterly*, **61** (1), 83–8.

Drew, D. and Reeves, B. (1980) Learning from a television news story, *Communication Research*, **7** (1), 121–35.

Easton, D. and Dennis, J. (1969) *Children in the Political System*, New York: McGraw Hill.

Eisenstadt, J. W. (1984) Studies in sociability, unpublished MS, quoted in Gamson (1992).

Eliasoph, N. (1990) Political culture and the presentation of a political 'self', *Theory and Society*, **19** (3), 465–94.

Ellsworth, E. (1989) Why doesn't this feel empowering? Working through the repressive myths of critical pedagogy, *Harvard Educational Review* **59**(3), 297–324.

Etzioni, A. (1993) *The Spirit of Community: The Reinvention of American Society*, New York: Simon and Schuster.

Fairclough, N. (1989) *Language and Power*, London: Longman.

Ferguson, B. (1985) Children's television: the germination of ideology, in D. Lusted and P. Drummond (eds), *TV and Schooling*, London: British Film Institute.

Fiske, J. (1987) *Television Culture*, London: Methuen.

Fiske, J. (1989) *Reading the Popular*, London: Unwin Hyman.

Fiske, J. (1992) Popularity and the politics of information, in P. Dahlgren and C. Sparks (eds), *Journalism and Popular Culture*, London: Sage.

Fornas, J. and Bolin, G. (1995) *Youth Culture in Late Modernity*, London: Sage.

Fraser, N. (1989) What's critical about critical theory? The case of Habermas and gender, in N. Fraser *Unruly Practices*, Minneapolis, MN: University of Minnesota.

Furnham, A. and Gunter, B. (1983) Political knowledge and awareness in adolescents, *Journal of Adolescence*, **6**, 373–85.

Galtung, J. and Ruge, M. H. (1965) The structure of foreign news, *Journal of Peace Research*, **2**, 64–91.

Gamson, W. A. (1992) *Talking Politics*, New York: Cambridge University Press.

Gauntlett, D. (1997) *Video Critical: Children, the Environment and Media Power*, Luton: John Libbey.

Gerbner, G. and Gross, L. (1976) Living with television: the violence profile, *Journal of Communication*, **30** (3), 10–29.

Gergen, K. (1991) *The Saturated Self: Dilemmas of Identity in Contemporary Life*, New York: Basic Books.

Gibbins, J. (ed.) (1989) *Contemporary Political Culture: Politics in a Postmodern Age*, London: Sage.

Gilbert, R. (1992) Citizenship, education and postmodernity, *British Journal of Sociology of Education*, **13** (1), 51–68.

Gilbert, R. (1996) Identity, culture and environment: Education for citizenship in the 21st century, in J. Demaine and H. Entwistle (eds), *Beyond Communitarianism: Citizenship, Politics and Education*, London: Macmillan.

Gillespie, M. (1995) *Television, Ethnicity and Cultural Change*, London: Routledge.

Glasgow University Media Group (1976) *Bad News*, London: Routledge and Kegan Paul.

Glasgow University Media Group (1982) *Really Bad News*, London: Writers and Readers.

Golding, P. and Middleton, S. (1982) *Images of Welfare: Press and Public Attitudes to Poverty*, Oxford: Martin Robertson.

Golding, P. (1994) Telling stories: Sociology, journalism and the informed citizen, *European Journal of Communication*, **9** (4), 461–84.

Graber, D. (1988) *Processing the News: How People Tame the Information Tide*, 2nd edn., New York: Longman.

Greenstein, F. I. (1965) *Children and Politics*, New Haven: Yale University Press.

Gripsrud, J. (1992) The aesthetics and politics of melodrama, in P. Dahlgren and C. Sparks (eds), *Journalism and Popular Culture*, London: Sage.

Gunter, B. (1987) *Poor Reception: Misunderstanding and Forgetting Broadcast News*, Hillsdale, NJ: Erlbaum.

Habermas, J. (1962/1989) *The Structural Transformation of the Public Sphere*, Cambridge, MA: MIT Press.

Habermas, J. (1987) *The Theory of Communicative Action, Volume 2: Lifeworld and System*, Boston, MA: Beacon Press.

Harber, C. (1992) *Democratic Learning and Learning Democracy*, Ticknall, Derbyshire: Education Now.

Harcourt, K. and Hartland, S. (1992) *Discovering Readers*, Tunbridge Wells: Newspapers in Education.

Hart, R. (1994) *Seducing America: How Television Charms the Modern Voter*, New York: Oxford University Press.

Hartley, J. (1996) *Popular Reality: Journalism, Modernity, Popular Culture*, London: Edward Arnold.

Harvey, D. (1989) *The Condition of Postmodernity*, Oxford: Blackwell.

Hess, R. D. and Torney, J. V. (1967) *The Development of Political Attitudes in Children*, Chicago, IL: Aldine.

Hollander, N. (1971) Adolescents and the war: the sources of socialization, *Journalism Quarterly*, **48**, 472–9.

Holt, J. (1975) *Escape from Childhood: The Needs and Rights of Children*, Harmondsworth: Penguin.

Home, A. (1993) *Into the Box of Delights*, London: BBC Books.

Howitt, D. (1976) *Report of Pre-school Children and Television Project*, Centre for Mass Communication Research, University of Leicester, cited in D. Howitt *The Mass Media and Social Problems*, Oxford: Pergamon (1982).

Hunter, I. (1994) *Rethinking the School*, Sydney: Allen and Unwin.

Ichilov, O. (1990) Dimensions and role patterns of citizenship in a democracy, in O. Ichilov (ed.), *Political Socialization, Citizenship Education and Democracy*, New York: Teachers College Press.

Inglehart, R. (1977) *The Silent Revolution: Changing Values and Political Styles among Western Publics*, Princeton, NJ: Princeton University Press.

Iyengar, S. (1991) *Is Anyone Responsible? How Television Frames Political Issues*, Chicago, IL: University of Chicago Press.

James, A. and Prout, A. (eds) (1990) *Constructing and Reconstructing Childhood: Contemporary Issues in the Sociological Study of Childhood*, London: Falmer Press.

Just, M. R., Neuman, W. R. and Crigler, A. (1992) *An Economic Theory of Learning from News*, Research Paper R-6, Cambridge, MA: Harvard College.

Katz, J. (1993) The media's war on kids, *Rolling Stone*, 25 November, 47–9, 130.

Katz, J. (1996) The rights of kids in the digital age, *Wired*, 4.07.

Kerr, D. (1997) *Citizenship Education Revisited*, (IEA Civic Education Project: Abbreviated Phase 1: National Case Study: England), Slough, Berkshire: National Foundation for Educational Research.

Kinder, M. (1995) Home alone in the 90s: Generational war and trans-generational address in American movies, television and presidential politics, in C. Bazalgette and D. Buckingham (eds), *In Front of the Children: Screen Entertainment and Young Audiences*, London: British Film Institute.

Knight, G. (1989) The reality effects of tabloid television news, in M. Raboy and P.A. Bruck (eds), *Communication For and Against Democracy*, Montreal: Black Rose.

Kress, G. (1995) *Writing the Future: English and the Making of a Culture of Innovation*, Sheffield: National Association of Teachers of English.

Kunkel, D. (1993) Policy and the future of children's television, in G. L. Berry and J. K. Asamen (eds), *Children and Television*, London: Sage.

Laybourne, G. (1993) The Nickelodeon experience, in G. L. Berry and J. K. Asamen (eds), *Children and Television*, London: Sage.

Lichtenberg, J. (1991) In defense of objectivity, in J. Curran and M. Gurevitch (eds), *Mass Media and Society*, London: Edward Arnold.

Liebes, T. (1992) Television, parents and the political socialization of children, *Teachers College Record*, **94** (1), 73–86.

Liebes, T. and Katz, E. (1990) *The Export of Meaning*, Oxford: Oxford University Press.

Lindley, R. (1989) Teenagers and other children, in G. Scarre (ed.), *Children, Parents and Politics*, Cambridge: Cambridge University Press.

Livingstone, S. and Lunt, P. (1994) *Talk on Television: Audience Participation and Public Debate*, London: Routledge.

Lyons, M. (1995, November) Personal communication: Interview with the author.

Marshall, T. H. (1977) *Class, Citizenship and Social Development*, Chicago, IL: University of Chicago Press.

Miller, T. (1993) *The Well-Tempered Self: Citizenship, Culture and the Postmodern Subject*, Baltimore, MD: Johns Hopkins University Press.

Mills, C. Wright (1956) *The Power Elite*, New York: Oxford University Press.

Moore, S. W., Lare, J. and Wagner, K. A. (1985) *The Child's Political World: A Longitudinal Perspective*, New York: Praeger.

Morse, M. (1985) Talk, talk, talk, *Screen*, **26** (2), 2–17.

Murdock, G. and Golding, P. (1989) Information poverty and political inequality: Citizenship in the age of privatized communications, *Journal of Communications*, **39** (3), 180–95.

Myers, G. (1995) 'The power is yours': Agency and plot in *Captain Planet*, in C. Bazalgette and D. Buckingham (eds), *In Front of the Children: Screen Entertainment and Young Audiences*, London: British Film Institute.

Nava, M. (1992) *Changing Cultures: Feminism, Youth and Consumerism*, London: Sage.

Neuman, W. R., Just, M. R. and Crigler, A. N. (1992) *Common Knowledge: News and the Construction of Political Meaning*, Chicago, IL: University of Chicago Press.

Nichols, B. (1981) *Ideology and the Image*, Bloomington, IN: Indiana University Press.

Peters, J. D. (1993) Distrust of representation: Habermas on the public sphere, *Media, Culture and Society*, **15** (4), 541–71.

Pew Research Center for the People and the Press (1996) *TV News Viewership Declines* (news release), Washington, DC: Pew Research Center.

Philo, G. (1990) *Seeing and Believing*, London: Routledge.

Pilcher, J. and Wagg, S. (eds) (1996) *Thatcher's Children: Politics, Childhood and Society in the 1980s and 1990s*, London: Falmer Press.

Putnam, R. D. (1995) Tuning in, tuning out: The strange disappearance of social capital in America, Paper delivered to the American Political Science Association, October.

Reimer, B. (1989) Postmodern structures of feeling: values and lifestyle in the postmodern age, in J. Gibbins (ed.), *Contemporary Political Culture*, London: Sage.

Richardson, K. and Corner, J. (1986) Reading reception: Mediation and transparency in viewers' accounts of a television programme, *Media, Culture and Society*, **8** (4), 485–508.

Robinson, J. P., Chivian, E. and Tudge, J. (1989) News media use and adolescents' attitudes about nuclear issues: an American-Soviet comparison, *Journal of Communication*, **39** (2), 105–13.

Robinson, J. P. and Levy, M. R. (1986) *The Main Source: Learning from Television News*, Beverly Hills, CA: Sage.

Rose, J. (1984) *The Case of Peter Pan: On the Impossibility of Children's Fiction*, London: Macmillan.

Rubin, A. M. (1976) Television in children's political socialization, *Journal of Broadcasting*, **20** (1), 51–9.

Sancho-Aldridge, J. (1997) *Election '97: Viewer Responses to the Election Coverage*, London: Independent Television Commission.

Scraton, P. (ed.) (1997) *'Childhood' in 'Crisis'?* London: UCL Press.

Scruton, R., Ellis-Jones, A. and O'Keefe, D. (1985) *Education and Indoctrination*, Harrow, Middlesex: Education Research Centre.

Sears, D. O. (1990) Whither political socialization research? The question of persistence, in O. Ichilov (ed.), *Political Socialization, Citizenship Education and Democracy*, New York: Teachers College Press.

Sparks, C. (1988) The popular press and political democracy, *Media, Culture and Society*, **10** (2), 209–23.

Sparks, C. (1991) Goodbye, Hildy Johnson: The vanishing 'serious press', in P. Dahlgren and C. Sparks (eds), *Communication and Citizenship*, London: Routledge.

Sparks, C. (1992) Popular journalism: Theories and practice, in P. Dahlgren and C. Sparks (eds), *Journalism and Popular Culture*, London: Sage.

Stam, R. (1983) Television news and its spectator, in E. A. Kaplan (ed.), *Regarding Television*, Frederick, MD: American Film Institute.

Sternberg, J. (1995) Smells like teen spirit (not!): Generation X abandons the news, Paper delivered at the Australian Teachers of Media Conference: Adelaide.

Stevens, O. (1982) *Children Talking Politics: Political Learning in Childhood*, Oxford: Martin Robertson.

Times Mirror Center for the People and the Press (1990) *The Age of Indifference: A Study of Young Americans and How They View the News*, Washington, DC: Times Mirror Center.

Tulloch, J. (1976) Knowledge and the TV quiz show, *Screen Education*, **19**, 3–13.

Turner, B. (1986) *Citizenship and Capitalism*, London: Allen and Unwin.

Turner, B. (ed.) (1993) *Citizenship and Social Theory*, London: Sage.

Turner, B. (1994) Postmodern culture/modern citizens, in B. van Steenburgen (ed.), *The Condition of Citizenship*, London: Sage.

van Zoonen, L. (1991) A tyranny of intimacy? Women, femininity and television news, in P. Dahlgren and C. Sparks (eds), *Communication and Citizenship*, London: Routledge.

Walker, D. (1996) Young people, politics and the media, in H. Roberts and D. Sachdev (eds), *Young People's Social Attitudes*, Ilford, Essex: Barnardos.

Wartella, E. (1994) Producing children's television programs, in J. S. Ettema and D. C. Whitney (eds), *Audiencemaking: How the Media Create the Audience*, Thousand Oaks, CA: Sage.

Wexler, P. (1990) Citizenship in the semiotic society, in B. S. Turner (ed.), *Theories of Modernity and Postmodernity*, London: Sage.

Wilkinson, H. and Mulgan, G. (1995) *Freedom's Children: Work, Relationships and Politics for 18–34 Year Olds in Britain Today*, London: Demos.

Wober, M. (1980) *Television and Teenagers' Political Awareness*, London: Independent Broadcasting Authority.

Index